The author was born and brought up in Co Down, NI – of farming stock and Christian parents. His father was a farmer and his mother a nurse. He holds a diploma in theology from Queen's University Belfast; a diploma in theology from the Irish Baptist College; a BA degree from Open University; an MA degree from Magee College Londonderry; and a Doctorate degree from Queen's University Belfast.

He has three children and is a retired minister of religion. His interests are reading, hill walking, writing and enjoying nature.

To Frank
from Nigel
Son of David
Murphy - Nov 2023

[signature]

To parents – Dee and Jean.

Dr David Murphy

THE SCIENCE OF RELIGION IN THE SCIENCE OF LIFE

Evolution for Slow Learners

AUSTIN MACAULEY PUBLISHERS™

LONDON ∗ CAMBRIDGE ∗ NEW YORK ∗ SHARJAH

A CIP catalogue record for this title is available from the British Library.

ISBN 9781398476745 (Paperback)
ISBN 9781398476752 (Hardback)
ISBN 9781398476769 (ePub e-book)

www.austinmacauley.com

First Published 2023
Austin Macauley Publishers Ltd®
1 Canada Square
Canary Wharf
London
E14 5AA

The writer would like to thank Austin Macauley Publishers for their help and encouragement and in preparing this work for publication.

The writer owes so much to Queen's University, Open University, MaGee University, Irish Baptist College, Union Theological College.

The roots of Education run deep but the fruit is sweet.

Table of Contents

Introduction

"The eventual goal of Science is to provide a single theory that describes the whole universe," wrote Stephen Hawking in 1998. However, a single theory of the universe must include an adequate explanation as to how the universe came to life on at least one planet – planet Earth, why the earth was so conveniently life-facilitating, and the origin of the order the producing means in the form DNA and RNA that has within it all the necessary means to produce the biological complexity of intelligent life on earth, and then how inanimate matter was brought consciously to life and endowed with many different attributes of being and understanding.

We need to explain how matter was ordered sufficiently to bring into existence the biological complexity of living things and then how inanimate matter was endowed with conscious life and attributes of understanding different in nature and substance to all that which we understand physics to be. We don't need to be an Einstein to know that that which can be intelligently investigated must of logical necessity be ordered intelligently. But many different scientists can spend their entire lives intelligently investigating the universe and everything in it and suspect not for a moment that that which they can intelligently investigate of logical necessity needs first to be ordered intelligently.

This means that many scientists are operating within a monumental contradiction in terms because to a rational mind the universe and everything in it needs first to be ordered intelligently before it could be investigated intelligently and scientists ordered intelligently to reason intelligently before they could investigate anything intelligently. So it seems that some scientists do not really understand what they are doing when they engage in science or the significance of what they are investigating which they find to be more incredibly complex and ingeniously ordered than anyone had ever imagined.

A countless number of books have been written apportioning all that exists to the order-producing sum of nothing. While Einstein had occasion to remark that: "The harmony of natural law … reveals an intelligence of such superiority that compared to it, all the systematic thinking and acting of human beings is an utterly insignificant reflection." But we as human beings ordered intelligently to think intelligently are those who are morally obliged as rational beings to join cause to effect and apportion a world full of intelligently ordered things to an intelligent and sufficient cause and living things to a living life producing cause.

But for some, no matter how utterly complex those things investigated are or consciously alive they are revealed to be the cause that brought them into existence never gets beyond nothing. In this they are being incorrigibly unfaithful to that which they have been ordered to be as rational beings in an ordered world, and refuse to use their powers of reason with which they have been so richly endowed to apportion an intelligently world full of ordered things to an intelligent and sufficient cause, or living things to a living life producing cause. In this they have not only managed to deceive themselves but also mislead the bulk of humanity by arguing that if they stretch the evolutionary process out long enough all that exists can be explained in terms of the order producing sum of nothing. Whatever, this is, it is not science and on the bases of raw logic it cannot be.

Therefore, we argue that religion which begins with the idea of a wise creator is solidly grounded in rational thinking and is, in fact, a logical necessity for those who think logically and reason causally. What we need is not merely an intelligent and sufficient cause that can explain a world full of intelligently ordered things, but the ordered sum of living things so that we are a living reflection of that living life producing cause from which we have come, the nature of whom can be seen in all that we have been ordered to be endowed as we are with different qualitative attributes of being. Therefore, to provide a single theory that describes and explains the whole universe as argued by Stephen Hawking, we need to face to the logic of the cause involved in the light of the effects produced.

To understand the nature and purpose of our existence as human beings, we need to look within ourselves to determine that which we have been ordered be with different categories of understanding and qualitative attributes of being which when exercised appropriately enable us to know all that we were made and meant to know as human beings and to experience all that we were meant to experience as living entities who are a living reflection of that cause from which we have come. Life takes us beyond the working of a physical brain that no matter how materially complex cannot of itself explain the conscious reality of life as we experience it to be.

By reducing life to empirically based criteria leaves, the affective side of life out of the equation, when life represents a different kind of reality altogether to that of physics and determines who we are operating experientially as conscious beings in a physical world. So what we need is a science of the existence of man that does justice to who we are as complex living beings and all that this means in profound life defining terms.

Some people think that Charles Darwin in his *Origin of Species* postulating the theory that life had evolved by means of natural selection and had advanced from very small beginnings to become extremely complex living things. But we cannot in theory or in practice slow an order producing down to the point that it does not need to be explained in terms of an intelligent and sufficient cause and to do so is a fatal mistake. Whether or not we can always identify and understand all those order-producing steps of evolutionary progression down the long ages of evolutionary history they are all in place to produce the ordered and living sum of the effects produced no matter how slow and gradual that process may be. In fact, the more strategic steps we need to explain intelligently ordered things the more ingenious the cause must be.

Bertrand Russell argued that life is but an "accidental collection of atoms" and because of this: "Only within the scaffolding of these truths, only on the firm foundations of unyielding despair, can the soul's habitation henceforth be built." But life is no accident, and the more we apportion extremely complex and intelligently ordered things to an endless stream of accidents the more an intelligent mind is convinced that an endless stream of accidents has nothing whatsoever to do with it.

So, while many scientists like to boast that we live in the so-called age of reason, we show in our study that many scientists seem rather to have altogether abandoned it, while our inner reality of being whereby we live life and engage in science is left out of the equation altogether leaving us with a most distorted and dangerous understanding of reality. In fact, some scientists have a problem with the meaning and significance of science itself, with many wanting the luxury of using their intelligence to investigate the world and everything in it while at the same time denying that the world and everything in it has anything to do with intelligence an order producing cause of any kind.

By refusing to acknowledge the not inconsiderable evidence that life on earth evolved some theists are not taken seriously within the scientific world. But Charles Hodge and B.B. Warfield, eminent theologians, argued that Nature and the Scriptures should be read together in order to come to a balanced and holistic understanding of all that exists because they in the end are saying the same thing for those who have a mind to see it. With nature representing the order producing laws that govern the universe and God as a wise creator who is the mind behind these ingenious order producing laws which when added together represent a process of intelligent design indicative of and synonymous with the working of a wise creator. Therefore, we have what we call a science of religion in the science of life, in that intelligent life needs to be explained in terms of a living life-producing cause that is synonymous with the one theists call God.

Os Guinness, an eminent philosopher/theologian, has argued that Christians have been deeply sinful in their anti-intellectualism in which they refuse to accept the evidence for evolution operating over millions of years because they believe it ran against what they believe the Scriptures taught was a six 24-hour day creation. Colin Brown in his book *Philosophy and the Christian Faith* has declared: "It is not surprising, therefore, that friends and foes alike tended to think that Reformed evangelical theology had nothing to contribute to the intellectual debates of our time." While Francis Collins, director of the mapping of the Human Genome Project in his book *The Language of God*, argues that those who reject and ignore a broad and rigorous body of scientific data are: "effectively committing intellectual suicide."

The founder members of the Royal Society were by and large sincere theists who sought to study nature in all its forms so as to enlighten the mind by revealing something of the ineffable magnitude of the cause involved in the light of the ordered sum of the effects produced. So the more scientists increasingly discover the vast complexity of all that exists they are increasingly revealing how incredibly wise the creator of all things is. The only problem is that they then forget to give due credit to the creator of all things, but heap great honours on themselves for being so wise they were able to discover something of the ingenious means adopted by a wise Creator to order all things into existence.

John Newton saw no contradiction between God as a wise creator and good science, because science was increasingly revealing the vast complexity of all things confirming the existence of a wise creator who was the creative mind behind the ordered and living sum of all things. And as our maker has created us as living beings this leaves open the possibility he can communicate with us and us with Him in living life producing terms. Our very being is, after all, is a living reflection of that cause from which we have come and we can identify the nature of our creator by the attributes of being with which he has so richly endowed us as a species: and by granting to us the attribute of rational thinking we are logically compelled to conclude that we need such a being. Nothing comes from nothing, this is a fundamental and emphatic conclusion forced on us by means of reason.

We will show that in different ways under different headings theists have reason on their side and we need to use it to engage those who have got so sloppy in their reasoning they can apportion all that exists to nothing! So rather than being pre-occupied with the time-line theists should be showing that science by its very nature is revealing that evolution is a process of intelligent ordering of the most ingenious life producing kind. Only theists can provide scientists with a much-needed cause in the form of a pre-existing intelligence who can explain all that they are otherwise at a total loss to explain in a world of vast and varied complexity.

Socrates the Greek philosopher rightly believed that the chief dignity of man was to exercise their reason in search of the truth; while the God of the Bible never expects us to believe that which is not reasonable or rationally compelling. "Come let us reason together says the Lord," through the prophet Isaiah. Antony Flew may well argue that the onus of proof is on theists to establish the existence of God, and that we should begin our search from the presumption of atheism. But this is quite ridiculous and logically absurd because it is for atheists and evolutionary theorists to explain how intelligently ordered things both animate and inanimate can be explained outside of an intelligent and sufficient cause of any kind the whole idea of which is in fact a complete contradiction in terms.

So the question is not necessarily whether life evolved or not, but what kind of process evolution is in the light of all that issues from it by way of the vast complexity of intelligent life on earth. Therefore, we argue that the conflict between faith in a wise creator and good science is essentially a needless conflict because God can be regarded as, and is logically bound to be, the creative mind behind the order producing power of evolution operating to the order producing genius of Nature's laws. Laws that come alive within us to revel the living life producing cause, our creator really is waiting to receive an appropriate and meaningful response from us.

But theists do themselves no favours when they set the laws of nature as revealed by science against the testimony of the Scriptures when evolution operating to the laws of nature could well be, and seem to be, the means our creator used to create and science seems to be showing us how. The account of creation in Genesis can be seen as a true but simplified account of creation to accommodate a pre-scientific people in an unsophisticated age, while to argue that ultimately nothing of any order producing significance produced the ordered complexity of all that exists is totally unacceptable because it is wholly irrational and scientifically nonsensical.

Sadly therefore, theists have miserably failed to expose the fundamental irrationality that lie at the heart of the classical theory of evolution by being wholly preoccupied with defending a six day creation refusing to establish the fact that life needs to be explained in terms of an intelligent and sufficient cause no matter how long the process took. The highly respected theologian Charles Hodge believed that the Bible must be interpreted by good science and that nature is as truly a revelation of God as the Bible and we only interpret the Word of God by the Word of God when we interpret the Bible by good science because God is the author of both.

Peter Hicks points out that Francis Schaeffer as a conservative theologian was strongly committed to arguing within the laws of logic, which he defined as the science of correct reasoning, believed that conservative Christianity tended to retreat into a self-defeating form of anti-intellectualism, failing to see that evolution was as sure a way to the existence of an necessary and sufficient cause in the form of a wise creator as was a six day creation.

But some evolutionists of the anti-God anti-design kind have no means to explain the ordered complexity of anything so they must apportion the ordered sum of all things to an endless stream of luck taking them into the domain of fairy-tale stories which in the end everything is ultimately explained in terms of no cause at all. So under different headings we examine the logical connection between science and religion endeavouring to show that at every level these are bound together both logically and ontologically to produce a holistic science of life.

Chapter 1
Reason the Ground of Truth
and Understanding

When we begin to consider the nature of truth, it is important to remember that we as human beings are an essential and most important part of the truth we are trying to come to terms with and explain. Therefore, truth is not merely objective but subjective, with the inner world of the mind which is the most profound and important part of reality that needs, not only to be understood for what it is, but used as it was meant to be used if we are to know and experience all that we were made and meant know as human beings. We do not know how the brain was wired up to create in us all that we experience ourselves to be, but we cannot deny who we experience ourselves to be because we as finite beings cannot understand that which our maker has ordered us to be. Moreover, we must use all our attributes of being to know and experience all that we were made and meant to know as human beings of which reason and moral being are central aspects of who we are as human beings.

Reason informs us that we need an intelligent and sufficient cause to explain the ordered and living sum of our existence and the existence of all things for that matter. The fact that who we are and all that exists goes beyond our capacity as human beings to fully understand means that our creator is much wiser and exceedingly more creative than ourselves. Tens of thousands of scientists over the years have studied the heavens and the earth and still only partially understand it, while how a physical brain can produce in us a living self-conscious reality of being we experience ourselves to be is still a mystery. However, for science to work things have to be intelligently ordered or there would be nothing of any intelligently ordered significance for scientists to investigate and no one with the necessary intelligence to investigate anything.

Reason informs us that intelligently ordered effects whatsoever those effects may be must of logical necessity be explained in terms of an intelligent and sufficient cause or causes, and by investigating different effects scientists can draw rational conclusions in relation to the cause involved. If this were not the case, science would be rendered impossible because it would be utterly futile for scientists to go looking for causes in relation to different effects where no intelligent and sufficient causes exist. Science pre-supposes that we live in an intelligently ordered world full of intelligently ordered things to investigate or scientists would be wasting their time doing science. And, moreover, there would be no intelligently ordered minds to intelligently investigate anything.

John Gribbin sums up the scientific method by arguing that if a theory disagrees with the findings of an "experiment, it is wrong." But an experiment must be set up appropriately on the basis of reason and its findings judged on the bases of reason to see if they agree with a given hypothesis about a particular phenomenon or artefact under investigation, and the findings assessed on the bases of rational thinking in an attempt to understand the nature of the thing under investigation and therein to discover also something of the nature of the cause involved in relation to the effects produced.

If scientists were to make nothing but wild guesses unrelated to phenomenon or artefact under investigation they are never going to get to the truth about the origin anything. Scientists may make an educated guess as to the cause of a particular effect and rationally assess that hypothesis against the effect under investigation to see if they equate. Therefore, both our experiment and any conclusion drawn in relation to it must be based on reason and assessed in the light of reason and the necessary conclusions drawn with respect to the cause involved in the light of effects produced. But if the test bears no relation to the object under investigation then it's back to the drawing board in an effort to devise a test that hopefully will more accurately reveal the nature of the object under investigation and therein the nature of the cause involved.

Gribbin however goes on to argue that the universe is comprehensible to mortal minds because it is governed by a small set of simple rules. But if this is true, why does Gribbin go on to say that the scientific worldview is the greatest achievement of the human intellect, because if this is the case the world of science surely can't be all that simple. He quotes Einstein who once remarked that: "The eternal mystery of the world is its comprehensibility." (Gribbin 1998, p.3)However, the world is comprehensible to us because being ordered intelligently into existence it can intelligently investigated by us and the more we investigate it the more exceedingly complex and intelligently ordered we find it to be.

For Gribbin to suggest that the universe is made up of a small set of simple rules is to be singularly naïve when the earth and living things are so utterly complex after thousands of years of diligent investigation by the greatest minds on the earth, it is still but partially understood by us and this applies right down to simple living cells that are exceedingly more complex than anyone had ever imagined. Moreover, Gribbin is also wrong when he argues that physics is the most fundamental of sciences and all else is likened to a stamp collection. (Gribbin 1998, intro) The most important aspect of science is not physics but metaphysics; that is the existence of inquiring and intelligent minds without which there would be no science.

Therefore, to get to the truth about the origin of all things, we need to take account of ourselves as those doing the investigating. Socrates the Greek philosopher could see the importance of the soul as a reality in itself as the seat of consciousness and moral character and the driving force behind intellectual pursuits that guides and directs us in the pursuit of knowledge. This is why he urged people to "know thyself" because therein lay the most profound reality in the known universe that needs to be explained, a reality that makes science possible and compels us as rational beings to attribute intelligently ordered things to intelligent and sufficient causes, and the ordered and integrated sum of all things to an intelligent and sufficient cause in the form of a wise creator.

No house is better than the foundations on which it is built, and the scientific house is no better than its rational foundations and will come tumbling down if it deserts the ground of rational thinking and fails to draw the necessary and logical conclusions in which effects are explained in terms of sufficient causes and living things in terms of a living life producing cause. The "Logos" for Plato was: "A divine revelatory principle, simultaneously operative within the human mind and the natural world." Moreover, the mind and the intelligence we as humans use to do science cannot be defined or validated in empirically based scientific terms and represents a reality that takes us beyond the world of physics into the world of inner being that drives scientists with highly inquisitive and intelligent minds to do science, only to find that the universe and everything in it is ordered above and beyond what the collective minds of men can fully understand.

We would suggest that part of the reason why some scientists can so easily depart from the cause and effect logic of rational thinking is because reason and rational being cannot be set forth and examined in empirically based scientific terms so it is constantly avoided, taken for granted and never explained in terms that does justice to it. Therefore, the decision of the National Academy of Sciences not to accept the principle of intelligent design because intelligent design cannot be ratified in empirically based scientific terms is a rather deceitful ploy to avoid the idea that a world full of extremely complex and intelligently ordered living things needs to be explained in terms an intelligent and sufficient cause in the form of a wise creator. Then they call it science and we are meant to be impressed when long ago such have deserted the ground of rational thinking, and the reason for this seems to be that once they concede the principle of intelligent design the logic of an intelligent designer in the form of a wise creator comes logically and forcibly into play.

What is the point in doing science if we are not going to draw the necessary logical conclusions about intelligently ordered things perceived and explained in terms of a cause fit to explain them? It appears therefore, that the National Academy of Sciences fail to understand what science is all about and what scientists are doing when they do science. And this we would suggest is a devious stratagem to avoid the obvious, namely to avoid the compelling logic that behind an ordered world full of intelligently ordered things there is and has to be an intelligent order producing cause operating with the necessary means to bring order out of chaos and conscious life out of inanimate matter.

Therefore, the life sciences, of which intelligence is a part, is part of the faculties with which nature has so richly endowed us as a species so as to understand and draw rational conclusions about different things perceived. As rational beings, therefore, we are morally committed to apportion an intelligent and sufficient cause to things we can clearly see are intelligently ordered, extremely complex and some of which are endowed with the ineffable reality of conscious life. And still some don't seem get it. The extent to which we can think logically and reason intelligently sets us apart from the rest of the animal kingdom and that while they are intelligent in their own way they operate more to instincts than hard-nosed rational thinking and think not to draw rational conclusions about intelligently ordered things perceived. Science is based on the premise that because things are ordered intelligently they can be investigated intelligently and understood intelligently and this is why science has been so successful in its quest for knowledge and understanding of the world and everything in it even though there is much we still do not understand.

Richard Dawkins argues that the existence of life on earth represents "a huge improbability on a colossal scale", and there is no point it seems in which the odds get so extremely immense and massively vast even beyond all human understanding, that such things pass over from being a huge improbability on a colossal scale to a cause fit to explain them. The odds, as we shall see later in our study, of something made of some 200 parts falling into place by chance come out at more than the subatomic particles in the entire universe and Dawkins agrees with these odds and comes up with some illustrations of his own that bears out the impossible nature of these odds which forces him to introduce mechanisms of order producing genius which brings him back to a process of intelligent design.

However, the more complex and intelligently ordered things are understood to be the more ridiculous this explanation is until science of this kind is in danger of becoming completely farcical in which the effects are utterly marvellous but the cause involved never gets beyond "a huge improbability on a colossal scale." Natural selection was said to explain how living things came into existence and increased massively in complexity from simple beginnings to increasingly complex living things. But natural selection itself needs to be explained unless it is a form of magic doing that which is logically impossible and otherwise and incomprehensible. And what kind of magic is it that can bring order out of chaos and conscious life out of inanimate matter outside of an intelligent and sufficient cause? This kind of magic theists call God.

It was eventually discovered that ingenious mechanisms of order producing ingenuity in the form of DNA and RNA was the intelligent means by which natural selection was made possible. These have been likened to an architect's plans and a builder's skill, one to provide the necessary plans to produce intelligent life on earth and the other to follow those plans through to completion to produce intelligent life on earth. Who is the author of these life-producing plans and with the necessary means and materials to execute them so as to bring order out of chaos and living things out of inanimate mater? In fact chaos operating within chaos could only produce a never-ending round of self-perpetuating chaos.

To facilitate this lack of rational cause and effect thinking, scientists like John Gribbin must make everything to look so natural, simple and inevitable that life on earth doesn't need to be explained in terms of an intelligent and sufficient cause at all. This is why Gribbin, like so many other Darwinians and empirically based scientists, must reduce the coming into existence of life on earth to steps so small and simple they don't need to be explained in terms of an intelligent and sufficient cause. But steps no matter how small and simple never get so simple and inconsequential that they do not add up to an intelligent case sufficient to explain the ordered sum of that which is being produced. Gribbin in the end is himself forced to admit that: "This scientific world view is the greatest achievement of the human intellect" which means that things must not be so simple after all needing scientists of the highest calibre to work out and understand the ingeniously ordered sum of the effects produced. While there is so much we still do not understand with scientists playing catch-up with that cause that brought all things into existence and in which those scientists are still only scratching the surface. (Gribbin 2001, Intro.

The National Academy of Sciences believe that science and religion are "mutually exclusive" as different kinds of knowledge that must operate side by side in the world but which cannot be reconciled philosophically. But this is completely untrue. Science and religion are not merely compatible but logically and causally connected because we need an intelligent and sufficient cause to explain how a world full of intelligently ordered things came into existence from what before was in a state of primordial disorder and by means sufficient to turn disordered matter into states of highly ordered complexity and then endue inanimate matter with conscious life which represents a process of intelligent design behind which there is, and has to be, an intelligent order producing cause and life generating creativity. In fact, science and religion are joined at the hip by virtue of the fact that we need a God like intelligence to take a disordered world of primordial chaos and turn it into a world teaming with extremely complex living things and science is progressively showing us the ingenious means by which this was accomplished which has the finger prints of a wise creator all over it.

This includes the intrinsic essence of life itself infused as it is with the vital force of conscious being endowed with spiritual and qualitative attributes of being in which we as human beings are living proof of a living life producing cause at work in the universe because effects whatever their nature must be explained in terms of a cause that is able to explain them, and this puts us as conscious beings into living contact with that cause from which we have come as being relating to being and creator to creature made in the image of God. It seems pretty obvious the cause that ordered us into existence as rational beings expects us to reflect on the origin of our existence in the light of all that we have been ordered to be and to appreciate the attributes of being with which we are so richly endowed as a species and to use then to good effect in relation to our maker who endowed us with them and our fellowman with whom we to share this our planet we call earth.

Thus we as human beings must reflect something of the nature of our creator's own being in the ordered sum of who we are and the nature and purpose of our existence in the light all that we have been ordered to be as moral beings in an ordered world forever indebted to our creator. It's not enough to argue that living things survived because they were best adapted by natural selection to live within a particular environment. We must ask ourselves how living things were ordered and equipped to live within a particular environment which before was nothing but a disordered mass of disparate chemicals, a cause that can bring matter to life fully equipped to live of the resources of a particular environment.

Reason is something we were born with we did not think it up or work it out for ourselves, it was there just like one's life to be used to understand and intelligently interact with the world we live in and other living things. But how could we be ordered intelligently to reason intelligently by a process of blind randomness operating within the context of primordial chaos which could produce nothing but a never-ending process of regurgitated chaos. For scientists to be effective in their quest for understanding of the world and their place within, it requires two things: 1 – That we as human beings must be ordered intelligently to think intelligently and to be able to draw logical conclusions from the ordered sum of effects produced; 2 – The earth and everything in it must be ordered intelligently for us to be able to understand it intelligently, investigate it successfully and live within it meaningfully.

David Papineau points out in his book on Philosophy: "Our world is one of causes and effects things making other things happen." (Papineau 2004, p.20) Therefore, adds Papineau: "The notion of cause cannot be eliminated from our understanding of the world." (Papineau 2004. p.23)Therefore, for us as human beings, rational thinking is incorporated into our very act of thinking and perceiving and as a result we can take everything very much for granted and thereby fail to consciously perceive that the vast complexity of intelligent life on earth could possibly have come into existence by a process of blind and blundering randomness. So that an appropriate cause must of logical necessity be apportioned to a process on intelligent ordering which brings into being the vast complexity of intelligent life on earth no matter how slow that process might take.

Therefore, when scientists set out to investigate the world and everything in it they are implicitly or explicitly expressing the fact that the world and everything in it is ordered intelligently and for this reason it can be investigated intelligently, understood intelligently and described intelligently. But unfortunately, many scientists want the privilege of investigating the world and everything in it intelligently without apportioning an intelligent and sufficient cause to those things in an attempt to avoid the logic of intelligent design behind which there is and logically has to be an intelligent and sufficient cause in the form of an intelligent designer. So in the end for many scientists like Sean Carroll intelligently ordered things are just attributed to brute facts that don't need an explanation in terms of a sufficient cause. (Carroll 2016, p. Indeed, this may be a very convenient cop-out because it is certainly not good science or anything to do the cause and affect logic of rational thinking to examine different intelligently ordered things and to find them to be more ingeniously ordered and exceedingly more complex than anyone had ever imagined and then conclude that these have nothing to do with an intelligent and sufficient cause and are just brute facts.

It is somewhat hypocritical for taking credit for being able to work out something of the ingenious order producing nature of the means involved whereby living things were ordered into existence only to give no credit whatsoever to that cause that ordered all things into existence for people like Carroll to investigate and to discover how marvellously complex and intelligently ordered life really is and to then conclude that it is all down to Brute facts is a strategic cop-out to avoid what to an unprejudiced mind operating to the logic of sufficient cause is abundantly self-evident which is nothing but the blind leading the blind.

Richard Dawkins however like to ridicule theists because he believes that religion is not based in rational thinking, but Dawkins who attributes the ordered complexity of life on earth to no intelligent or sufficient cause at all is the who is being irrational. Dawkins illustrates what he believes is the gullibility of Christians to Thomas the Doubter who after Jesus challenged him to come and touch him where the sword pierced his side to verify that he was truly alive from the dead said to Thomas: "blessed are those who believe but have not seen." This means according to Dawkins, that what Jesus was saying to his disciples is that you don't need proof but just believe anyway.

But this is totally mischievous and wholly misleading because the proof of Jesus resurrection would come to those to whom Jesus revealed himself in clear unmistakable and tangible terms as alive from the dead including doubting Thomas, and their collective testimony would bear witness to the resurrection of those who were so utterly convinced of the resurrection they were willing to pay the ultimate sacrifice in their own martyrdom. Moreover, the blessings referred to by Jesus were not earthly glory or merely material proof of his resurrection, but the blessings of a good conscience and a sound mind before God, peace that passes all understanding and hope that springs eternal in a world which has the effrontery to believe that nothing produced the ordered sum of everything and all it has to offer mankind is a philosophy of despair, to eat, drink and be merry for tomorrow we die.

While Kenneth Miller assures his fellow theists that there is "no reason for believers to draw a line in the sand between God and evolution." (Cited in Witham 2002, p.5) This is because evolution is an order producing cause of vast life producing significance not unlike and synonymous with the idea of a wise creator. But many evolutionists turn against their own theory of evolution by ultimately apportioning its working to nothing of any intelligent order producing significance at all when all the time and down the ages it has produced a world of extremely complex and intelligently living things calling out from the bowels of reason for an explanation in terms of an intelligent order producing and life generating cause. As the eminent scholar Frederick Copleston rightly argues: "I cannot see how science could be conducted other than the assumption than that of order and intelligibility in nature."

But Bertrand Russell trying to evade the logic of sufficient cause argues that: "… a physicist looks for causes; that does not necessarily imply that there are causes everywhere. A man might look for gold without assuming that there is gold everywhere; if he finds gold, well and good, if he doesn't he's had bad luck. The same is true when the physicist looks for causes." (Cited in Metaphysics: The Big Questions 1998, p.436f) But this argument is deeply flawed and is highly misleading. The point is that people do not suppose that gold being a rare commodity is to be found everywhere a person might look for gold, but we can be absolutely sure that the world and everything in it (including gold wherever it is found) needs to be explained in terms of an intelligent and sufficient cause. This is why scientists have been so successful in discovering causes for so many different things because they are there to be found in a world of ordered complexity. And things that we can understand intelligently we can be assured have been ordered intelligently whether or not we can always explain the specific nature of the cause or sequences of inter-related causes involved.

Darwinians like to argue that 'natural selection' somehow explains how evolution operates to produce intelligent life on earth, but it has never been explained how evolution by natural selection operates effectively to do this leaving all that exists a mystery unexplained, but which to an intelligent mind is abundantly self-evident in that intelligently ordered things need to be explained in terms of an intelligent and sufficient cause and living things in terms of a living life producing cause. As we will see later in our study, even Darwin was befuddled by the whole process of natural selection and even thought that somehow it operated to produce intelligent life on earth outside of an intelligent and sufficient cause of any kind. The mystery of course was eventually explained with the discovery of DNA and RNA as an ingenious mechanism of order producing excellence which has been referred to as the language of God because it had the order producing power within it to explain the vast complexity of intelligent life on earth.

The only thing that now needs to be explained is the order producing genius of DNA, that can not only produce the biological complexity of life on earth, but the life generating genius of conscious being that rises up within us to confront us with evidence of a living life producing cause as work in the universe. The ability to reason effectively is generally referred to as intelligence and is more formally referred to as I.Q. That is the ability to understand the logical relationship between different effects in relation to their causes because intelligently ordered things do have intelligent and sufficient causes and this is why scientists go looking for them: they just conveniently forget to add up to an intelligently constituted sum of them and fail therefore to see that they add up to a process of the exquisite design and mind-boggling creativity.

Mathematics can be regarded as abstract reasoning which in its simplest form numbers can be added together to produce conclusions that are regarded as logically and self-evidently true. Thus $2 + 2 = 4$ – not because someone arbitrarily says so, but because it is logically self-evident as a conclusion drawn from the facts as represented in the symbols themselves. Galileo once remarked:

26

"I do not feel obliged to believe that the same God who has endowed us with reason and intellect has intended us to forgo their use." (Cited in Southwell 2013, p.26)

But some evolutionists, we would argue, want to evade the whole course of rational thinking when it suits their reductionist purposes and anti-God proclivities; and, in fact, some have turned this aversion into an art form by using every possible means and subtle semantic verbiage to avoid the idea of sufficient cause when it comes to explaining a world full of intelligently ordered things. As a result we end up with a theory in which the ordered sum of everything is attributed to the order producing sum of nothing and therein we find ourselves in a never-never land of causal absurdity where the ordered complexity of life on earth came into existence by means that are the very antithesis of the ordered sum of their existence. In fact, to abandon reason in this sure way is to abandon truth itself.

Moreover, such things as intelligence, love, joy, peace, goodness, hopes, aspirations and the need to keep promises etc. etc. cannot be validated in empirically based scientific terms. So are we to abandon such values and virtues that take us to the heart out existence as human beings because they cannot be validated in empirically based scientific terms which is an insult to the sacredness of life and the one who is the author of it.

We have what is referred to as inductive reasoning in which conclusions are drawn from certain inferences drawn from observation. So we might see white swans on a thousand different occasions and conclude that all swans are white only to find that some swans are black. Therefore, we must be careful about drawing conclusions about the way we perceive different things to be because there could be differences we haven't yet perceived, but when perceived adds to our understanding of those things all of which need to be explained in terms of sufficient cause. We have the example of the farmer who faithfully feeds his chicken every day for a whole year and then the next day the chicken expecting to be fed is picked up by the farmer and taken home to his wife to cook for the Sunday lunch. This is what David Hume referred to as the problem with inductive reasoning. But it is not so great a problem at all because unknown to the chicken the farmer had this in mind all along and had the chicken realised this it would well have had good reason to do all in its power to escape.

And we can also conclude that all swans of whatever colour are of the same species and that all need to be explained in terms of an intelligent and sufficient cause and if we want to know why some swans are white and some are black ask a geneticist and they will explain it to you. Therefore, there are still causes for all these things including why some swans are black and some are white and likewise, there is a good explanation as to why the chicken after being fed faithfully by the farmer for so long eventually became part of the Sunday lunch. But unfortunately for the chicken it was not aware of this fact because if it had it might have taken occasion to *flew de coup*, but the cause was always there waiting to happen in the mind of the farmer. Therefore, there are causes for all such things whether or not we are aware of those causes or not.

Then we have deductive reasoning in which the premises logically entail the conclusion and to fail to draw such conclusions is to go completely irrational. Thus we can say that all John's children have ginger hair, so that James being a son of the same John must logically have ginger hair. To say otherwise would be a complete contradiction in terms. So if we were to claim that intelligently ordered things came into existence by means that have nothing to do with an intelligence or an intelligent and sufficient cause of any kind this also would be a complete contradiction in terms and nothing to do with the truth as it pertains to the origin of those things. So with deductive reasoning the conclusions are logically entailed in the premises themselves as illustrated in the above example.

Modern science seeks to understand hidden causes that lie behind the origin of different things and they do this by means of observation, investigation and experimentation because that believing such causes exist they set their minds to find them. If such causes did not exist scientist would be wasting their time looking for them. But in the modern world of anti-God mentality many scientists after they discover many of the ingenious means and methods by which different things were ordered into existence, they then endeavour to explain the order producing efficiency of these means away so that they mean nothing in terms of an intelligent and sufficient cause leaving us within a monumental contradiction in terms in which nothing is ultimately explained. When we add conscious life to the reality that needs to be explained we need a cause that can explain how a physical brain can produce something which physics by definition cannot of itself explain. So we come face to face with evidence of a life producing cause at work in the universe the ultimate expression of which is ourselves as human beings the cause of which and purpose of which can be discovered in that which we have been ordered to be.

Thus the cause and effect logic of rational thinking is invariably applied to man-made things, but when it comes to mankind itself and a world of exceeding more complex things this logic is not only avoided but flagrantly denied turning the cause and effect logic of rational on its head to avoid the idea of a wise creator to whom we owe everything and as moral beings ultimately answerable. All right thinking people regard life as precious and sacred with it and those who commit murder are guilty of a serious crime. But how could life be precious and regarded as sacred if it ultimately constitutes nothing but an elaborate piece of chanced irrelevance, an ordered compendium of inanimate matter which by definition cannot have attributes of qualitative being, feelings, hopes and aspirations that take us beyond the world of physics?

So what is life trying to tell us in terms of sufficient cause and the origin from which we have come in the ordered and living sum of who we are, rational beings, inordinately complex, consciously alive, in possession of attributes of being we regard as precious, hopes and desires we possess as a species? The fact is that we need to exercise all these attributes of being to know and experience all that we are made and meant to know as human beings. Sean Carroll in his book the *Big Picture on the Origins of Life*, Meaning and the Universe itself ends up arguing that there are things that have no reason they are "just brute facts – things that are simply true, with no further explanation possible." (Carol 2017, p.42)

However, the ultimate brute fact is the ordered and living sum of who we are and experience ourselves to be as human beings, we must have a cause or we wouldn't be here thinking about it, and now that we are thinking about it we must surely use all our attributes of being to experience all that we were made and meant to know as human beings, and as rational beings reflect on the origin from which we have come in the light of all that we have been ordered to be. Science must operate along all of these fronts if we are to know and experience all that we were made and meant to know as human beings. It is a brute fact that anything less is a form of reductionist absurdity in a vain attempt to avoid the idea of a wise creator to apportion the ordered sum of all thing to brute fact needing no explanation by way of an intelligent and sufficient cause. As Plato has argued: "Logos was a divine revelatory principle, simultaneously operative within the human mind and the natural world, and to discover *kosmos* in the world was to reveal *koemos* in one's own soul."

To reduce life to constructions of corporeal substance that fell into place by a process of blind randomness is to abandon the ground of rational thinking altogether and effectively negate the world of being that transcends all that we predicate of the mundane sum of empirically based reality. We are endowed with a rich legacy of being which not only needs to be explained, but used if we are to know and experience all that we were made and meant to know as human beings. Consciousness itself, feelings, attributes of being, rational thinking and different categories of understanding peculiar to our existence as human beings cannot be explained in empirically based scientific terms but need to be explained on their own ineffable life defining terms that govern our thinking and represent who we are as a species.

But empirically based science wants to restrict verifiable reality to sense based physical facts which effectively negates and nullifies the life world and all that we are as moral beings of profound life defining substance and significance operating experientially in a physical world. Richard Tarnas rightly argues that materialism failed to take account of the subjective phenomenology of human consciousness and man's sense of being as a personal volitional entity different in nature and character to the unconscious impersonal world of physics. (Tarnas 1996, p.362)

There are things that are presupposed in the doing of science, namely a living conscious reality of being without which there would be no one to do science, and intelligence by which we can draw the necessary conclusions in relation to the intelligently ordered sum of things perceived. In fact, reducing reality to empirically based things wipes out the whole of science because the very act of engaging in science and the means by which it is carried out cannot be validated in empirically based scientific terms. However, whether they like to admit it or not, scientists are operating within the presupposition that things are intelligently ordered and men of letters should know that if things were not intelligently ordered they could not be intelligently investigated or intelligently understood by us.

Therefore, what we need is a thoroughly consistent philosophy of life, a science of the existence of man and all that this implies in term of sufficient cause. Bryan Magee admits that Carl Popper held that all of us must inevitably hold metaphysical beliefs about the world whether we like it or not. But more to the point, it is completely impossible not to hold metaphysical beliefs about our own reality of being through which we live life and consciously engage with the world of physical things. Magee rightly argues that the inner world of being: "is indubitable in a way that the objective (world) is not and can never be." (Cited in Magee 2000, p.118) This is because the inner world of being represents who we are as conscious beings and it is obviously impossible to deny who we experience ourselves to be and when we add to this the world we experience by means of our senses we have what could be referred to as a holistic science of reality as it really is.

David Hume, sceptic and philosopher, argued that we cannot tell how particular effects are produced and gave the example of one billiard ball hitting another billiard ball causing it to move as it does. But Isaac Newton demonstrated to us the laws of motion and how this worked. How an object remains at rest until a force acts upon it, the acceleration of the ball impacted is proportional to the force of the cause involved, so when object A is impacted by object B it causes an equally opposite reaction in object B. So there is after all a perfectly good explanation as to why a billiard ball impacting another billiard ball moves as it does. But this is what those using their powers of reason knew in principle all along but could not explain it in precise technical terms.

Kant has aptly argued that we attribute a cause to a given effect because the reason we possess as a species informs us that we must, so that everything that happens of logical necessity must have a cause sufficient to produce the nature and sum of the effect or effects produced. Scientists go looking for these causes convinced that they are there to be found, but some in their ill-motivated naivety attribute the order producing sum of all things to no intelligent cause at all so that chance, luck and good fortune can explain the order and living complexity of all things which is neither rational or convincing because change is no explanation for the coming into existence of the ordered complexity of anything, and our luck soon runs out when it comes to producing extremely complex things by randomly moving disordered matter about, while good fortune favours those who think intelligently and act accordingly.

If we were to throw a ball across a room, a cat would immediately dash after it, but if we as human beings saw a ball come rolling across a room, we would also look to see who threw the ball, knowing that as rational beings such a cause exists. We would even go further and know that the ball needed an intelligent explanation by way of sufficient cause as does the cat that darts after it. Two elements contribute to knowledge, sensory perception of the physical world and our different faculties of understanding that determine how we understand and relate to that world. As living beings, we need to be explained in terms of a living life producing cause, because we represent a living life producing effect endowed with different faculties of being and attributes of understanding. We are moral beings which mean that the cause that ordered us into existence must be a moral being and knows how to confer this attribute of being upon us even if we cannot understand how the brain was ordered to make us moral beings.

It is not unreasonable to suppose that by creating us moral beings our maker is giving us notice that he as a Holy God and will one day judge the world in righteousness. And if events did not have intelligently constituted causes everything would be in a state of perpetual chaos and confusion would reign on the earth and there would be no one with the ability to intelligently investigate anything and there would be nothing of any intelligently ordered significance to investigate.

So reason is the governing principle that regulates the universe and our understanding of it as rational yet finite beings in which our knowledge of it is always expanding. Bryan Magee speaking of Carl Popper points out that: "we should put faith in reason and make that our supreme regulative ideal." (Magee 2000, p.234) While Jim Baggott argues in his book *Farewell to Reality:* "That we are not uniquely privileged observers of the universe we inhabit. We are not at the centre of everything." (Baggott 2013, p.23) However, it seems that we are special enough to be able to investigate the world and everything in it and by means of reason to know that a world full of intelligently ordered things owes their existence to an intelligent and sufficient cause.

In fact, nature has put us at the very centre of things by conferring intelligence upon us enabling us to think intelligently and reason causally to see that things that are ordered intelligently need to be explained in terms of an intelligent and sufficient cause and that living things need to be explained in terms of a living life producing cause and that makes us privileged indeed and confers great responsibility on us to reason logically and think causally ensuring to apportion intelligently ordered things to intelligent and sufficient causes.

While monkeys are special in their own way, they do not do science or intelligently investigate the world they live in as we humans do, they take everything for granted and think not to enquire into the origin of anything or think to apportion intelligently ordered things to an intelligent and sufficient causes or an ordered world full of intelligently ordered things to a wise creator.

So we must decide whether to go with the monkey or step up to the line as rational beings as we are ordered and ordained to do and face up to the fact that behind the vast of complexity of all that exists there is an order producing and life creating intelligence in the form of a wise creator at work in the universe.

But some want to have the privilege of investigating an intelligently ordered world full of intelligently ordered things without apportioning these things to an intelligent and sufficient cause which is an abdication of their moral responsibility as rational beings. The cause that ordered us into existence as rational beings obviously wants us to know that we owe our existence to an intelligent life producing cause and by reflecting on our existence as human beings we can reflect on the kind of cause from which we have come and the purpose of our existence as human beings. Perhaps it is Baggott who wants to remove us as human beings from the centre of the picture who as rational beings are honour-bound to conclude that intelligently ordered things owe their existence to intelligent and sufficient causes and living things to a living life producing cause.

As sentient beings, we are part of the world's intrinsic truth and this is why we need to also look within ourselves to see who we really are as living beings in order to better understand the kind of cause from which we have come, and therein discern more clearly the purpose of our existence. This is exactly what Plato urged his followers to do, while in more general terms, Einstein saw great significance in the fact that the world is intelligible to us, because he realised that the world and we ourselves must be intelligently ordered or we couldn't intelligently investigate it or intelligently understand it terms of sufficient cause which would render science rather a wasted exercise because there is little point in investigating things intelligently to understand how they originate and operate if ultimately they owe their existence to nothing of any intelligently ordered significance.

Carlo Rovelli thinks that: "We are an integral part of nature; we are nature, in one of its innumerable and infinitely variable expressions." (Rovelli 2015, p.74) But what kind of a cause must nature be, that it can produce an ordered world and then fill it with extremely complex living things in which we seem to be living expressions of nature's own being. Rovelli goes on: "If we are special we are only special in the way that everyone feels themselves to be, as every mother is to her child." (Rovelli 2014, p.65) But if this statement means anything it means that we are special in the cosmic sense because Mother Nature has ordered us intelligently to think intelligently and therein to realise that we are her offspring are indeed special. But what ungrateful children to give no honour or respect to that cause that ordered us into existence and breathed life into our mortal bodies. To avoid this some seem to go conveniently obtuse when it suits their anti-design purposes in an attempt to avoid coming face to face with the logic of a sufficient cause in the form of a wise creator.

If someone was to ask us for proof that something that we understand intelligently was ordered intelligently, we would know that there was something horribly wrong with their thinking because to an intelligent mind this fact is abundantly self-evident. As Paul Johnson argues: "The best ally of theology was natural philosophy... The visible marks of extraordinary wisdom and power appear so plainly in all the works of creation that a rational creature will seriously reflect on them cannot miss the discovery of a deity." (Johnson 1976, p.334)

While John Locke argued, that those who depart from reason are bound to sink into confusion and that a rational creature that will but seriously reflect on the works of creation cannot miss the discovery the existence of a deity and that the mind cannot be generated by a purely material cause. (Cited in Johnson 1976, p.336)For those who fail to apportion as intelligently ordered world full of intelligently ordered living things to no intelligent and sufficient causes at all are not only being irrational, but as rational beings are being morally irresponsible because we as rational beings are morally obliged to apportion intelligently constituted effects to intelligently constituted causes and living life producing effects to a living life producing cause. The ordered nature of the effects produced reflects the nature of the cause involved both with respect to physical effects and metaphysical effects. In fact, those who abandon reason in the search of the truth have effectively abandoned the very foundations of truth itself.

Stephen J Gould regards the intelligence of Homo sapiens, "as an ultimate in oddball rarity." But as ordered beings endowed with intelligence we are not an in oddball rarity, but the evidence of an intelligent and sufficient and sufficient cause at work in the earth and expressing their mind and purpose in that we have been ordered to be. While David Hume, in spite of his oft times convoluted and sometimes contradictory semantics, recognised that reasonable and intelligent people find themselves led to a belief that there must be some sort of designer of the world, and shortly before his death he added a passage to his work indicating that the cause and causes of order in the universe probably bear some remote analogy to human intelligence. (Cited in the *Pimlico History of Western Philosophy* 1999, p.459)

It is not difficult to see that those theorists who deny the idea of a wise creator find themselves in a catch twenty-two situation in that while being forced to admit that life on earth is extremely complex and intelligently ordered and can be investigated intelligently, but they have nothing of any intelligent order producing significance to explain the ordered complexity of anything and have to revert to explanations that are both irrational and ridiculous. Thus, we would argue that as Hodgson expresses it: "The resort to God is not a cloak to cover ignorance but the logical consequences of the nature of our knowledge and the nature of the universe as discovered by empirical science." (Hodgson 1994, p.193)

An evolutionist's last line of defence is to explain life on earth in terms of natural selection, but natural selection is anything but natural if behind if there is no order producing power behind it to bring into being the vast complexity of life on earth. Referring to the first primitive life forms that appeared on the earth without any previous history or means to explain them Richard Dawkins writes: "It is as though they were just planted there, without any evolutionary history. Not surprisingly Philip Johnson argues that the Cambrian explosion is the greatest problem facing the theory of Darwinianism." (Cited in Blanchard 2000, p.96) But this affirmation is only wrong because it is not the only and greatest problem facing Darwin evolution, because how ingenious mechanisms of order producing genius kept appearing within evolution as if out of nowhere to carry on producing increasingly more ordered and complex living things is an ongoing mystery of life producing creativity that has never been satisfactorily explained. Nor has it been explained how out of the raw chemicals of the earth physical in its form and inanimate in nature each life-form has its own unique nature of being as a living entity and is not like some wound up clock motor inanimate in its form and featureless in nature.

Aristotle regarded his intellectual pursuits as moments of happiness that accompanies a god's activity of contemplation: "The kind that surpasses all others in every respect because it nurtures the more divine element in humanity." (Cited in the *Pimlico History of Western Philosophy* 1999, p.65)

Chapter 2
Deserting the Ground of Rational Thinking

It could be said that the mind is the ground of our knowing and reason is the basis of sound understanding. The universe is set up on the basis of reason and that is why scientists have been so successful in their investigations of the universe and everything in it. Even David Hume to whom many cynics and sceptics take cover accepted that causality was the cement of the universe and is what holds the world together and enables us to investigate it intelligently. It could be said that we in our own right are microcosms of that intelligence that ordered us and all things into existence. But it is argued by some that to postulate the idea of God as the origin of intelligent life on earth solves nothing because it leaves God unexplained. But why must we be able to explain God as the creator of all things before we can conclude that we need such a creator to bring into existence things we can clearly see as rational beings are extremely complex and intelligently ordered and that goes beyond our human comprehension to fully understand?

We as human beings ordered intelligently to reason intelligently have every right, and are morally obliged, to conclude that an ordered world full of intelligently ordered things owe their existence to a cause sufficient to explain the ordered and living sum of their existence. Therefore, we whose existence gives clear evidence of a wise creator do not have to explain our creator for us to know that such a creator exists any more than we have to witness and understand everything about the working of our car and the factory in which it was produced to conclude that it was built in a factory by means of purposeful intelligence by a manufacturer with the intelligence and knowhow to produce it. So we need a cause that can explain all that we predicate of ourselves as complex living entities both biologically and ontologically with an ordered brain and a living self-conscious mind that necessitates a living life producing cause at work in the universe.

As human beings ordered intelligently to think intelligently, we can clearly see that all that exists far exceeds our finite intelligence to fully understand and that we must therefore, of logical necessity, apportion the ordered sum of all things to a cause that far exceeds our own intelligence, a first and sufficient cause who can explain the ordered and living sum of all things. We cannot explain God, but as rational beings we can see the need for such a being who can explain what we know needs to be explained and that exceeds our ability to fully understand. So it is quite ridiculous, therefore, to reject the existence of a wise creator because we cannot explain Him. It is a bit like refusing to accept the existence of computers because we do not fully understand how they work.

Emanuel Kant has rightly argued that cause and effect relations are absolute and eternal and cannot be reversed, and this applies to life on earth because our maker is not the author of confusion but of an ordered world and a sound mind, intelligent beings ordered intelligently to think intelligently who can see clearly that we live in an ordered world that stretches beyond our own finite mind to fully comprehend. So when our finite human intelligence runs out of road we are looking into an infinity of wisdom beyond our finite minds to fully understand. This is where we bow our heads in thankful wonder and stand in awe at the ineffable reality of all things, and if we love life give praise to Him who granted it to us. Peter Hodgson rightly argues that the order producing power of nature can be regarded as a process of "God's self-revelation." (Cited in Hodgson 1994, p.193) The only alternative is to argue that nothing brought into existence the intelligently ordered sum of all that exists which is not a rational statement and no explanation for the ordered sum of anything and is an insult to that intelligence from which we have come and to whom we owe our very existence.

Scientific theories are not wild speculations we are informed: they are grounded in careful observation, controlled experiment, rational deduction to determine the nature their working and to come to some appreciation of the nature and their origin, How is it then that when scientists by careful analysis discover something of the ingenious means by which intelligent life was ordered into existence they seem to refuse to apportion this to a process of intelligent design or to an intelligent and sufficient cause of any kind? They seem to think that when they have discover how something operates or came into being that this is one less thing we need God to explain. But this is nothing but vain presumption born out of prejudice. Scientists may well by means of their intelligence discover how different things operate and even came into being, but they did not bring into existence those things so they still need to be explained by means other than themselves.

This is not merely very poor science it is a sloppy piece of thinking totally lacking in appreciation for that cause that brought into being an ordered world full of intelligently ordered living things. As we have seen Shaun Carroll in his book *The Big Picture on the Origins of Life, Meaning and the Universe* accepts that while he admits that cause and effect relationships are now a present fact, we do not need to apportion these order producing relationships of vast order producing significance to an intelligent and sufficient cause of any kind:

> The secret here is to accept that such questions may or may or may not have answers. We have every right to ask them, but we have no right to at all to demand an answer that will satisfy us. We have to be open to the possibility that they are brute facts, and that's just how things are.
> [Carroll 2017, p.45]

This explanation may satisfy an idiot or a monkey, but not a rational human being endowed with the attribute of an intelligent mind who knows as surely as reason can teach it to them that effects have causes commensurate with the nature of the effect in question. Its only when it looks like God is the cause that theorists begin to have problems was cause and effect thinking. For everything else there is a cause with Carroll arguing that cause, everything else Carroll therefore, couldn't be more wrong when he argues that: "There are good reasons why things often seem to happen for reasons – and also reasons why that's not a bedrock principle." (Carroll 1917, p.42) Carroll is obviously trying desperately to squirm out the principle of sufficient reason (or sufficient cause) to a world where there are no causal foundations, a 'just is' world of magic, myths and fairy-tale stories in which the universe and everything it are just brute facts that mean nothing and come from nothing. This represents a zombie type of science.

But when it comes man made things it is a different story – thus Carroll writes: "Purpose and meaning in life arise through fundamentally human acts of creation rather than being derived from anything outside ourselves." Carol 2017, p.11) But do intelligent human beings who are capable of such acts of creativity not also need to be explained. And do we not represent a creative force in their own right that point to a first cause, an uncaused cause that can explain the ordered complexity of all that exists. A living life creating cause of whom we are

38

a living finite reflection? Reason argues that this is the case, while Carroll is really presupposing the very thing that needs to be explained.

Carroll goes on to argue that we have no reason to believe that reason is a bedrock principle governing the universe. But if reason is not a bedrock principle governing the universe by what principle do intelligently ordered things appear on the earth when reason dictates that such must be explained in terms of an intelligent and sufficient cause? If the universe and everything in it did not operate to reason and the principle of sufficient cause all and everything would be in a state of perpetual confusion and we as human beings would be a mindless extension of that confusion.

When we desert the ground of rational thinking, we can apportion everything to anything or nothing at all. This may seem to be a good way to avoid the idea of a wise creator whom we as moral being may have reason to fear, but this is to bury one's head in the sand for fear of facing up to the truth of what is going on in the real world governed by reason and operating to an order producing intelligence of immense and profound order producing significance. If reason did not underlie the universe we would be a confused mess: or rather, we would never have come into existence at all. The only things that might have come into existence outside of an intelligent and sufficient cause are people like Carroll because they seem to be erratic, confused and all over the place when it comes explaining intelligent life on earth. Even when we are unable to explain the precise origin of certain complex effects, we as rational beings still know both intuitively and rationally as surely as reason can teach it to us that it owes its existence to a cause fit to explain it consistent with all that we predicate of it.

So when theorists fail to apportion effects to appropriate and sufficient causes, they are running against the logic of rational thinking into a bog of mindless confusion. Such order producing effects could not possibly be apportioned to luck or an endless stream of happy coincidences from what before was a state of primordial disorder. And we know that things are intelligently ordered when we can reason intelligently about them, while we cannot make an intelligently coherent statement without engaging our powers of reason and if we were to stop using it will be a sad day for mankind.

Bertrand Russell argued that: "The reason that physicists have ceased to look for causes is due to the fact, there are no such things. The law of causality, I believe, is a relic of a bygone age." So what then are scientists doing when they engage in science? Moreover, if Russell is right this would render all scientists redundant, all policemen out of a job and all inventors' very poor people indeed. Papineau bringing us back down to earth again rightly argues that: "However, we should not assume that because science does not mention something, it doesn't exist …" The notion of cause cannot be eliminated from our understanding of the world. (Cited in Papineau 2009, p.22 and 22) Why are we might ask, are some scientists so afraid to apportion intelligently ordered things to intelligent and sufficient causes when this is the very thing they are getting paid for? The writer would suggest that it is because they are trying to avoid something, namely that when they do so they are immediately confronted with the logic of a wise creator to whom they owe everything and expects us to be faithful to that which we have been ordered to be. God is the elephant in the science lab that many are trying to avoid.

Shaun Carroll goes on to argue with respect to cause and effect relationships: "The secret here is to accept that such questions *may or may not have answers.*" (Carroll 2017, p.45) How very convenient and appallingly naive this statement really is and is clearly an attempt to evade the obvious to avoid the inevitable. The brute fact is that the universe and everything in it are intelligently ordered and this is why we can as rational beings make sense of it, intelligently investigate it and increasingly understand the ingeniously ordered nature of it where effects have causes and are not just brute facts with no significance, but brute facts that need to be explained and be attributed to causes that can explain them. It seems that some scientists who regard themselves as so academically smart and intellectually accomplished are operating to a contradictory agenda that originates from a deeply prejudiced mind.

This broader ontology typically associated with atheism is naturalism writes Carroll. (Carroll 1988, p.11) But it is natural for a combine harvester to thresh corn and it is natural for something like wheat to exist that needs to be threshed, but both the wheat and the combine harvester still need to be explained and this is done by explaining the factory in which the harvester was produced and a most creative mind that put the order producing information into the wheat in the form of DNA to produce ever more wheat. So what is natural in this case seems to be supernatural, a creative mind operating effectively on the earth to bring order out of chaos and breathe life into inanimate matter.

The brute fact that we as rational beings do not merely have the right to ask as to the origin of the universe and intelligent life on earth, but the right to demand an explanation sufficient to do justice the ordered and living sum of all that exists. If everything in it is but brute facts and owes their origin to nothing of any order producing significance why does Carroll take some 430 pages writing about nothing when there is not a lot one can say about nothing. But if such theorists were to erect a chicken-coop in their back garden they would feel greatly offended if we were to suggest that it was a brute fact that needed no explanation.

Moreover, empirically based scientific facts no matter how complex cannot explain the conscious reality of a living mind endowed with qualitative attributes of being by which and through which we live life and meaningfully operate in the world of physics. Consciousness in not an empirically based phenomenon that we can define, verify or detect by our senses, we cannot see it smell it, touch it, taste it, hear it or taste it. We cannot define it or identify it as we would a physical object, no matter where we look in our physical body we cannot find it even in the neurons of the brain, yet it is sacred, sensitive, the control centre of our existence, endowed with a will that controls our actions, feelings, desires, hopes, and aspirations, the very essence that constitutes our personage in other words sentience. A world of conscious being not quantifiable in physical terms, a mystery of all mysteries that takes us beyond the world of our senses, a body of knowledge and understanding that is me. Embodied spirits a sacred soul, and as one has well said: "What shall a man give in exchange for his own soul."

What we must do to be fair to ourselves is to take the sum of who we are and experience ourselves to be, body, mind and spirit and apply rational thinking to it and ask ourselves the question, from what kind of cause have we come that can explain all that we experience ourselves to be? To join spiritual being to rational thinking and gain some approximation of the brute fact might as to who we are and from whence we have come. This would seem to be a zombie type kind of thinking unworthy of the term science and to live life behind a wall of ignorance for fear of coming face to face with the logic of a wise creator. Carroll wants to stop where he wants to stop and leave the order producing laws of nature and the life generating power of evolution hanging precariously from an exceedingly long series of skyhooks.

Those who like to boast in the reason-based nature of their evolutionary paradigm in the end have to turn to the beggarly elements of luck, chance and an endless stream of happy coincidences because they have no other means to explain the ordered complexity of anything. In the world of crime detection as few as three coincidences could mark someone out as a person of interest in relation to a crime, and if there were four or five coincidences that tie the suspect to the crime this may well be sufficient to convict. But with some evolutionary theorists the order producing coincidences go endlessly on within an never-ending stream of order producing efficiency to fill the whole earth with complex living things and some do not suspect for a moment that this might have something to do with an order producing intelligence of vast life producing significance at work in the universe.

Therefore, those who boast that their theory is based on reason will do everything in their power to avoid it when it suits their ill-motivated prejudices against the idea of sufficient cause especially when that cause begins to look like the work of a wise creator. In this, the rational cause and effect logic of rational thinking is abandoned and lady luck seems to be working overtime in a frantic endeavour to do what luck by its very nature could not possibly do. What we end up with is a science or religion in the science of life, with physics being the junior partner in this relationship.

We would suggest that the unwillingness to consider in holistic terms the implications of the deep realities of our being is based in no small way to prejudice because such people are not willing to consider a theory that is fully consistent with the rudiments of rational thinking until by a process of mindless reductionism life is explained away and we are left with the shell and no substance. Then we wonder why life is increasingly regarded as cheap and violence for some against the human person is little more than a physical act against an accidental conglomeration of physics that fell into place by a long series of happy coincidences. It is surely unscientific to attribute the order producing laws of nature to a host of unexplained brute facts and happy coincidences that produced an intelligently ordered world and then filled it with intelligently ordered living things.

So for some all that exists is an endless stream of free lunches the size of the universe and everything in it, but free lunches of this order producing magnitude cannot be regarded as free, there is a price to pay by way of sufficient cause but those who refuse to pay could be regarded as free-loaders looking for something for nothing and then calling it science. For scientists to begin their search for the truth about the origin of an ordered world full of what we know to be extremely complex living things by presupposing that such things cannot possibly have anything to do with an order producing intelligence tells us more about their biased preconceptions than their ability to think rationally and reason causally. How do such theorists explain their own intelligence if they were not ordered intelligently to think intelligently?

Henry Plotkin argues in his book *Evolution in Mind* that: "Scepticism about the strength of natural selection abounded" and this was because we as human beings who pride ourselves in their rational capacity find it difficult to believe in: "a theory in which chance plays such a central role, and was always going to run into strong opposition." (Plotkin 1998, p.26f) In other words, chance doesn't sit well with an intelligent mind as the means to explain the existence of exceedingly complex and intelligently ordered things. Moreover, what is the point in doing science if scientists are not willing to draw logical conclusions about the ordered sum of complex things and apportion them to a necessary and sufficient cause? Such scientists are stuck in their own reductionist delusion and have forsaken the ground of rational thinking altogether in which effects have causes and the cause in terms of intelligent life on earth must be sufficient to explain all that we predicate of the effects produced both physically and metaphysically, biologically and ontologically, empirically and spiritually. And even if the incremental steps are so small and gradual they cannot be discerned with the naked eye, nevertheless when added together are capable of producing the ordered sum of the living the whole whatever that whole may be from a worm to a human being.

If we were to ask an average member of the public what evolution is and what is its significance in terms of cause, they would very likely answer by saying that living things evolved so slowly and imperceptibly over such an extremely long period of time this means that life does not need to be explained in terms of an intelligent and sufficient cause or credited to the work of a wise creator. In other words, everything just tumbled into place over such a long period of time until the first living things appeared on the earth like some form of powerful enchantment and kept on becoming ever more complex by what theorists like Richard Dawkins describe as a sequence of events "of immense improbability on a colossal scale."

But there seems for some that there is no point in which the odds of producing a living creature like ourselves by chance that the odds become so utterly improbable the idea becomes completely ridiculous. Such sink into a kind of base superstition ever propagated by a prejudiced mind to avoid the idea of a wise creator because as moral beings their conscience is pricking lest God comes looking for them. And as we shall see even Richard Dawkins admits: "that we can have a little luck but not too much," but with the standard theory of evolution the luck just goes endlessly on with no point where it must be considered in which luck becomes so utterly ridiculous we must consider an alternative explanation that can explain what luck by its very nature could not possibly explain. But for some the process of evolution was so slow and gradual the idea of sufficient cause has been lost in translation so that we have a world filled with intelligently ordered things animate and inanimate that came into existence by means that are so utterly ludicrous it becomes a form of base superstition.

Natural selection was said to be the means by which evolution operated to produce intelligent life on earth, but this meant nothing in real terms because it has never been explained how natural selection actually operated to bring into existence the vast and ever increasing complexity of intelligent life on earth. We might consider a factory in which things like combine harvesters are being produced by an ever so slow process of assembly, but we would never consider that because of this that the process is not operating to a process of intelligent ordering put in place by a wise and purposeful manufacturer. Should we slow the process down so that it took a hundred thousand years to produce one combine harvester, we would still say that it was a process of intelligent ordering as opposed to process of blind randomness even if the process was moving so slowly we could scarcely discern any sign of design. We would judge the process by what is being produced in the light of the total disorder that once existed.

Such a machine would have up a million parts counting every part big and small and every nut and bolt. The odds of this process of assembly falling into place by chance are virtually incalculable. Something of these massive odds can be better understood when we know that for 100 things to fall into place by chance to produce something of some ordered significance are 10 with 158 noughts after it which is a number so utterly vast we can scarcely conceive it. And yet a single living cell has millions of parts and the human body is made up of some forty trillion cells each a world of complexity in their own right. So evolution by natural selection is only natural when all the ingenious means are in place and operating effectively to produce the vast complexity of different living things.

Moreover, it would be an exercise in utter futility for scientists by means of intelligence to go looking for such causes to explain intelligent life on earth where no intelligently constituted causes exist. If we were to blindly strike the keys of our typewriter, how long would it take before we would get a well-written book and eventually get something like the Encyclopaedia Britannica. But one shouldn't waste their time trying it because it has been well and truly tried by giving monkeys typewriters and it simply doesn't work, about half a line was as far as they got every now and again before things regressed back into nothing but gobbledygook. In fact, evolutionary theorists take for granted the raw and varied complexity of chemicals as found in the Periodic Table out of which different components of a biological body are formed and then fitted together to form the ordered, intricate and varied complexity of the living whole. As we now know, DNA operating in conjunction with RNA is the means by which this is accomplished and which have within themselves the necessary coded information of how to turn the different chemicals into different biological components of living things. As Michael Behe, whose expertise in biochemistry prompts him to unequivocally state that biochemically macroevolution is impossible outside of a process of intelligent ordering of the most incredibly sophisticated kind? This we will be examining more closely in a later chapter.

Therefore, we have a universe set up with all the necessary and immense complex mix of chemicals that when ordered precisely together can to produce the biological complexity of different living things so that the cosmic stage was set up with the necessary means and materials that when ordered appropriately could produce the proteins that make up the biological complexity of intelligent life on earth. Moreover, just as intelligently ordered effects require intelligent and sufficient causes, so intelligently constituted causes that produce intelligently ordered things represent the working of an antecedent intelligence set up and operating efficiently to produce intelligent life on earth, pointing us to the idea of a wise creator.

But according to some scientists, a chanced upon Big Bang happened some thirteen or so billion years ago that just happened to have all the necessary raw materials in the form of a rich and varied mixture of chemicals to produce all that now exists, and that there was such a rich concentration of these chemicals on the earth to bring about the right conditions to sustain life should it ever appear, and then within the earth different mechanisms and means appeared like mini factories of vast order producing efficiency appeared set up and equipped with the necessary means and mechanisms to bring into existence all manner of living things out of the chemicals of the earth, and then these different things of different kinds came to life with their own nature of being to fill the whole earth with a wide variety of living things. And then mankind the most intelligent and sophisticated of the species by means of intelligent investigation increasingly discovered some of the ingenious means by which nature operated to accomplish this process of order producing ingenuity many decided that as moral beings they wanted to be beholding to no one and accountable to no one claimed the glory for their ability to discover something of how life was ordered so spectacularly into existence, but decided to give no credit whatsoever to that cause from whence they and all things had come. In professing themselves wise they had become fools.

The Greek philosopher Plato referred to the source of cosmic order as *Nous;* that is a creative mind behind the phenomenal complexity of the natural order. Michael Behe in his book Darwin's Black Box writes about the irreducible complexity of a human cell which biological evolution has failed to explain in terms of sufficient cause and which is far beyond the possibility of blind chance to explain.(Behe, p.34) Some of these ideas show just how far some who boast in their rationally based theory of origins have drifted from the cause and effect logic of rational thinking and by tampering with the evidence they go onto talk about how ultimately nothing produced the ordered sum of everything. We now know that even the simplest living cells are extremely complex in their own right, but some have this peculiar idea that if you leave primordial chaos lying around long enough it will somehow morph into extremely complex living organisms made up of trillions of living ordered and integrated cells that are not just indescribably complex but consciously alive.

Matthew Alper accepts that: "One of the fundamental principles of science is that every action has an effect": and "This in turn means that every effect has a cause." However, if every effect has a cause what is the cause of those order-producing effects that combine so ingeniously to produce intelligent life on earth in ever increasing degrees of ordered sophistication? Alper goes on to affirm that at the age of twenty-one he decided to place his faith in the physical sciences because he had plenty of evidence for a physical universe but nothing whatsoever to believe in any spiritual reality. (Alper 2006, p.22–24)But who does he think he is, is he nothing more than a complex configuration of inanimate matter? Is he not in fact a living conscious being of some considerable intelligence and spiritual significance and life-defining complexity? If he is not, how is he going to intelligently engage in science and draw the necessary conclusions about things perceived and then goes on to write a book about it?

And if he insists in pursuing this empirically based way of thinking he really doesn't qualify as a human being at all and is devoid of that which is needed to be a scientist which is the spiritual quest of an inquisitive mind for knowledge and understanding, a being endowed with intelligence that if he but would listen to it insists on explaining intelligently ordered things in terms of an intelligent and sufficient cause and living things in terms of a living life producing cause. By holding exclusively to the world of physics and rejecting the genuineness of the life world with its spiritual reality of being and intelligent attributes of understanding, he is left with nothing wherewithal to engage in science or to draw the necessary conclusions with respect to the ordered complexity of his own existence and different complex things so perceived. This is the scientist that forgets to take account of himself, and who fail to realise the significance of what he is doing when he engages in science!

Or if Alper is devoid of a self-conscious living spirit and limits reality to empirically based physics says to a girl friend or wife 'I love you' he is only going through the motions with no genuine feelings and saying no more than 'I love you with all my blood-pump' which is hardly going to impress. So is Alper a physical entity dead to the world of the spirit and a chanced upon object the significance of which would make him something akin to an inanimate object? It seems that Alper needs is to be introduced to himself as a living self-conscious being of vast ontological significance, and cannot hid from himself forever and might waken up one day to find himself confronted with that life generating cause that ordered him into existence and to give account of himself as a moral being. But like Adam and Eve he is in hiding not only from God but from himself.

Love, joy, peace, goodness, hopes, aspirations, of different kinds as well as moral being are all spiritual attributes within which we live and move and have our being and through which we can relate in kind to other living people and to Him who endowed us with these attributes of being. As the effects are so the cause will be, we are spiritual being of profound life defining substance and significance with and different attributes of being and we must use them all if we are to know and experience all that we were made and meant to know as human beings. A.R. Peacock and P. Davies argue, physics and chemistry cannot give a full account of living things. (Cited in Thompson 2000, p.53) But not only can physics and chemistry not explain life as we experience it to be, far less can it explain the coming into existence of conscious life by randomly moving inanimate matter about.

When we understand evolution for what it really is we can identify it as the way a wise creator operated to produce intelligent life on earth with the whole earth being set up like a great cosmic factory with all the necessary means and mechanisms to produce intelligent life on earth. But the process of evolution is so methodically slow some evolutionary theorists don't seem to have noticed this yet and think that everything just tumbled into place by an endless stream of happy coincidences which is neither scientifically credible or a logically possible which turns this kind of science into a form of cosmic farce and scientists who think this way operating within what is a monumental contradiction in terms.

In fact, the idea that luck could produce a world full of extremely complex and intelligently living things is much worse than those who in past ages attributed the laws of nature to the mythical gods of ancient world which, although were poor explanations, were at least an attempt by those who at least knew that we need an explanation for different effects and occurrences. But modern scientists know full well how incredibly complex life is right down to a single living cell but go on attributing it all to luck leaving us drowning in a sea of superstition.

Moreover, many scientists are so completely naïve they believe that when they explain something of how nature operates and life on earth came into existence that this is one less thing we need God to explain which means that God becomes the God of the gaps. But this is only so much presumptive nonsense because while scientists by means of intelligent investigation can discover something of how life on earth came into existence scientists had nothing to do with it, these order producing means were put in place by someone other than themselves, for them as intelligent beings to investigate and discover how incredibly complex life really is and how wise is the creator of all things. The honour for the existence of intelligent life on earth which scientists now have the privilege of investigating belong to another much wiser than them, but some theorists mix themselves up with him.

So when scientists uncover the laws that hold the universe together and bring into existence intelligent life on earth they are but discovering ingenious order producing laws that someone has put in place for them as intelligent beings to discover and which when added together represent a process of order producing ingenuity indicative of the work of a most wise creator which warrants a humble and appropriate response from us. Even the intelligence by which scientists use to investigate intelligently ordered things in an intelligently ordered world is granted to them by that cause that ordered them into existence so they can neither take the credit for their own existence or those things they successfully investigate by means of their God-given intelligence.

Matthew Alperagain argues that science is able to account for the process of evolution operating over "three and a half billion years without the aid or assistance of any transcendental force or being: *The origin of evolution without God!*" (Alper 2006, p.45) But if scientists by using their God-given intelligence can come to some approximation of how evolution operates to bring into exist intelligent life on earth, then the same intelligence demands of us, and them, that we apportion this process to an intelligent and sufficient cause of such order producing magnitude it is synonymous with that of a wise creator. Or is he wiser than that cause which not only created him but all things. The very laws of nature come alive within us in that which we experience ourselves to be and some haven't the savvy to appreciate what they have got and the humility to say thanks. What Alper is saying is like going into a factory in which something like motor cars are produced and investigating the order producing means involved and then saying that now we know how motor cars are produced we do not need to be explained in term of a wise manufacturer and perhaps so arrogant as to think we do not have to pay the price for the privilege of owing one.

One thing is certain, we are never going to produce an intelligently ordered living thing by randomly moving inanimate matter about should shuffle thus for all eternity. A blind and blundering watchmaker operating to no purpose is about the best some evolutionists can come up with to explain the vast complexity of intelligent life on earth. In fact, the ingenious mechanisms evolutionary scientists now introduce to explain intelligent life on earth represent a process of the most exquisite design and God-like creativity so that some end up denying the very things they are describing. So Alper's claim is just a naïve piece of wishful thinking wholly divorced from the logic of rational thinking.

Life must first be intelligently ordered before it could be intelligently investigated, and as we human beings had nothing to do with it someone much wiser than ourselves ordered it into existence for us as intelligent beings to investigate, appreciate and enjoy. This means that Alper's form of science ultimately explains nothing and in fact becomes the very antithesis of an intelligent explanation for intelligent life on earth. Only theists can be good evolutionists because only they have the perfect explanation for what is otherwise an intractable problem for those who have nothing to explain the ordered complexity of anything in a universe they insist is empty of intelligence.

As Leibniz argues: "Nothing happens without a cause" and this is a fundamental prerequisite for rational thinking and an essential criteria for doing science! To get some 40 to 60 trillion living cells ordered together to operate as a single unit of organic complexity is no mean feat especially when we remember that evolutionists have not explained the origin of a single one of these exceedingly small but complex living cells let alone how they all came together to produce the ordered and integrated complexity of a complex living whole. In fact, some scientists do not seem to understand that the moment they begin to investigate by means of intelligence the world and everything in it, they are presupposing that the world and everything in it is intelligently ordered or it could not be sensibly investigated or intelligently understood by us.

It is suggested that some people prefer a supernatural explanation for life on earth but that science sticks to naturalistic explanations. But what when the so-called naturalistic explanations clearly indicate that behind the ordering into existence of intelligent life on earth there are ingenious order producing laws of nature that together represent a process of the most exquisite design behind which we have a right to assume is a super-natural mind of God-like intelligence. Therefore, that which is natural seems by all accounts represents a process of order producing ingenuity and life producing creativity. And when this process of life producing creativity passes beyond human understanding as it undoubtedly does, it represents that which is indeed supernatural beyond the finite mind to fully understand.

This is possibly why Paul Davies a thoroughgoing evolutionist has suggested that: "... science offers a surer path to God than religion." (Cited in Strobel 2004, p.286) While the philosopher John Locke insisted, that we need a mind first way of thinking because only an intelligent mind of massive order producing proportions could initiate an elaborate process of intelligent ordering that fills the whole earth with enormously complex and intelligently ordered living things.

Some so-called philosophers like to argue that to apportion life on earth to a pre-existing intelligence we have to explain that vast series of causes, which they liken to turtles piled on top of one-another which means we have explained nothing because we still have to explain the turtles. But we do not have a long line of causes leading nowhere we need to postulate a first and sufficient cause that able to explain all the order producing events that brings into being all that now exists. So the turtle analogy is seriously flawed as is the thinking of all those who fail to link all the effects produced in a world of vast complexity to as intelligent and sufficient cause. Theists, therefore, are the only true scientists! Moreover, we as the creature do not need to be able to explain all that our creator is to know that we need such a creator to explain the order sum of all things. But what arrogance to suppose that we as creature can stand in judgment over their creator when it is much more likely that it is our creator who will ultimately stand in judgement over us as the moral and intelligently ordered beings he has created us to be.

If we want to produce something like a cement mixer, we have to have someone with the creative vision to conceive of such a thing, an intelligent mind to work out the means to produce it and then the ability to order the necessary means together with great precision before we have our cement mixer. In terms of living things such a process represents an intelligent mind-first process in the form of a wise creator who provides the necessary materials in form of chemicals and then puts in place with the necessary means to order them all together produce intelligently ordered living things from what before was once a disordered composition of chemicals. If we were to produce a car in an instant as by some great magic, we would undoubtedly be hailed as a wonder worker endowed with great powers, but if we were to build a factory and by a slow and meticulous process of assembly produced many thousands of cars over many years this would still represent a process of order producing genius emanating from the working of a most creative mind. Moreover, time cannot get evolutionists off the hook because no matter how long we stretch the process out we still need an intelligent mind operating to the necessary means to produce intelligently ordered and extremely complex living things.

Moreover, it is rather naïve for scientists to insist that different commodities produced by human beings from a bailer to a ball point pen must invariably be credited to an intelligent and sufficient cause in the form of an intelligent mind and then believe that those people with the intelligence to produce such things and much more besides have their origin in something as utterly ridiculous as nothing or to a mindless process of meaningless irrelevance. Since the beginning of the earth some four and half billion or so years ago to the present day, not a single sweaty mouse, a paper clip, or a safety pin came into existence until someone with the necessary intelligence and purpose of mind acted to produce such things, even though all the basic raw materials were available on the earth to produce such things.

It is utterly inconceivable that we need an intelligent mind and intelligent means to produce such simple things out of the raw chemicals of the earth but we in which every cell of our bodies is immensely more complex than the most sophisticated things made by human beings came into existence by a process that has nothing to do with intelligence or a sufficient cause of any kind. It is a generally accepted fact that only life can produce life, or as one scientific description goes: "Modern biology teaches that living things can only arise from other living things by a process of reproduction." (Cited in Silver 1998, p.239) Again Professor Brian Silver points out that: "Intelligent beings can purposively bring together chosen chemicals under carefully controlled conditions, but this is very different from accounting for the *spontaneous* formation of living systems in an inanimate world empty of intelligence." (Silver, 1998, p.139)Bill Bryson points out that even a single amoeba cell has 400 billion bits of genetic information which is enough information to fill 80 books of 500 pages each the odds of their coming together by chance are so utterly inconceivable it is reckoned to be completely impossible. (Bryson 2003, p.366)

Living cells can replicate in order to perpetuate their existence, which is something of such wonder we call it a miracle adds Bill Bryson. It is like producing a motor car with the ability to replicate its own existence and for that replicated car to do the same and so and so forth. As Richard Dawkins is forced to admit: "To get an idea of the size of these protein machines, each one is made of about 6000 atoms, which is very large by molecular standards. There are about a million of these large pieces of apparatus in a cell, and there are about 2,000 different kinds of them, each kind specialised to do a particular operation in the biological chemical factory." (Dawkins 1988, p.121)

So at the root of evolution we have a marvel of order producing wonder and life producing profundity operating like a most ingenious life producing process more inspiringly ingenious than the most ingenious man-made factory admits Richard Dawkins. While Nick Lane reminds us that we need a continuous flux (or flow) of energy to promote self-organisation and: "This continuous flux of energy is precisely what is missing from the primordial soup. There is nothing in the soup that can drive the formation of the dissipative structures that we call cells, nothing to make these cells grow and divide, and come alive, all in the absence of enzymes that channel and drive metabolism." (Lane 2016, p.95)

So living things do not only need order producing means but immense amounts of order producing energy to order them all together to produce the ordered sum of the living whole. Brian Silver goes on to argue that: "It stretches even the credulity of a materialistic abiogenesis fanatic to believe that proteins and nucleotides (DNA and RNA) persistently emerged simultaneously and at the same time within the primeval soup." (Silver 1998, p.347) Proteins are large organic compounds that go to makeup the biological complexity of a physical body, but if primitive cells contained only proteins they would have no future because proteins cannot replicate and for this we need nucleotides (DNA and RNA) which are independent complex systems needed for replication to take place. Silver goes on to point out that: "I do not know the origin of life, those of us who hold, like I do, that life emerged spontaneously from inanimate matter are, we must admit, at a distinctly embarrassing disadvantage: we have not come up with a convincing mechanism for abiogenesis." (Silver 1998, p.339)

Silver goes on to argue that dead matter cannot become living without coming under the influence of matter previously alive. "This seems to be as sure a teaching of science as the law of gravitation … life must have been in the universe for all past time, either that or we must turn to the finger of God in the Sistine Chapel, and after reading this chapter you may well conclude that this is our only hope." (Silver 1998, p.39)But of course, many evolutionists are not willing to admit to any such problems with the standard theory of evolution and pretend that their theory of evolution is so logical and compelling, simple and inevitable when outside of an intelligent and sufficient cause it most certainly is not. For this reason, the academic Os Guinness reproaches some Christians for being anti-intellectual and not engaging the modern world of atheistic materialism on rational terms to point out the wide range of inconsistencies that lie at the heart of their interpretation of evolution. And for this he argues: "we are beginning to pay the price." (Cited in Noll 1995, p.23)

When we apply the logic of rational thinking to evolution, we find ourselves up to our necks in a process of intelligent ordering behind which there must of logical necessity be a most ingeniously creative mind operating to achieve a preconceived purpose. Moreover, no matter what way anti-design evolutionists and reductive materialists try to explain how evolution works outside of a process of intelligent design they invariably find that it is riddled with contradictions, confused thinking and explanations that simply do not logically stack up and some of these we have already pointed out and others we will be examining in later chapters. So what is the source of this life producing genius emanating so prodigiously from within evolution, because until this is explained nothing is ultimately explained?

But many anti-design evolutionists need to throw off the yoke of rational thinking in order to avoid the idea of sufficient cause which when reason is applied looks suspiciously like the one theists call God. We can see through our physical eyes and we can see through the eyes of our understanding operating to the principle of sufficient cause which demands that intelligently ordered things must be attributed to intelligent and sufficient causes. While those who abandon the cause and effect logic of rational thinking are really deceiving themselves and are liable to believe anything. Such people can see through their physical eyes but the eyes of their understanding are tight shut so that in seeing they do not understand and would prefer to remain cosmologically blind than to see that which they seem determined to avoid.

One W. K. Clifford, for instance, has argued that it is always wrong to believe that which goes beyond the evidence and gives the example of a ship owner who fails to ensure that his ships are seaworthy because he hasn't adequately inspected them to know that this is indeed the case. So if one of his ships sinks as a result of his negligence the ship owner is guilty of any lives lost as a result. This thinking is often extended to matters of religion in which it is wrong to believe in God without the relevant and appropriate evidence.

However, apart from the fact that this wrongly implies that there is no evidence for the existence of a wise creator: here we have an illustration some use to deny the existence of a wise creator where they believe there is no such evidence for such a creator who go on to believe in a theory in which the ship of life on which they sail does not have as much as an intelligent designer, was thrown together by means of blind randomness, was launched without a sea-worthy certificate from a responsible body, has no competent captain at the helm, no rudder to guide it on the high seas and no lifeboats to rescue those that are left to drown as a result of such mindless stupidity and moral irresponsibility when boat sinks as it most surely will.

Charles Colson points out that nature becomes a substitute deity for Darwin as his son William could affirm: "As regards his respect for the laws of nature, it might be called reverence if not a religious feeling. No man could feel more intensely the vastness and inviolability of the laws of nature." (Cited in Colson 1999, p.95) In other words, the laws of nature represent the ingenious order producing means behind the order producing genius of evolution. But what kind of order producing genius does nature represent that it can bring into existence the immense complexity of life on earth complete with a conscious reality of being ordered intelligently to think intelligently? Is nature in this case not exactly like and synonymous with the one theists call God? Therefore, evolutionists cannot escape the idea of a wise creator by attributing life to the laws of nature when the laws of nature are operating to an order producing creativity indicative of the working of such a creator.

Darwin was not happy with the idea of randomness as an explanation for life on earth and in: "Notebook B sees Darwin cast in an almost Newtonian role, articulating how the elegance of natural laws acting in creation would glorify rather than diminish God." (Spencer 2009, p.52) But because Darwin could not see how nature was operating to produce intelligent life on earth he would sometimes express doubts about the kind of process evolution was, and it would be another century before the ingenious mechanism of DNA was discovered to show us how evolution actually operates to do what Darwin was at a total loss to explain and without which there would be no evolution at all.

Mary Shelly has said: "Supremely frightful would be the effect of any human endeavour to mock the stupendous mechanism of the creator of the world." What kind of science is it that some can assume that they are so highly intelligent and creatively ingenious and then regard the origin from which they have come of being so inherently stupid and singularly inept? What ultimate use is science if scientists haven't the wisdom to understand who they are and the significance of what they are doing when they engage in science, namely investigating by means of intelligence a world full of intelligently ordered things for which we need a most incredibly ingenious order producing cause?

Originally, the highest quality of man was seen in his ability to reason so that the more intelligently ordered scientists discovered the world and living things to be the more incredibly ingenious they believed the cause to be. Thomas Nagel may well argue that Darwin enabled secular culture to heave a great sigh of relief, by apparently providing a way to eliminate purpose, meaning and design as fundamental features of the world. But apart from the fact that science does no such thing, in his keenness to get rid of the idea of a wise creator Nagel doesn't seem to realise that his boast is wholly self-defeating and most depressingly self-negating, because it is utterly self-defeating to be happy to be living in a world that is devoid of all purpose, meaning and signs of design which would make life so utterly meaningless and futile that it were better we had not lived at all. Moreover, purpose, hope and understanding is found in that which we have been ordered to be and those hopes and aspirations programmed into our very being lift us above the world of a mundane materialism and mindless obscurantism.

Therefore, it is not too much to claim that the narrow and self-imposed limitations of an empirically based scientific worldview failed miserably to engage the larger intellectual challenge of life and how to explain it. This has profound implications for the relationship between science and religion in which religion has at its core the idea of a wise creator as the natural and logical explanation for the coming into existence of intelligent life on earth. The following is a description of how Cox and Forshaw describe the scientific method and how they look for a new law to explain how things operate: "First we guess it. Then we compare the consequences of the guess to see what would be implied if this law that we guessed is right. Then we compute the result of the computation to Nature with experiment or experience, compare it directly with observation to see if it works. If it disagrees with experiment it is wrong" (Cox and Forshaw, 2008, p.41)

But it is worth noting that the idea of intelligence, discernment, and reason based judgment is conspicuously absent from this analogy. Scientists do not begin their investigation of how nature works by a wild and thoughtless guessing game. It is always (consciously or unconsciously) an educated guess and then using their intelligence in relation to the subject matter under investigation and therefore devising an experiment that is going to determine by means of intelligence if their hypothesis about it is right or wrong. If our assessment about a particular subject matter is not arrived at by setting up of an appropriate experiment on the basis of reason and assessing the findings on the basis of reason, we are never going to come to a rational and appropriate understanding about anything. In fact, if this were not the case we might as well ask a zombie to do the guessing for us.

Scientists do not get Nobel prizes for being good at mindless guessing games they do so for being smart. Cox and Forshaw readily admit that Einstein as a scientist was a genius that will be remembered as long as there are humans in the universe, but one cannot be described as a genius by playing wild and mindless guessing games and not using our intelligence to draw rational conclusions about our scientific investigations.

But the above analysis is a subtle attempt to avoid the idea that things are intelligently ordered and to understand how nature operates to accomplish her ingenious designs we need to use our intelligence to draw logical conclusions with respect to our findings about those investigations. Van Huyssteen writes: "The crucial question now is whether theology in any way exhibits rationality comparable to the rationality of scientific reflection." (Van Huyssteen 1997, p.41) The fact is that theology by postulating the idea of a wise creator is not merely comparable to the rationality of good science, but supplies the rational basis that explains why there are so many intelligently ordered things for scientists to investigate and intelligent minds to do the investigating.

It is argued that Darwin's theory of natural selection proposed that that complex and intricate life forms could arise simply from blind processes of random variation plus the struggle for survival, without the need to posit any guiding intelligence. Here we have the magic formula which is supposed to explain how evolution works but when examined ultimately explains nothing. It goes without saying that a blind process of random variations within the context of primordial disorder could not possibly produce the ordered complexity of anything. Add the this struggle for survival referred to here which is wholly misplaced, because nothing could struggle to survive before it exists, and for inanimate matter to come alive and struggle to do anything we need a process of order producing intelligence and life-generating creativity before we have the survivable complexity of a living anything.

So, the above explanation is a kind of a mirage in which some think they see something which in this case is a successful struggle to survive when nothing of any order producing significance is taking according to them to explain the ordered complexity of anything and in the end represents nothing but of a piece of semantic confusion and wishful thinking. Moreover, Plato insightfully argued that truth is not introduced into the mind from without, but led out from within so that the mind finds revealed within itself knowledge both of its own nature and the world as revealed to the mind by means of our senses. Thus, the mind in all its fullness is the primary reality that determines how we perceive the world outside of us without which we would be conscious of nothing. Both these aspect of reality need to be explained in their own right, with the mind determining, not only that we perceive but how we perceive and understand different things perceived. While reason being part of that intrinsic nature of being demands of that we apportion to intelligently ordered things perceived to an intelligent and sufficient cause and our own reality through which we perceive being to living life producing cause. In this we have holistic and inclusive understanding of reality as it is for us as human beings.

But empirically based scientists who fail to take account of themselves have a totally distorted view of reality and often fail to use their rational faculty of being to assess the origin of things perceived and the mind through which they perceive them and so they have a totally distorted view of reality. So as Richard Tarnas writes: "Socrates resolute attention to his mind and soul, to moral virtue as well as intellectual truth, the world order was contracted and revealed." (Tarnas 1991, p.37) And in this we have an all-inclusive and comprehensive science of life.

Chapter 3
Evolution Lost to Reason

The philosopher Immanuel Kant has argued that the law of causality is eternal and absolute, and that self-conscious experience is the result of two separate faculties, the faculty of sensibility and the faculty of understanding. (Cited in Hundert 1990, p.22) In other words, our senses reveal to us the nature of the world of physics while our reality of being constitute who we are as those doing the perceiving with many different categories of understanding through which we understand, experience and interact with different beings and things perceived. Intelligence, and the cause and effect logic of rational thinking, is an essential part of those attributes of being we possess as a species, and when we fail to use it we are going to draw all the wrong conclusions about different things perceived and attribute everything to anything or to no cause at all.

Therefore, life comes as a package deal and determines how we understand and respond to things perceived operating to different attributes of understanding that constitute a different kind of reality altogether to that of empirically based physics. Empirically based physics join with a qualitative reality of being to constitute life as we experience it to be. However, our own reality of conscious being is even more profoundly real than objective facts about the world of physics and without which we could not consciously experience anything. All reality for us is a subjective experience because it determines that we perceive and how we experience the world of empirically based reality and how we respond in different to ways to different things perceived. From within our own reality of being, we make a life for ourselves that is consistent with different attributes of understanding in the pursuit of existential fulfilment, purpose, peace and happiness. Therefore, as the old adage goes – *"Cogito, ergo sum"* I think therefore I am.

Sean Carroll tries to make much of the fact no one has explained how mind and body coalesce, conform and interact one to the other. But one doesn't have to understand how mind and body operate together to form that united and interconnected reality we call life. We cannot without endangering our credibility, authenticity and even destiny as sentient beings deny who we experience ourselves to be. Physics by its very nature cannot explain who we experience ourselves to be, why we regard life as sacred, why we make laws and rules to protect life and punish those who wantonly take the lives of others? We have no greater proof of anything than who we experience ourselves to be in all its life defining fullness, and on it observation of and interaction with the physical world depends. To wilfully deny who we as conscious sentient beings constitutes a form of ontological suicide. It seems that Carroll would deconstruct himself to call his prejudiced soul his own.

So we must move beyond objectivity argued Hegel, to *ontology,* a science of the existence of man, and to phenomenology, the study of living experience that takes us to the heart of who we are as human beings. There is nothing of which we are more certain than who we experience ourselves to be, but part of that experience is characterised not merely sense based information but desires, hopes and aspirations intrinsic to who we are as human beings. Reason operates within this world of being as our guide in everything so as to achieve our different goals, needs and purposes with conscience acting as our moral compass and reason operating to enable us to execute different decisions made.

As rational beings we must be consistent with the logic of rational thinking not merely was respect to decisions made, but in the more general sense with respect to the origin of our own existence as intelligently ordered beings in an intelligently ordered world which is highly suggestive that we owe our existence to an intelligent and sufficient cause whose purpose in creating us is revealed in the different categories of understanding with which we have been so richly endowed. To combine reason, moral being and human volition together it would seem that moral integrity is a large part of what life is really all about. In other words, life is not just taken up with thoughts about things but our moral integrity as human beings and most people would agree with this assessment with moral integrity being the most crucial component by which we judge the integrity of our fellow human beings.

The purpose of something is determined by that which it has been ordered to be, a pen is made for writing, a car for driving to get us where we want to go, and a human is made for living according to and consistent with our many different attributes of being with which we have been so generously endowed as a species. So we could reasonably assume that our maker has put us on notice by endowing with volition and moral being and is obviously concerned about how we live our lives as moral beings. But for some to claim that human beings ultimately came from nothing of any order producing significance so there is no one to thank and no purpose to life does not concur with the evidence. Because that cause has endowed us with a modicum of intelligence that demands of us that we apply it to the ordered complexity of all things, and also to the ordered and living sum of who we are, and therein to know the origin from which we have come and why we are on this earth.

It's within our own reality of being that we seek for truth. Reason draws our attention to the fact that effects must be explained in terms of a cause, or a vast series of interconnected causes, that are able to explain the ordered sum of the effects produced. While with living things, the cause must be able to explain the ordered and living sum of the effects produced, and the different aspects of being with which we have been so richly endowed as a species out creator has shared something of His own being with us his creatures, made in his image as the Scriptures affirm. In other words, we can recognise the essential attributes of God in that which we have been ordered to be. While we need to be able to explain all there is to an aeroplane and how it works for it to get us where we might want to go.

Jerry Fodder argues that the goal of psychology should be to describe the programme that constitutes the mind, not the physical materials that happen to be running the programme. So to describe the mind, we need only describe the programme as in the form of own consciousness of ourselves and we can leave the details about the software out of the story. The mind with its different attributes of understanding accompanied with different hopes and aspirations can be reduced to all that we understand the working of a physical brain to be. Moreover, the brain does not only need to be described, it needs to be explained, and how out of all that we understand the brain to be it is producing more by of life producing effects and qualitative attributes of understanding that the brain as we presently understand it to be cannot possibly explain.

Therefore, there is a certain mystery to life with respect to the programmes of life as experienced from within, but, nevertheless, the mind behind this mystery reveals its purpose in the nature and of those attributes with which we have been endowed and that when they are faithfully embraced and used as they were meant to be used we fulfil the purpose for which we were created and find ourselves at peace within ourselves and in communion with that cause from which we have come. Scientists cannot explain how the brain generates consciousness let alone that conscious reality of being divided as it is into different qualitative attributes of understanding through which we engage the world around us, other people and things in nature and our maker who granted them to us.

The idea that the brain fires 40 times per second does not explain who we are as human beings, or that the brain is made up of 80 to 120 billion neurons and a thousand-million million synapses does not of itself explain who we experience ourselves to be as conscious living beings of profound ontological substance and significance. We do not assess the significance a bus merely by the many different parts that go to make up its existence, we assess it by what it has been ordered to be and to do, namely as a mode of transport that enables us to get us where we want to go. The brain generates, by means we still do not fully understand, a living self-conscious mind with many different attributes of understanding that takes us on the journey of life and by the diligent and effective use of these we know all that we were made and meant to know as human beings. Things moral and things spiritual, things practical and things theoretical, things physical and things metaphysical, things logical and thing mathematical, things social and things psychological the sum of which when used appropriately brings into contact with the One who endowed us with these attributes of being.

But if we fail to use all our attributes of being as they were meant to be used, we are in danger of being defective as human beings and failing to realise our full potential as a species. Or as one theorist has put, of becoming a plaster cast of a man all form but no substance. Science, if it is anything, is the quest of rational beings seeking to understand the origin and significance of their existence and the existence of all things both in physiological and existential terms that place where mind and matter meet. But it seems that in the post-modern world many theorists have lost all sense of meaningful dialogue about the origin from which they have come and end up apportioning the ordered sum of all that exists to no intelligently constituted cause at all leading to what could be regarded as a crisis of identity operating within what they are informed is a purposeless vacuum of mindless nothingness.

So what we need is an all-inclusive science of life if we are to get to true understanding of reality as it is for us as human beings. Truth is not merely about something outside of us but includes the reality that is us and what we were made and meant to know as sentient beings. Sean Carroll recounts how meeting a fellow scientist on an aeroplane on their way to a conference in Bozeman, Montana and asked him what he thought on the matter of the nature and purpose of life, to which he answered: "That's easy The purpose of life is to hydrogenate carbon dioxide." (Carol 2017, p.260) But such a remark is somewhat flippant with respect something as profound and serious as life and one cannot help wonder that if the pilot of the aeroplane was to speck over the intercom to say *Brace–Brace-Brace we are about to crash,* his hydrogenate carbon dioxide might well take on a life of its own with fear and apprehension that his hydrogenate carbon dioxide could not explain. Of if he had a child that was knocked down by a bus and seriously injured he might well be endowed with a good dose of reality beyond what his naive and flippant description of life in the above statement could possibly explain.

We live in the so-called age of reason and reason demands that things of whatever sort that we can intelligently reason about must be ordered into existence by a cause that can explain them. Moreover, it is the cause that is of primary and superior importance while the effect is the benefactor and recipient. But some in spite of their supposed scientific prowess break this rule on a daily bases by failing to do justice to this spectacular order producing creativity of life generating excellence by failing to apportion to it a cause worthy of the precious and ineffable nature of it. Then we wonder why for many life is looked upon as cheap and the individual regarded as more like a mundane thing than a sacred being. Paul Davies states that:

"I am … impressed that by the extraordinary ingenuity and harmony of the laws of physics. It is hard to accept that something so elegantly clever exists without a deeper purpose … I have no idea what the universe is about, but that it is about something I have no doubt."
[Cited in Blanchard 2000, p.275]

However, the origin and purpose of the universe can best be seen and understood in the spectacular nature of the effects produced from the starry hosts above us to the moral being within us. We as human beings are the crown of creation are have endowed with the gift of rational thinking so that we can see the nature and purpose of the cause involved in the nature of the effects produced. Reason does not operate in a vacuum but is informed from within our own nature of being from the psychological, rational, psychological, aesthetic, epiphanic, moral and the spiritual so that the world speaks its meaning through human consciousness. To reflect on the living sum of who we are and to realise that we owe our existence to a living life producing cause whose nature and purpose is reflected in all that we have been ordered to be and with different categories of being and understanding through which we can relate to Him. The purpose of a factory can be seen in the end produce of that which the factory produces and as living rational beings we are the end product and God our maker is waiting and expecting an appropriate response from us.

Or is it that we don't want to see it least we be obligated to our maker to love and obey Him and do all in our power to please Him. You despisers you wonder and perish said God to his ancient people who often disappointed Him for a lack of a worthy response to Him in spite of the much evidence he had given to them of his will for them and goodness toward them. So the most pertinent question a human being could ask is who they are in the light of all they have been ordered to be and therein decide the kind of cause that brought them and all things into existence and therein gain some clear approximation of the origin from which they have come and the purpose of their existence.

* Bryan Magee could confidently affirm that: "the subjective is indubitable in a way that the objective world can never be."

* While Socrates's resolute attention to his mind and soul, to moral virtue as well as intellectual truth the world order itself had been contacted and revealed.

* The Deity recognised by the philosopher Rousseau was not an impersonal first cause, but a God of love and beauty whom the human soul could know from within. That religion was intrinsic to the human condition. Man's actual nature – his feelings, his depths of impulse and intuition and spiritual hunger that transcended all abstract formulae.

* For Richard Tarnas, through science man had served God's greater glory, demonstrating the mathematical beauty and complex precision of the stupendous order reigning over the heavens and the earth.

* Plato described knowledge of the divine was implicit in every soul so that the philosopher must permit himself to be inwardly grasped by the most sublime form of Eros that universal passion and to restore a former unity, to overcome the separation from the diving and become one with it.

* Then said another: Seek and you will find knock and the door will be opened unto you, for he who seeks will find and to him that knocks the door shall be opened unto him.

Plato urged people to look within themselves to recognise that truth that lay within and not merely that truth that led in from without by means of the senses. Thus, he urged people to "Know Thyself," because only by knowing who we are can we truly determine the origin from which we have come. The above is all part of the Science of life and we will never find God until we use all the means at our disposal by which to do so.

As living entities ordered into existence to be moral beings, it is reasonable to conclude that the origin that brought us into existence is a moral being and has a moral purpose in mind when he created us and calls us to make, or learn to make, the right choices between the two opposing forces of good and evil. In this, our integrity or otherwise as human beings is determined and our character as human beings is revealed by the decisions we make in this respect. But when it is insisted that the only verifiable truth in the universe is that which can be validated in empirically based terms the inner world of moral being is therein qualified out of existence to be of no more significance than an accidental conglomeration of chemicals that fell into place for no good purpose.

There is no truth so close to us as who we experience ourselves to be and no other truth reveals as much to us as to the origin from which we have come and the purpose of our existence. But because conscious life cannot be examined under a microscope in a laboratory or moral being set forth as a physical object verifiable in empirically based terms it is said that such things are not real predicates at all. Therefore, life in all its fullness is explained away because it cannot be validated in empirically based scientific terms so that we know so much about the world of empirically based things but so little of ourselves, who we are or why we are here. Therefore, as Tarnas again reminds us:

In contrast to the Greeks' implicit emphasis on an integrated multiplicity of cognitive modes, the order of the modern cosmos was now comprehensible in principle by man's rational empirical faculties alone, while other aspects of human nature, the emotional, aesthetic, ethical, volitional, relational, imaginative, epiphanic, were generally regarded as irrelevant or distortional for an objective understanding of the world.

So Knowledge was primarily not about ultimate purpose, moral integrity, spiritual fulfilment or personal liberation but in intellectual mastery of the material world. (Tarnas 1998, p.287) Sean Carroll argues that to say that the universe *had a beginning* is not the same as saying that the universe *popped into existence.* He believes that it is right to say that the universe popped into existence, but incorrect to say that it had a beginning, because the former does not imply a thoughtful creation, but the latter does. So for Carroll the universe and all that this implies just popped up out of nowhere, but for theists it has a cause fit to explain it and all that ensued from it. (Carroll 2017, p.199f)

Moreover, empiricists could be said to be dead to the world of the spirit and some mockingly claim that there is no ghost in the biological machine rendering us nothing more than empirically based subjects passing through this world on a journey from nothing to nowhere. Thus the life world, the world of the spirit, is stripped away and denuded of real substance and significance in scientific terms. Even something like pain cannot be ascertained or validated in empirically based scientific terms which means that empirically speaking doctors are being paid under false pretences and we are the ones doing the paying.

Daniel Dennett argues that Darwin showed us how to reverse the whole course of rational thinking, by showing us that things naturally evolved by a process of natural selection without the need for an intelligent and sufficient cause of any kind. So, in his book *Darwin's Dangerous Idea*, Dennett argues that we should expect to find: "all sorts of excellence, worth and purpose that can emerge, bubbling up out from mindless, purposeless forces." (Dennett 1995, p.65)It is easy to see that here we find that the effects are so utterly marvellous full of excellence, worth and purpose, but the cause is so utterly pathetic it can be regarded as no cause at all. So the cause is the very antithesis of the ordered and living sum of the effects produced. So Dennett rejoices in the belief that Darwinian evolution, "is a wonderful way of thinking that inverts the whole course of rational thinking" so that we no longer need a process of intelligent ordering or the working of an intelligent mind to produce the vast complexity of life on earth. (Dennett 1996, p.65) But this of course is not merely a new way of thinking, it is a most devious and dangerous way of thinking because the whole idea is based on the belief that somehow natural selection could do that which is logically impossible and bring order out of chaos by means that has nothing to do with an order producing process so that the means are the very antithesis of

66

the ordered sum of the effects produced and this seems to be what it means to be intellectually fulfilled atheist.

In fact, scientists have discovered many of the ingenious mechanisms of order producing complexity which constitute an order producing process of marvellous and momentous creativity, but these mechanisms are explained away as a long series of happy coincidences. We now know we need DNA and RNA are mechanisms of ingenious order producing intelligence, but for some it seems that DNA the intelligent life producing information and RNA the mechanisms that take that information and turns it into the biological complexity of living things all of which appear like magic out of nowhere replete with information that in the case of human being has enough information that would fill books of Encyclopaedia Britannia size stacked one hundred and forty foot high. But even this does not explain how conscious life in all its qualitative profundity can appear within the biological complexity of an ordered body or even the ordered sum of a physical brain. Adding physics to physics and physical brain cells to physical brain cells add-infinitum does not of itself explain how the qualitative reality of a conscious mind is produced.

To equate the vast complexity of a physical brain with conscious life is arguing that if we had enough electric wire we could produce electricity which is not correct. No matter how much electric wire we might have it is never of itself going to produce electricity because the two things are intrinsically different. But electricity can travel down electric wire, so consciousness can travel across the synapses of the brain but is intrinsically different from all that we know and understand the synapses and neurons of the brain to be. Electricity has to be generated by powerful generators using magnets to send electrons down the wires to power many different things and produce light. So life is very different from all that we know a physical brain to be, so that there is mystery here, an underlying spiritual dynamic at work that brings the brain to life and produces categories of understanding and different attributes of being.

Michael Behe, in his study of evolution, found that when he searched the relevant literature on evolution to find how natural selection actually works he discovered to his astonishment that "the 'how' was always missing." (Cited in Strobel 2004, p.194) The physical brain in itself is a work of art and cannot possibly have fallen into lace by chance, and although scientists can say that DNA in conjunction with RNA explains it, but this explains nothing because these are miniaturised biological factories that need to be explained and are more ingeniously creative than all the man-made factories put together. We now know that evolution is operating to the life producing genius of DNA and RNA which was not discovered until about hundred years or so after Darwin's theory of evolution was published. And now that DNA has been discovered many theorists don't want to admit that this completely changes the nature of evolution.

But Daniel Dennett rejoices that things of excellence, worth and purpose can come 'bubbling forth' in manifold abundance from a process that is 'mindless, purposeless and meaningless', so the origin of life is turned into a form of sophisticated gobbledegook full of fine-sounding words that mean absolutely nothing in terms of an intelligent and sufficient cause. To put it in mathematical terms, you could take any number no matter how huge and add it to another number no matter how massive and with evolution you never get beyond nothing. So some want a world full of free lunches and pay for nothing by way of sufficient cause and feel they have nothing to give thanks for by way of an intelligent and sufficient cause or anything akin to a wise creator to whom they owe everything. Moreover, we reiterate, inanimate matter irrespective of how it is ordered cannot explain the subjective phenomenology of conscious life and our sense of being as a personal volitional entity different in character from the unconscious impersonal world of physics.

Only theists can explain intelligent life on earth in all its different complex forms by postulating a cause operating within nature in the form of a wise creator who has both provided the raw materials within the furnaces of the universe by which to produce the biological complexity of life on earth and supplied the mechanisms of order producing genius by which to order those raw material into the biological complexity of different life forms and then to infuse these forms with conscious life. We now know with the help of electron microscopes how immensely complex living things biologically speaking really are right down to the simplest living cell.

However, our self-conscious reality of being is an essential part of our existence and needs to be explained in terms consistent with the experiential nature of the effects produced, and this reveals to us something about the nature of the life generating cause involved and why we are on this earth. A moral reality of being reveals to us that our creator is a moral being and knows how to confer this attribute of being upon us, and as those with the capacity to love our maker is endowed with this attribute of being and knows how to confer this attribute of being upon us and on down through the wide range attributes of being we possess as a species. Even the attribute of rational thinking is an attribute of being conferred on us by our creator who obviously wants us to use it to good effect for our own advantage, and to know that we need to explain our own existence in terms of a living life producing cause synonymous with the idea of a wise creator theists call God.

But unfortunately this is the point when many theorists go, not only nose blind, but brain dead, or conveniently obtuse to avoid that which is otherwise staring them in the face. Some unfortunately, are locked into a world of empirically based sterility which as inanimate matter is devoid spiritual contend and qualitative substance of being that constitute the life world as we know it and experience it to be. Moreover, it is within this spiritual reality of being that we can relate to other living beings and to that life producing cause from which we have come as spirit answering to spirit and life engaging life. Therefore, we are an ordered compendium of biological complexity within which we have a living self-conscious mind of vital living life defining reality. The life that is within us has a huge say as to who we are, determining what we are capable of knowing and defining the origin from which we have come.

We can have a relationship with this living life producing cause from which we have even fellowship in kind. To miss this or misunderstand it we are in danger of missing the profound significance of life and what life is really all about. The reason that is within us is all the time trying to get us to see this, and to draw rational conclusions with respect to our existence in terms of a living life producing cause. This is why God through the prophet Isaiah could challenge the children of Israel: "To come and let s reason together says the Lord" in order to repair what was a broken relationship. But some for their own reasons don't want to reason with their maker even He who conferred reason upon them. While some are so busy playing god, they have no time for Him who really is God.

Therefore, the mind adds its own essential elements of ontological reality to the world of empirically based data and both combine to produce a holistic reality of life as we experience it to be. And when all our faculties of being are deployed, the intellectual, volitional, emotional, sensory, imaginative, aesthetic, spiritual, moral, and sacred, we find ourselves within something that is truly ineffable, something of some profound life defining truth and ontological significance and in this mankind has some very important decisions to make if we are to reach our full potential as human beings.

As we will see in more detail later in our study, that Richard Dawkins in his book *The Blind Watchmaker* admits that: "we can accept a certain amount of luck in our explanation but not too much." But Darwinians attribute so much to luck they are in danger of sinking in a sea of superstition where luck is the main ingredient and chance is the underlying explanation for the existence of intelligent life on earth. And again Dawkins argues that to claim that evolution is completely random is not a theory he would regard as meaningful. (Dawkins 1988, p.307) So what is going on here? It seems that even Dawkins is confused about his own theory of evolution because it isn't chance and it isn't intelligent design so what other options do we really have? Evolutionists of this kind find themselves describing much but explaining nothing and end up in a tangle of mindless confusion.

Daniel Dennett's contribution to this debate is to argue that life came bubbling forth in manifold abundance from purposeless forces of meaningless irrelevance and mindless irrationality and then argues: "Give me Order and time, and I will give you Design." (Dennett 1998, p.65) But of course, Dennett cannot explain order any more than he can explain design and he certainly cannot do so by reversing the whole course of rational thinking in which life came bubbling forth by means that are the very antithesis of the ordered and living sum of its existence. A process of blind randomness within the context of primordial disorder could not in theory or in practice produce the ordered complexity of anything, and all we would ever get would be a process self-perpetuating chaos.

"Let me start with regularity, the mere purposeless, mindless, pointless regularity of physics," he argues, "and I will show you a process that eventually will yield products that exhibit not only regularity but purposive design." (Dennett 1995, p.65) But what order producing regularity could emanate from a process that is purposeless, mindless and pointless? Dennett is just playing about with words in a desperate attempt to avoid the idea of purposeful design which is needed to explain intelligently ordered and exquisitely designed living things. As far as the writer is concerned, here we have an explanation in the form of sophisticated gobbledygook masquerading as science.

Dennett rejoices in the fact that he is following Darwin whom he believes shows us how evolution can reverse the logic of rational thinking to produce intelligent life on earth where no intelligent order producing cause exists. But Darwin never established any such thing and it has never explained how natural selection turned a world of disordered chemicals into the ordered complexity of living things. Darwin did suspect that the laws of nature were the secret behind the order producing power of evolution but because he could not identify the means involved he at times doubted it and in his confusion wondered if life could originate by chance from a warm muddy pool in which chemicals could combine to produce the first living things. But even if this were so it turned out to be means so spectacularly ingenious they could not be detected with the naked eye in the form of genes which have billions of letters of order producing information on how to build living things out of the chemicals of the earth. We now know that the secret of life lay in the life producing genius of the genome the order producing power of which has never been explained, and cannot possibly be explained by randomly moving disordered chemicals about.

But many evolutionists like Dawkins and Dennett have not taken account of this game-changing fact and still naively believe that evolution by natural selection, operating to a process of blind randomness, could somehow produce intelligent life on earth with an ontological reality of conscious being attached. Evolution comes to life within us and challenges us with something truly ineffable, giving evidence of a living life-producing cause at work in the earth and even more especially within us.

Moreover, one doesn't have to be an Einstein to know that it is a logical impossibility for a process of blind randomness to produce extremely complex and intelligently ordered living things from what before was in a state of abject disorder. But the idea that an order producing 'regularity' could emanate from a process of blind randomness adhered to by Daniel Dennett is completely impossible but the idea is still thrown into a convoluted mix of ideas by many evolutionists to give the impression that somehow an order producing regularity could emerge from a process of blind randomness in the hope that others would not notice the mindless obfuscation that lies at the heart of their theory of evolution. So either Dennett has his head screwed on back to front or his brain is wired up the wrong way round.

Dennett rejoices in what he believes is: "Darwin's strange 'inversion of reasoning' was a new and wonderful way of thinking completely overturning the mind-first way of John Locke." (Dennett 1995, p.65) But of course Darwin showed us nothing of the sort he was just ignorant, or wants to ignore, the ingenious means going on within the process of evolution some of which later evolutionists have now discovered to be both marvellous and ingenious. But even from within the logic of rational thinking, it should have been obvious to any right thinking person that there was more going on within evolution than a process of blind and blundering randomness oscillating aimlessly within primordial chaos.

Even God would not, and by his very nature could not, reverse the course of rational thinking because he is not the author of confusion and that is exactly what we get when we reverse the inviolable logic of rational thinking and attribute intelligently ordered effects to means that are diametrically opposed the intelligently ordered complexity of the effects produced. So the term 'regularity' used by Dennett in the above quote is just a word thrown into the mix to give the impression that some kind of order producing regularity could come bubbling forth from a process of mindless irrationality and purposeless irrelevance.

This kind of double think in grammatical terms is referred to as a 'crafty conflation', that is two ideas brought together as if there was a logical connection between them, when in Dennett's case they most certainly is not. In other words, in the real world no order producing regularity could arise from a process of meaningless irrelevance and the mindless machinations of blind randomness. Dennett is not merely operating within a paradox which is an apparent contradiction, he is operating within a monumental contradiction in terms in which the cause is the very antithesis of the ordered and living sum of the effects produced which is cosmologically absurd and scientifically naive.

Therefore, to understand Dennett's theory of evolution we must dispense with rational thinking altogether and learn to think irrationally in order to discover how evolution works to bring into existence a world of complex living beings and things. But when we forsake the moral high ground of rational thinking we are in very dangerous territory indeed and one that is destined to lead those who follow it astray in which they are destined to draw all the wrong conclusions about the origin of life on earth and the ultimate purpose of it.

The plain fact is that it is the order producing links within the process of evolution which enable scientists to intelligently investigate the world of different living things and identify those order producing links that bring into existence intelligently ordered living things. If this was not the case, scientists would be wasting their time examining different things to find the connecting links whereby different things were ordered into existence where no such links exist. Moreover, if we as human beings were not ordered intelligently to think intelligently, there could be no science and everyone would be running about like headless chickens in a world of mindless randomness and order-less confusion.

When evolutionary theorists use the instrument of an intelligent mind to investigate the world and everything in it, they are already implying that the world and everything in it is ordered intelligently and for this reason can be investigated intelligently. But some seem to be so cosmologically blind they cannot see this and some who seem to be so inherently prejudiced don't seem to want to see it. One evolutionary theorist's seem to think that: "Absolute ignorance is fully qualified to take the place of Absolute Wisdom" when it comes to explaining a world and everything it. (Cited in Dennett, 1995, p.65) While John Locke argued that it is just as: "impossible to conceive that even bare in cogitative matter should produce a thinking intelligent being as that nothing should of itself produce matter." (Cited in Dennett 1995, p.26) Locke rightly argues, *Ex nihilo nihil fit* – from nothing – nothing comes. Unless that is we want to reverse the whole course of rational thinking give up on science altogether and quietly go insane.

Michael Behe again has pointed out that what we have is the 'irreducible' complexity of life on earth in which everything has to be ordered into its own order producing place and functioning effectively with every other part before we have the ordered and viable complexity of anything whether it is a living cell or a mousetrap. Richard Dawkins is fully aware of the impossibility of things falling into place by luck to produce highly complex things and writes: "You don't need to be a mathematician or a physicist to calculate that an eye or a haemoglobin molecule would take from here to infinity to self-assembly be higgledy-piggledy luck." (Cited in Lennox 2007, p.154) How then were infinitely complex things ordered sufficiently to come into existence if luck and a process of blind chance was out of the question and there is no wise creator to do what a process of luck could not possibly explain. And this applies to a single haemoglobin cell as Dawkins later admits, not to mention the vast ordered and integrated complexity of living things.

Dawkins admits that we can have a little bit of luck but not too much, but if this is the case what is that contingency other than luck that is needed to produce the manifold complexity of intelligent life on earth? But the answer to this question has never yet been addressed let alone explained, and in the case of human beings we are made up of some 50 or so trillion living cells each of which is massively complex in its own right and the chances of coming into existence by luck are beyond impossible.

The environment might be able reject permutations of matter that were not ordered sufficiently to come into existence come alive and survive within a particular environment, but this could never explain how complex living things were ordered sufficiently into existence to come alive and survive within a particular environment. Randomly moving disordered chemicals about is not going to cut it should shuffle thus for all eternity. We might spray our vegetable patch all we like with weed killer but we are never going to get a good harvest until we plant good seed that will bear good fruit. And if evolution was a process of blind randomness, as some say it is, it could not possibly have anticipated or foreseen what any environment was like in order to prepare living things suitably equipped to live of the resources of a particular environment.

Darwin's finches on the Galapagos Islands developed different beaks, but this doesn't explain how any bird came into existence on any island fully equipped to live of the available resources of that environment. And if such a bird was not fully equipped with the right beak to forage for the food on a particular island and the appropriate metabolic equipment to turn that food into energy to survive it would never have come into existence as a viable living thing. Living things once sufficiently ordered and adequately equipped to live within a particular habitat could come into existence and survive, but those that were not so ordered could not, but how could something as complex as a bird come into existence where no bird producing intelligent was at work to bring it into being?

As Michael Behe rightly points out, the entire bird had first to be ordered in every essential detail to be able to come alive and survive within a particular environment. But how could such birds came fully ordered and adequately equipped to come alive and survive within a particular environment if evolution was operating to a process of blind randomness and could not have known what any environment was like or have the ability to equip living things to live within a particular environment even if it did? Richard Attenborough seems to make the same mistake time and time again when he implies that all things just tumbled into place and adapted to the environment in the most wonderful of ways without referring to any form of order producing intelligence. Only once did the writer hear him quoting Darwin who at the end of his book on the Origin of Species wrote:

Thus, from the war of nature, from famine and death, the most exalted object which we are capable of conceiving, namely the production of higher animals, directly follows. There is a grandeur in this view of life, with its several powers, having been originally breathed by the creator into a few forms or into one; and that whilst this planet has gone circulating on according to the fixed law of gravity, from so simple a beginning endless forms most beautiful and most wonderful have been, and are being evolved.

People, not least young people, need to know that there is a credible origin to life in order for it to have meaning and purpose, but the impression is so often given that evolution is just one never-ending sequence of happy coincidences behind which there is no real meaning or purpose. For life to be worth preserving, it needs to have a rational explanation in order to have purpose worth preserving. Evolution has been described as a struggle for survival, but who or what was doing all this struggling when nothing could struggle to do anything before it exists? It is obvious that something else was operating within evolution or acting intelligently upon the process to do what a process of blind randomness struggling aimlessly within primordial chaos could not possibly do, and making an exceedingly good job of turning the raw chemicals of the earth into the viable complexity of living things ordered sufficiently and suitably equipped to live of the resources of a particular environment.

And when it comes to the working of an intelligent mind, John Locke is undoubtedly right when he affirms that it is inconceivable that incogitable (unthinking) matter could produce the ordered sum of anything let alone extremely complex living things not only ordered sufficiently to survive within a particular environment, but ordered intelligently to think intelligently which enables us as human beings to go on to produce intelligently ordered things in our own right. How could an intelligent mind be ordered into existence to think intelligently by a process of mindless randomness and meaningless irrelevance? We have already noted that if disordered matter was being rearranged by means of blind randomness it could never produce the viable complexity of a living thing and the odds prove to be so astronomically vast the whole idea is ridiculous as even Richard Dawkins in one of his more senior moments is willing to admit.

Some philosophers have rightly argued that what we grasp by means of reason is as real as that which we perceive by our senses. So if we see something that is intelligently ordered we by means of reason we are compelled as rational beings to apportion it to a process of intelligent ordering behind which there is an intelligent order producing cause. In other words, we cannot by means of our physical senses (sight, hearing, smell, taste and touch) prove that intelligently ordered things need to be explained in terms of an intelligent and sufficient cause, but the rational thinking of an intelligent mind that we humans deem ourselves to have demands that we do. And when scientists limit verifiable reality to empirically based facts they negate the life world without which we would be material objects as opposed to living things dead to the world and even to themselves.

We perceive many different things by means of our senses but we absorb these facts into an intelligent mind endowed with different attributes of understanding which enables us to make sense of these facts and as rational being know that we need an intelligent and sufficient cause to explain the ordered and living sum of them. But Daniel Dennett, trying again to desperately justify his own irrational back to front way of thinking quotes Philo who argued: "What peculiar privilege has this little agitation of the brain which we call thought that we must thus make it the model of the whole universe?" (Dennett 1975, p.30)

This is another way of saying that just because we as human beings operate to a mind first way of thinking (in other words intelligence) in which we first need an intelligent mind to produce intelligently ordered things this doesn't mean that this principle has to be applied to the way that nature works and evolution operates to produce extremely complex and wonderfully designed living things. This means that the universe and everything in it could have come into existence outside of an intelligent and sufficient cause of any kind and that we as intelligent beings could came into existence by means that are the very antithesis of the intelligently ordered sum of our existence. In other words, just because we as human beings know that we need an intelligent manufacturer to produce things like motor cars this doesn't mean that this is the way nature works to produce infinitely more complex living things. Now Dennett is insulting our intelligence!

In this, Dennett is clutching at straws and is making a fool of himself by deserting the ground of rational thinking in which the vast complexity of intelligent life on earth doesn't need a cause, or the effect comes before the cause which is to get thing arse about face. By endowing us with reason and intelligence, our maker has given to us the means to make the idea of his existence a testable hypothesis so that if we find that life on earth is extremely complex and intelligently ordered we as rational beings are honour bound to attribute it to an intelligent and sufficient cause in the form of a wise creator. And if we fail to do so we are destined to fall headlong into a monstrous delusion of cosmic confusion in which reason is turned on its head so that nothing of any order producing significance produced the order sum of all things. Dennett is trying desperately to avoid the obvious to keep a sinking ship afloat.

But such theorists insist on taking the credit for their own creations but give no credit whatsoever to that cause which created them and who gave them the ability to be creative in our own right. We as human beings are microcosms of that creative genius that ordered us into existence so that there is a direct causal link between our own existence and a wise creator who gives clear evidence of his order producing genius in that which we have been ordered to be.

Therefore attributes of our own being reflect something of the nature of that living life producing cause from which we have come and provide the means by which we can relate to Him who has made us in his own image. But God, by creating us as autonomous beings has given us the right to choose because a forced relationship is neither a happy or genuinely fruitful one. So we must make the most of the evidence God has given to us of his existence both from within us and in an ordered world full of intelligently ordered things and to make a response as living entities to that living life producing cause that ordered us into existence and in this we are made complete and ontologically fulfilled as a species.

Evolutionists like Dennett who are so keen to accuse theists of being irrational find themselves up to their necks in a world of mindless irrationality and not a little confusion in which they deem themselves intelligent but go on to argue that they originated from a process of causal irrelevance and mindless irrationality. But this is not science; it is a confabulation of mindless obscurantism masquerading as science in a frantic effort to avoid the truth that behind the ordered and living sum of all things there is a most ingeniously creative mind operating to a purpose that can be discerned in the ordered and living sum of all that exists. We must hold to reason as the true and authentic way to the truth if we are to avoid ending up believing in the most deviously concocted falsehood ever contrived by the minds of men.

Moreover, if nature's way has nothing to do with the logic of cause and effect relationships, why do such scientists go on to use their intelligence to investigate the world and everything in it when according to them this would be an exercise of utter futility in a world they believe is not intelligently ordered at all. This is a complete obfuscation that makes no sense by way of an explanation for intelligent life on earth.

Dennett also argues that extremely complex and intelligently ordered living things can be reduced to order producing contingencies so 'small and stupid' they don't represent a process of intelligent design at all. But this simply doesn't work because stages of change that produce intelligent ordered things never get so small and simple that they don't need to be intelligently ordered to produce intelligently ordered things. In fact, the opposite is the truth, because the smaller and more insignificant the basic elements of change the more intelligence and order producing ingenuity we need to order them all together to produce different complex things. We might reduce a watch to its ever so small and apparently insignificant parts, even to the atoms that go to make up the existence of those parts, but we still need an intelligent watchmaker to bring all those parts together to produce the ordered and complex sum of the watch.

All that we as human beings have created is due to the working of intelligent minds with the creative vision to conceive of useful artefacts and follow that creative vision through to completion by adopting the necessary means by which to do so. In the four or so billion years since the earth came into existence not as much as a sweaty mouse, a pair of plastic scissors or a game of tiddlywinks came into existence until human beings by means of intelligence thought them up and deployed the appropriate means to produce them. But even when the all that exists goes beyond our ability as human beings to understand some still don't get it: and go on to attribute the intelligently order sum of all things to nothing of any order producing significance or to never-ending series of happy coincidences.

Our creator has shared something of his own nature with us by creating us rational beings who can think logically and produce many different things in our own right, and by diligent investigation of the facts we can increasingly discover something of the ordered complexity of all that exists and can appreciate more fully how incredibly wise is our creator. But the irony of all this is that when scientists discover by means of intelligence how something was ordered into existence they then conclude that it does not then need to be explained in terms of an intelligent and sufficient cause other than themselves. But theorists like Daniel Dennett wants to argue that all sorts of things: "Of excellence, of worth and purpose can emerge, bubbling up out of mindless purposes forces." (Dennett 1996, p.66)Thus, it came to be accepted by some evolutionists like Dennett that order and design were two distinct and separate things with order being simply regularity or a pattern operating within the physical world, while design being something planned and operating for a purpose. But it is obvious that if this regularity and pattern of things operating within physics was producing extremely complex and intelligently ordered living things that the intelligently constituted means must of logical necessity be within that process bringing us back to a process of intelligent design.

This is like a child shown round a motorcar factory and because they cannot logically see the clear pattern of purposeful design operating within the many order-producing mechanisms of the factory to produce motorcars they do not see it as a process of purposeful design. It is just some form of regularity or pattern of things they do not understand that means nothing in terms of an intelligent and sufficient cause. But in thinking this they are wrong. The intelligently constituted means are within the factory to produce that which is being produced. So Dennett's strange inversion of rational thinking, as he calls it, is only a figment of his imagination born out of pre-determination of mind to avoid the idea of a wise creator at all costs. But scientists continue to use this worn-out piece of obscurantist thinking so that in professing themselves to be wise some have indeed become fools, And then to add insult to ineptitude some go on to write books on how ingeniously creative nothing is.

Dennett goes on to argue that design is a flawed bridge between science and religion and that nature's way could be due to a process that has nothing to do with intelligent design. (Dennett 1995, p.30) But if this is the case let Dennett explain what this other way in which intelligently designed things could come into existence by means that have nothing to do with intelligence or a process of intelligent design so that we can be greatly enlightened. But of course he doesn't do this because he can't, and neither can anyone else because the whole idea is nothing but a complete piece of obscurantist thinking unworthy of the name science.

The idea of God as a wise creator is the only conceivable bridge between what was a disordered world and the ordered and vast complexity of all that now exists. But Dennett, it seems, is going to set the world to rights by abandoning the whole course of rational thinking and rejoicing in what he believes is Darwin's "strange inversion to reasoning" that was "a new and wonderful way of thinking" in which nothing of any order producing significance produced the ordered complexity of everything. But it cannot be much consolation for evolutionists to be informed that the Darwinian way of thinking inverts the whole course of rational thinking which is a sure way to end up believing anything no matter how irrational or ridiculous. In the end, evolutionary theorists who deny that evolution has anything to do with an intelligent and sufficient cause must apportion intelligent life on earth to a never-ending sequence of luck, to a process of blind and blundering randomness, to an immense improbability on a colossal scale, or to nothing at all. Such explanations are bought at a very high price, even the price of truth itself, because truth can never be discovered by abandoning the ground of rational thinking.

A monkey though a complex and intelligently ordered creature is not competent in the art of abstract thinking as we human beings are and can get away with taking much for granted and drawing no rational conclusions about their own existence or the ordered complexity of all that exists. But we as intelligently ordered beings endowed with intelligent minds are without excuse. So we must decide whether to go with the monkey or stand up as rational beings and use our faculty of reason as it was meant to be used and recognise that extremely complex and intelligently ordered beings and things don't come into existence by means of a long series of happy coincidences, some form of cosmic magic, luck on a gargantuan scale, or by a process of mindless randomness or by means so small and stupid they don't need to be explained in terms of an intelligent and sufficient cause. Isn't it interesting that those who boast that we live in the age of reason are the first to abandon it when it comes to avoiding the idea of a wise creator?

In fact, some have never considered the vast and incomprehensible nature of the odds involved to produce even the simplest things. This can be confirmed by giving monkeys typewriters in which they never got beyond half a line no matter how long they typed. In the case of evolution, we need books of information encyclopaedic size stacked 140 feet high to hold the necessary information to produce a living person from amino acids, and even with this it fails to explain consciousness and all that this means in living life defining terms. Even the simplest living cell requires millions of genetic letters such as the simple amoeba which has 400 million bits which would take 80 books of 500 pages each to contain. Therefore, there is an awful lot of wishful thinking going on when some apportion an ordered world full of intelligently ordered living things to a process of blind and blundering randomness.

Richard Dawkins in his book *The Selfish Gene* in one of his more thoughtful moments readily admits that the idea of chance producing the ordered complexity of a living person is out of the question should you shake our biological cocktail shaker for the entire length of the existence of the universe and even then you would not succeed. (Dawkins 1989, p.16) Dawkins is forced to admit that the idea that life could have appeared on the earth by pure chance is not only wrong but not even an explanation he would regard as meaningful. (Dawkins 2006, P.309) This we will be examining more fully in a later chapter. While Richard Tarnas seems right when he suggests that there is a: "growing recognition that modern science's mechanistic and objective conception of nature was not only limited but fundamentally flawed." (Tarnas 1996, p.405) John Locke argued that reason is natural revelation that reveals to us to by means of reason that the nature of the thing produced reflects the nature of the cause involved. He writes: "The visible marks of extraordinary wisdom and power appear so plainly in all the works of creation that a rational creature who but seriously reflect on them cannot miss the discovery of a deity."

We cannot deny who we experience ourselves to be as living self-conscious beings operating in an empirically based world, and we need a cause that can explain the ordered sum of both. Moreover, just as the mind with its attributes of understanding takes us beyond the world of physics so the cause from which we have come necessitates a cause that takes us beyond the world of physics into a world of being ontologically rich, spiritually enlightening, morally endowed and guided by reason. But reason does not operate within a vacuum but within an ordered world and a living mind that when joined gives us a holistic philosophy of life. But it seems that some are lost to reason both within an ordered world and the experiential reality of a thinking mind that determines that we perceive and how we perceive and understand the world and our place within it.

Bryan Magee has pointed out that by restricting reality to empirically based criteria: "wiped out the whole of science." (Magee 1988, p.57) "This is because science represents the effective working of intelligent and inquisitive minds the reality of which cannot be identified or verified in empirically based scientific terms. Hegel used the word *Giest* which is translated mind or spirit which he regarded as the ultimate reality that determines who we are and how we interact with the physical world of sensibly perceived things and other living beings endowed with their own unique nature of being. So does our inner world of being constitute nothing by ways of verifiable reality because is cannot be established in empirically based scientific terms? Edmund Husserl has argued that for each of us there is one thing whose existence is indubitably certain and that is our own conscious awareness of ourselves; therefore if we want to build a conception of reality of rock-solid foundations, this is the place for us to start." (Cited in Magee 2001, p.210)

While Descartes puts thinking at the heart of our knowing with his *cogito ergo sum* theory which means: "I think therefore I am." Therefore, the existence of which we have immediate and indubitable proof of is our own conscious reality of being, and to demand proof of our inner reality of being is like someone demanding proof of their own existence and the life they are actually living. Therefore, empirically based science is not equipped to address this most crucial and important aspect of our existence as human beings because it leaves untouched who we are as conscious beings of profound ontological truth that takes us to the very heart of our being by which we live life and engage in science.

Professor Susan Greenfield one time Professor of Pharmacy at Oxford University argues that: "Clearly we need to know what is happening in the real brain, and yet the big question that the scientists are still ducking is how the actual feel of emotions, raw consciousness no less, is accommodated in a physical mass." (Greenfield 2001, p.50) While Bryan Magee sees what he believes are the inadequacies of the empiricism of the Oxford philosophers to penetrate into the truth of the inner world of being and argues that the self-imposed limitations of empirically based science: "disregarded the very language that penetrated most deeply into human experiences and our understanding of it." (Magee 2000, p.136)

Therefore, the most important part of knowledge is self-knowledge, even though we cannot understand how matter can generate qualitative states of being and feelings that affect us profoundly as human beings, but neither can they be denied without negating the conscious and living essence of ourselves. The fact is that we do not decide who we are or how we operate as living entities, that was decided by that life producing cause that brought us into existence and what we do with that preordained nature of being determines our integrity or otherwise as human beings.

If space explorers were to find the rusty remains of a combine harvester on Mars, empirically based theorists would immediately conclude that this was irrefutable evidence that intelligent life once existed there. But if they were to find the skeletal remains of a human being, even the one who by ingenious means produced the combine harvester, to some this would mean absolutely nothing but a piece of chanced upon irrelevance. The fact is that even the simplest living bacteria cells are so small that ten million of them could sit on a pinhead according to Richard Dawkins, and each one is more complex than a combine harvester. But it seems that some evolutionary theorists are not willing to apply the same causal logic to the ordered sum of their own existence as they do to things produced by us as human beings that seems wholly inconsistent and more than a little hypocritical.

Atheism does not start with the denial of God but by refusing to stay closely to the logic of rational thinking that demands such a cause to explain an intelligently ordered world full of complex living things. It is little wonder that C.S. Lewis argued that empirically based science leads to 'the abolition of man' because it denies the very things that underpin our humanity. While Ludwig Wittgenstein argues that: "Philosophers constantly see the method of science before their eyes, and are irresistibly tempted to ask and answer questions in the way that science does, namely to empirically based terms. This tendency ... leads the philosopher into complete darkness" and this we would suggest is because it leaves the inner world of being out of the question of reality which in turn leaves us in a world of mundane banality devoid of ontological substance and life-defining significance.

Professor Steve Jones describes life as a series of successful mistakes when it seems that he is the one who is mistaken because the idea of successful mistakes when it comes to life on earth is really a contradiction in terms and represents a desperate attempt to avoid apportioning the vast complexity of intelligent life on earth to an intelligent and sufficient cause. Mistakes produce errors not order. (Cited in Thompson, 2005, p.33)The Royal Society as an institution was committed to scientific investigation to ascertain the origin and nature of different things originally believed to be the work of God as the prime mover. But this attitude was gradually eroded under the guise of reason-based science in which it was thought that science could explain all that exists without the need for an intelligent and sufficient cause in the form of a wise creator.

But science was all the time using reason to come to a better understanding of the origin and nature of different things and every time they discovered the origin or working of something this was one less thing they needed God to explain, as opposed to reckoning up all the ingenious means whereby all things came into existence to discover how creatively ingenious the creator of all things. Such a conclusion is not science at all in any logically coherent sense, and is in fact an insult to science and an affront to reason and somewhat disingenuous for those who like to boast that science is based in reason when reason dictates that intelligently ordered things of logical necessity owe their existence to an intelligent and sufficient cause. As Bryan Magee aptly points out, the Oxford philosophers who operated to empirical verification wiped out the whole of science because science itself was a metaphysical research phenomenon that could not be validated in empirically based scientific terms.

Such theorists are not merely building their grand evolutionary edifice on a foundation of sinking sand, they find themselves unable even to explain the sand by way of chemical complexity on which they are trying to build. Life is not a dead letter but a living spirit with its own unique story to tell so that what we need is an in-ward turning of the soul to discover the kind of beings that we really are and to use it to experience all that were made and meant to know as human beings.

Ravi Zacharias has rightly pointed out that the idea of God's non-existence permeates almost every major discipline in secular universities and operates to a philosophy of life that delights in the fact that students now glorify in the fact that the university enabled them to become intellectually fulfilled atheists. But to be an intellectually fulfilled atheist one must conclude that nothing brought into existence the ordered sum of everything. Such thinking does not produce intellectually fulfilled atheists but self-deluded beings who because of the fact that life on earth is so inordinately complex they have lost the thread of order producing genius running through the whole of creation and have so thoroughly confused themselves in the ineffable complexity of it all they no longer know who they are, from whence they have come, or why they are on this earth. (*ig-no-ra-tioelen-chi*)

Chapter 4
The Search for an Authentic Science of Life

When we talk about life in the personal sense we are talking about consciousness and what we are conscious of as human being from within ourselves as ordered and integrated self-conscious beings with a wide range of faculties of understanding accompanied by feelings hopes and aspirations we possess as a species. The question has often been asked what is consciousness and how does the brain generate it. First of all, we know exactly what consciousness is and being more specific being conscious of ourselves because we experience it every waking moment of our lives. We dare not diminish or by a process of ontological reductionism limit conscious life to the working of a physical brain because if we do so we commit a form of ontological suicide. There is nothing more certain of who we experience ourselves to be and it cannot be made to equate with all we know the physical brain to be. Many scientists would reduce the existential reality of the mind to the working of the physical brain, but one only has to reflect for a moment to realise that these two things do not equate in real terms either objectively or experientially.

Michio Kaku in his excellent and thought provoking book *The Future of the Mind* refers much to the working of mind and as follow this line reasoning we discover that he is not really talking about the mind at all but about the physical brain and the massive complexity of its functioning but not the mind as we experience ourselves to be. He goes into considerable discussion about the brain and how it functions to control our decisions and operates to move the body in response to different decisions made by a living self-conscious mind. He quotes Rita Carter, author of mapping of the mind, who argues that: "Emotions are not feelings at all but a set of body-rooted survival mechanisms." (Kaku 2014, p.34) "But the question must be posed as for whom these survival mechanisms are meaningful and genuine felt realities made in response to different inner feeling and emotions. This is never explained, and it seems that physical substance as inanimate matter no matter how complexly arranged is not really interested in something like survival. There is something in this analogy and Kaku seems to realise this because he eventually asks the question: what do we mean by consciousness anyway?" (Kaku 2014, p.40)

Kaku then talks about the consciousness of robots which are not self-conscious of themselves with different feelings and emotions as sentient beings have because if this were the case to throw one in the scrapheap to buy a more powerful and efficient one would not only be cruel but should a capital offence against a living thing. They, therefore, should be sent to an old peoples' home for computers. One analogy of consciousness is that it is an: "… emergent phenomenon, miraculously arising out of the collective action of billions of neurons." The problem with this picture adds Kaku: "is that it says absolutely nothing about how this miracle occurs." (Kaku 2014, p.33) The brain is the exceedingly complex mechanism that responds to the direction of the mind as the control centre of our decision making, but the mind is a world of ontological reality characterised by different motivations, emotions, desires hopes and aspirations as yet unexplained in spite of all that understand about the workings of a physical brain. The idea put forth by Carl Sagan that: "the mind is the consequence of its anatomy and physiology" which is as simplistic as it is offensive, and even if this were the case, it transforms completely what we understand physics to be and what our present understanding of our anatomy can explain. Kaku explains that: "Others have given up trying to define consciousness, and try simply to describe it" which in the light of dilemma over it seems the best option. (Kaku 2014, p.42)

Some people still believe that Miller and Urey in their experiments in 1953 produced life in a test tube. But as Christopher Lloyd aptly puts it: "Yet Urey and Miller had not actually produced life itself in a flask, rather they had created some the ingredients of life" biologically speaking, namely a few amino acids. And the means by which they did so they did by using their God-given intelligence and not by operating blind to no good purpose. Moreover: "To this day no one has been able to produce an actual living cell out of lifeless chemicals in a laboratory so the debate about the first moment of life's incarnation still rages on." (Lloyd 2012, p.19–20) It is reckoned that it is impossible to produce amino acids from a realistic atmosphere of early earth, but even if it were possible we are still incredibly far from creating a living cell. We still have to get the right kinds of amino acids to link up to produce a protein molecule and that would still be a long way from a living cell. There needs to be dozens of protein molecules again in the right sequence to create a living cell. The gap between non-living chemicals and even the most primitive living organism is absolutely tremendous explains Brian Silver. And when we talk about living organisms here, we are not taking about something that is consciously alive but living in terms of metabolism – complex interactions going on within the cell.

The sheer complexity of such cells is astonishing, even the synthesis of chemical elements alone is amazing and these have to be ordered very precisely to produce the biological complexity of the simplest living things and we now know that this is achieved by means of the order producing information contained with DNA and RNA that can read that information that turn amino acids into proteins of which the vast biological complexity of living things are made up of trillions of livings cells each one immensely complex in its own right.

There are over three billion letters that make up the human genome that contain the necessary information of how to produce the ordered and intricate biological complexity of a human being. Even if a few of these letters are missing or not arranged in the right order it can have disastrous consequences which will not result in a viable replication. As Professor Brian Silver reminds us: "The gap between an aqueous solution of these molecules in a single living cell is stupendous," let alone complex organism made up of billions even trillions of living cells. Silver goes on to point out that the term organic chemistry is misleading since it means nothing more than the chemistry of molecules containing carbon atoms. We need a highly organised system of molecules to produce something like a simple amoeba cell containing a huge number of molecules coexisting in a flexible but mechanically stable package-the cell. (Silver 1998, p.322)

The variety of chemical reactions occurring in cells is enormous. All these reactions have to be coordinated in the cell and between cells otherwise the organism would self-destruct or never be ordered sufficiently to come into existence as a viable living thing at all. (Silver 1998, p.326) Moreover, Silver asks, how does a single cell know how to develop into a coordinated mass of cells having different structures and functions? Some seem to think that when they hear the term organic we are well on our way to producing complex living things when we can see from the above description this is certainly not the case. As Silver again points out, it is astonishing the way in which living organisms are adapted to the environment, the emergence of life itself, the fact that it is almost incredible that the universe should have developed so as to allow the formation of living matter and all this has led many theorists to suppose that the emergence of live and of men and women cannot have been an accident. (Silver 1998, p.337)

The secret of course was revealed, as least biologically speaking, in 1953 when the ingenious mechanism of DNA and RNA was discovered and which is as hard to explain as life is to explain without them. But when the genome was discovered by 1953 by Crick and Watson this in itself proved to be a sophisticated biological factory of life producing creativity of gargantuan proportions operating to turn amino acids into a rich variety of living things ordered and integrated into a viable living whole: "to produce the glorious and miraculous assembly of the first living cells." Moreover, while forty or so simple amino acids that were needed to produce a single primitive cell the Miller experiment produced two – adds Silver. But even if we had a universe crammed full of amino acids this in itself would be a dead end because we need nucleotides (DNA/RNA) as independent systems to order amino acids into simple living cells or would have led precisely nowhere.

As we will see later in our study, Silver points out that: "It stretches even the credulity of a materialist abiogenesis fanatic to believe that proteins and nucleotides persistently emerged simultaneously and at the same point in space from the primordial soup." Nucleotides, DNA and RNA as exceedingly complex mechanisms of order producing genius had to appear as a two part process of order producing genius at the same time and place to produce living cells, So the idea that physical chemical forces could by themselves bring about a living organism is not merely mistaken but altogether stupid argues Arthur Schopenhauer. Silver accepts that we as intelligent beings can bring different disorganised things together to produce intelligently ordered things but: "This is very different from accounting for the *spontaneous* formation of living systems in a universe empty of intelligence." (Silver 1998, p.339)While: "the gap between an aqueous solution of these molecules and a living cell is stupendous." (Silver 1998, p.345)

So what is the origin of the altogether ingenious mechanisms whereby the first simple cells came into existence, and the mechanisms that ordered millions of these living cells together to produce living things of massive complexity? "There are no systems more ordered than the living cell and its components," adds Silver. And we need to explain how literally trillions of living cells were ordered intelligently to produce even the simplest living things in the animal kingdom. Therefore:

> The basic problem facing anyone who is looking for the origin of life is to account for the formation of a complex, very highly organised, life-sustaining and life replicating system out of a mixture of chemicals that, certainly in the early days of the soup, displayed none of these characteristics. [Silver 1998, p.350]

But even this is light years removed from something we regard as consciously alive and it has never been explained how conscious life can be generated by all that we know about the working of a physical brain. Then these cells have to able to replicate, that represents a massively complex mechanism within massively complex mechanisms that not only had the means to come into existence but the means to produce exact replicas of themselves. Then millions, even trillions, of living cells had to be ordered together to produce complex living things of ever-increasing degrees of ordered sophistication. How could two different extremely complex halves, male and female, representing two different halves that go to make a massively complex whole that can come together in perfect harmony to produce progeny in kind? Such couldn't possibly have fallen into place by chance and needed massive amounts of intelligent coordination to produce two immensely complex halves that could come together in perfect harmony to produce offspring in kind and which represents a marvellous feat of biological engineering.

This process could be likened to two different manufactures producing two halves of a spaceship to send men to Mars which would require a process of massive coordination and planning afore-thought for this to work. But even this is nothing compared to the massive complexity of living things with human beings made of trillions of living cells and each producing half of the complex biological code in the of a genetic information code to produce a new living human being. Such biological engineering is ineffably sublime and awesomely inspiring, and then for that new human being to come consciously alive in a way the biology in itself cannot explain.

Even something as simple as collagen which represents an exceedingly small part of a living thing is made up of 1,055 miniature parts in which the odds of falling in to place by chance are, "quite frankly, nil," argues Bill Bryson.

(Bryson 2003, p.351) To explain this Bryson points out that this is equivalent to having 1,055 spinning wheels in a kind of slot machine with each wheel having 20 different symbols on each wheel and for those spinning wheels after being set in motion by pulling a handle on the machine in which every 1,055 of these wheels would stop at the exact same symbol. The odds of this happening to produce what is an exceedingly minute part of a living thing is beyond enormous and even if we reduce the spinning wheels to a mere two hundred (as opposed to 1,055), the odds explain Bryson represents 1 followed by 260 zeros after it. This is more than six times the estimated atoms in the entire universe and this is to produce just an exceedingly small part of the biological complexity of a living thing.

It is little wonder that Bryson reminds us that each one of these hits represent a miracle in its own right so that: "By all the laws of probability proteins should not exist." (Bryson 2006, p.351) Proteins we would remind the reader, is that complex chemical composition that goes to makeup the biological complexity of living things. DNA operating with RNA is the means that can turn amino acids into the biologically complexity of living things and when life started it advanced so swiftly that some like Lord Kelvin thought that perhaps the formula of life landed on the earth on a meteorite from some distant planet in the universe.

But of course, this shows signs of desperation: and no matter from where life originated it still needs to be explained. But for some, this couldn't have anything to do with the working of a wise creator even though no other explanation is forthcoming or realistically possible. For some two billion years or so, bacteria was the only form of life on the earth and then when oxygen levels sufficiently to allow for more complex living cells these began to appear with organelles (*little tools*) and other mechanisms such as mitochondria encased in a sack and with the ability to take in food and execrate the waste. Full-blown cells such as *protists* are wonders of design compared to simple bacteria with a single amoeba cell consisting of some 400 hundred million bits of genetic information which has been worked out would take about 80 books comprising of 500 hundred pages to hold that information. Then those cells began to multiply and organise themselves to become multi-cellular creatures of ever increasing complexity.

It was only in the Cambrian period about 540 million years ago we have more complex life forms coming into existence which reduces the times-pan considerably to produce living things with limbs, gills, nervous system and a brain of sorts which seemed to appear at this time having little to no evidence of gradual development over time. Then more complex animal life forms evolved right up to human beings made up of trillions of living cells each of which made up of twenty thousand different proteins.

We are, of course, an engineering marvel of ordered complexity and we haven't even got to the point of how inanimate matter was turned into the conscious reality of a living mind that could rationally reflect upon its own existence and respond in many different ways to different things perceived according to different categories of understanding inculcated into our existence. Even Richard Dawkins accepts that the idea of a haemoglobin cell coming into existence by chance is unthinkable, while Matthew Cobb writes: "All complex multi-cellular organisms on Earth are what are known as eukaryotes: they have complex cellular structures including a nucleus that houses the chromosome, organelles for synthesising proteins and above all mitochondria which are small energy-producing structures that enable eukaryotic cells to become up to a million times larger than cells without mitochondria, and that allow for cells to combine to form multi-cellular organisms. Rather than a gradual process there appears to have been a single event of mind-boggling improbability, for it involved two life-forms interacting in a most unusual way", to produce cells that are self-replicating. (Cited in Aliens 2016, p.159)Darwin describes evolution as: *"The Preservation of Favoured Races in the Struggle for Life."* But the struggle for life is an extremely complex business as we have seen even at the lowest of level living cells which couldn't have been a random process operating aimlessly within primordial chaos. So what enables living things to be so favoured as to be ordered sufficiently to come into existence as viably complex living things and to live of the resources of a particular environment? We have a struggle to survive, when nothing could struggle to survive before it exists, while inanimate matter could not struggle to do anything except it was being acted upon by the hand of an intelligent order producing cause. Natural selection is anything but natural unless and until the necessary means are deployed to make it natural and so to bring all the necessary means together to bring order out of chaos and living things out of inanimate matter.

And when scientists discover the means by which life was ordered into existence they find that these represent incredibly ingenious means of order producing significance. But rather than regarding these as the work of an order producing intelligence they are credited to no intelligently constituted cause at all and by some to a never-ending process of happenstance or an process of luck operating from the beginning of time to the present day. But happenstance of this order producing magnitude is no explanation at all and effectively means that the origin of life on earth is not explained in any intelligently constituted sense and takes us into the area of what could be referred to as fairy-tale physics.

Darwin himself seems to have been somewhat confused about the significance of his own theory of evolution which on the one hand he rejoices in the power of nature's forces to perform such a feat of biological engineering, but on the other hand could be somewhat confused and his head in a "muddle" when it came to explaining the life producing workings of evolution that seemed to bring into existence living things seemingly without sufficient cause. In his *Autobiography* he writes: "The old argument from design in nature, as given by Paley, which formerly seemed so conclusive, fails now that the law of natural selection has been discovered." (Cited in Brown 2001, p.6)But we now know that all the time natural selection was operating to order producing mechanisms of vast order producing efficiency in the form of DNA as the effective means to bring order our of disorder and living things out of inanimate matter. So just as motor cars are not explained until we explain the factory in which they are produced so we haven't explained life on earth until we explain the origin of the DNA factory in which they were produced.

The fact is that it turned out to be something Darwinians were missing and perhaps something some still didn't really want to see – namely DNA the order producing code of life and RNA the means of using that information to produce what it was setup to produce. Reason itself should have caused Darwin to be cautious before he flew in the face of reason and the irrefutable logic of rational thinking which demands that intelligently ordered effects demand intelligent and sufficient causes and when we desert the logic of rational thinking we are sure to find ourselves on the wrong side of the truth. And when the life producing genome was discovered that explained how evolution actually works to produce intelligent life on earth (at least biologically speaking) it turned out to be an order producing cause of ingenious life producing creativity which takes us back to a process of intelligent design.

Therefore, when Darwin concludes that, there seems to be no more design in the natural selection than in the way the wind blows he is completely wrong because it was always there but he just couldn't see it. (Cited in Brown 2001, p.6) It is obvious that Darwin and the scientists of his time knew nothing of the order producing genius of the life producing genome, but nonetheless it was all the time operating within evolution to produce intelligent life on earth. So Darwin in the above conclusion and those who followed him were completely wrong in this respect because, all the while, there was an order producing mechanism of ingenious order producing ingenuity operating deeply within the workings of evolution.

But Darwin as a professional naturalist and supposedly an intelligent man should have at least suspected that there must be more going on within the process of natural selection than a process of blind randomness oscillating erratically within the context of primordial disorder. He should have held fast to the rock of rational thinking in which effects have causes and intelligently ordered effects of logical necessity do have and must have a cause fit to explain them. But in his apparent naivety Darwin just assumed that everything was falling into place like clockwork with no intelligent agent of ordering in sight, but Darwin should at least have held his counsel rather than abandoning so quickly what reason was trying to teach him.

It seems however that some like Daniel Dennett wants to hold onto the myth of natural selection was operating blind and that it can somehow turn abject disorder into the ordered complexity of living things without the operation of an intelligent and sufficient cause of any kind. Sometimes, of course, as we have indicated, Darwin sometimes refers to the laws of nature as the source of this order-producing phenomenon but he doesn't follow this idea through with any degree of consistency so as to attribute these order producing laws to an order producing cause of life creating excellence. As a Grey who was an American scholar with whom Darwin was constantly in correspondence was trying to convince Darwin that the order producing significance of these laws represented a process of the most exquisite design because as a result of them the ordered complexity of living things was the end result.

Some just naively assumed that things evolved and just took it all for granted that it was natural for this to happen without explaining how, or seriously pondering the means that made it natural. But as a result, every cynic, charlatan and God defying atheist has jumped on the evolutionary bandwagon thinking that they had found a way to circumvent the idea of sufficient cause in the form of a wise creator when all they had was an ill-thought-out theory that failed to deliver and left them hanging from one very elaborate skyhook. Darwin cannot be blamed for not knowing about the ingenious mechanisms of DNA and RNA as the ingenious means whereby primordial chaos was transformed into intelligent life on earth, but as a rational being in which cause is logically related to effect he should at least have held his ground as opposed to abandoning it so quickly so quickly. But Darwin was no philosopher and often admitted that his head was in a "muddle" when it came to the question of evolution and metaphysics, while considering the origin of an eye made him feel ill. (Spencer 2009, p.88)

Moreover, how the biological complexity of a physical body was infused with conscious life and all that this involves by way of qualitative attributes of being is a whole different question which we will address in a later chapter. Voltaire spoke of a 'rational religion' or a 'natural religion', a rational religion supposedly is one is one that calls for an adequate explanation for the immense complexity intelligent life in the form of a wise creator, while natural religion is something that comes naturally to us as rational beings. Michael Behe in his search through evolutionary journals and periodicals found that no matter how evolution by natural selection was referred to the 'how' was always missing which means that evolution by natural selection was never really explained.

However, 'natural selection' is only natural if there is the wherewithal within it to produce intelligent life on earth just as it is natural for a washing machine factory to produce washing machines because it has all the necessary means and mechanisms in place to produce them. So before DNA was discovered evolutionists argued that natural selection outside of any intelligent order producing cause was somehow bringing into being intelligent life on earth. But still many Darwinians have not adjusted their theory of evolution in the light of this massive game-changing fact.

Natural selection was illustrated by Darwin by arguing that something like birds were ordered sufficiently to come into existence and survive within a particular environment and those that were not died out. But how could a process of blind randomness devoid of intelligence, sight or foresight plan or purpose know what any particular environment was like in order to bring into existence living things ordered and suitably equipped to live on the resources of a particular environment? There is nothing natural about evolution by selection if the means are not available to produce the ordered complexity of living things. Natural selection as described by Darwin was at best a refining process it is not a creative process, it can cull those things not sufficiently ordered to survive but as originally conceived it has no means to bring into being those different extremely complex life forms sufficiently ordered to survive within a particular environment.

Mel Thompson refers to those who believe that evolutionists argue that: "…developments in 20th century biology, showing the basis of evolution to be random genetic mutation, make the idea of a vital force redundant." (Thompson 2000, p.100) But the idea of random genetic mutations is complete nonsense because genetic mutations are anything but random and operate to the life producing formula contained within what we now know to be DNA and the order producing power of RNA to carry out with great precision those life-producing instructions within DNA. And as we have already noted, the life producing information within DNA is as hard to explain as life it to explain without it.

Moreover, how did evolution operating as many evolutionists argue, outside of an order producing intelligence of any kind produce male and female to perpetuate the species each massively complex in their own right but coming together in perfect harmony from a different gene sequence to produce offspring in kind? This represents double-act of order producing ingenuity that could not possibly have taken place by chance in which two versions of the same species came into being and come together in the most ingenious way to produce offspring in kind. The chances in terms of odds of this happening by chance are beyond zero – cosmologically impossible. There are those who argue that religious language is misused when it pretends to be scientific. But religion is the ultimate science because it supplies us with an intelligent order producing cause in the form of a wise creator that can explain that which evolution is at a total loss to explain and provide the necessary means to bring order out of chaos and breathe life into inanimate matter.

The Royal Society where intellectuals who joined is association to celebrate the discovers of science and used this to celebrate the fact that such laws were a real and silent witness to the existence of a wise creator so that natural philosophy was an ally of religion and reinforced faith in the idea of wise creator as the mind behind the ordered complexity of all things. While to reject that which logically compelling is but foolishness masquerading as science! Science cannot operate within a vacuum and needs an intelligently ordered world full of intelligently ordered things to reason intelligently about and different attributes of understanding that defines the scope of our understanding.

In fact, the truth is that evolution is so spectacularly successful it comes alive within us to confront us with clear evidence of a living life producing intelligence at work in the universe and expresses itself in all that we have been ordered to be as living entities of profound ontological truth. Therefore, the inner world of being has its own truth to tell as a living expression of that cause from which we have come and has the stamp of a wise creator indelibly etched upon it. But as has Peter Watson referring to Giambattista Vicoa seventeenth century scholar argued that the internal life of mankind can be known in a way over and above that of the physical world of our senses while human culture is truer and more profoundly real than knowledge of the world of physics but: "Man has been too busy looking outside himself to notice." (Watson 2005, p.826–7)

Our own reality of conscious being represents a profound revelation in itself whereby God reveals and communicates to mankind that portion of truth that he has laid within the reach of our natural faculties of understanding. The science of life in all its different disciplines, inner experiences, different categories of understanding are given expression in many different language games as Ludwig Wittgenstein puts it, each with its own truth to tell with regards to different aspects of that subject matter we call life. So just as we do not play chess according to the rules of rugby so we need different terms of reference to describe different attributes of understanding that give expression to different experiences, desires and instincts, hopes and aspirations emanating from within us and that constitute who we are as a species. Therefore, religion as a language game is forced upon us by the natural and compelling propensities of our own heart and the cause and effect logic of rational thinking in which living life defining effects need to be apportioned to a living life producing cause commensurate with all that we experience ourselves to be.

But by reducing reality to empirically based science, some have cut themselves off from the author and giver of life who communicates to us through attributes of being with which he has so richly endowed us as a species. A true and authentic science of life must therefore include all that we experience ourselves to be as sentient beings that take us beyond the world of empirical based reality into the life world that is multi-dimensional in its scope, existentially dynamic in its nature, purposive in its working and qualitative in its significance. But reducing truth to empirically based reality removes all sense of sanctity and sacredness from life and extinguishes those hopes and aspirations to which the human heart aspires.

Jesus warned us not to fear those who can kill the body but He who controls the destiny of the soul, but some seem to have convinced themselves that they have no soul and dance around the totem pole of science and sing praises at the altar of an empirically based idolatry. Thus Daniel Dennett believes that vitalism has been reduced to the trash heap of history unless you are willing to believe that the world is flat. This of course reduces Dennett to an object as opposed to a living subject because we need a vital life producing cause to produce a vital living producing effect. But one can well imagine that if someone was to hit Dennett over the head with a big stick for no good reason that the gangling cells of his physical brain would make a response of vital indignation that could not be explained if his brain was nothing more than a physical entity operating on in an empirically based world.

Dennett is vital enough to with great fervency of spirit and vivacity of mind to declare on the origin of all things and then argues that his existence and the existence of all things have nothing to do with a vital order producing cause of any kind. Therefore, he whose origin represents the order-producing sum of nothing wants to act as if he were very God pronouncing on the origin of all things, so it seems that some professing themselves wise have indeed become fools. Alfred North Whitehead regarded materialism as fundamentally wrong-headed, because when we reduce reality to empirically based matter this leaves unexplained the conscious reality of life through which we experience, interact with and dynamically engage with the world of other people and things.

Some argue that there is nothing in the mind that was not first in the senses, but what good are senses and the empirically based information they convey to the brain if the brain is not ordered intelligently to decipher that information and turn it into categories of understanding that make sense to us and then to make an appropriate response to it. We have an input from our senses and an input from within our own inner reality of being which combine to produce the sum of the human experience that moves us and motivates is in the world of other beings and things. This is where empirically based facts meet the ordered and living sum of who we are to constitute life as we experience it to be.

The plain fact is that empirically based reality is consciously absorbed into a living mind and understood according to different attributes of understanding, thus we might see a flower and regard it as a thing of beauty, smell it and be enthralled by its fragrance, buy a bunch of them and give them to someone as a token of our affection, grow them for the love of it, or sell them to make money and wonder how the DNA originated to bring such a thing of beauty out of the raw chemicals of the earth.

It has been argued that metaphysics go beyond the powers of empirically based science to validate or explain, but why should reality be limited to empirically based criteria when if this were the case we could consciously perceive anything or intelligently understand it. Our mind is presupposed in the act of perceiving and in the act of living and adds its own qualitative dimension of reality to that which we experience by means of our senses. This is why Alfred North Whitehead regarded materialism that split the notions of purpose, value and meaning from scientific explanation as fundamentally wrong-headed. (Cited in Stokes 2006, p.123) While Richard Tarnas believes the empirically based world view: "… seemingly failed to account for the subjective phenomenology of human consciousness and man's sense of being as a personal volitional entity different in character from the unconscious and impersonal world of inanimate matter." (Tarnas 1991, p.352)

It is rather unfortunate that some cannot acknowledge themselves to be vital living entities of some considerable qualitative significance from a chanced upon conglomeration of inanimate matter. Science is doing mankind no favours when it reduces the vast complexity of life on earth to a chanced upon arrangement of physics. So we must move beyond objectivity and look within where the secrets of life are revealed and develop a theory which represents an authentic science of life. Jim Baggott admits that physicists get a little twitchy when confronted with too many coincidences and goes on to argue that in the six fundamental constants of the universe without which we would not have a life-permitting world at all and which seems more than a mere coincidence.

Baggott argues that: "some physicists have dismissed fine-tuning as a non-problem and argues that it's a case of mistaking ignorance for coincidence?" (Baggott 2013, p.150) That is we are just unaware of the causes involved and chalking it up to coincidences. But how would knowing the causes mean that we do not need to explain these causes and the incredible order producing power of them? They all cannot be regarded as mere coincidences. As we have noted, Richard Dawkins willingly admits that we can have a little bit of luck but not too much, but with evolution outside of an underlying cause we seem to have an endless stream of luck which reads more like an elaborate fairy-tale story that breaks all the laws of logic and the principle of sufficient cause. The big bang was not just any old bang but one with the right balance of variables and constants that was just right to produce a life permitting universe part of which was the carbon atom which came in being by such a delicate and complex balance of unlikely interacting variables that Sir Fred Hoyle the highly acclaimed Astrophysicist admitted that it shook his atheism to the very foundation.

While if the Big Bang was not strong enough, it would have resulted in a big crunch collapsing in on itself through the forces of gravity, and if too strong it would have resulted in a big flop in which gravity would not have been strong enough to draw together the cosmic effects of the big bang in which there would have been no universe as we know it at all. But it was within the furnaces of the universe (giant supernovas) that many of the elements necessary for life were formed. All these and much more represent more than a host of happy coincidences and if one order-producing component had been missing life would have been rendered impossibly.

The position of the earth in relation to the sun making it conducive to life, spinning at the right speed, the right moon to act as a stabiliser to keep the earth from wobbling out of control, away from the dangerous asteroid belt, not too hot and not too cold, the right tilt to maximise the sun's heat, gravity to keep our feet firmly on the ground, the right type of water (as opposed to hard water), the right amount of oxygen, the right chemicals to produce all manner of different things, the protective ozone layer around the earth, soil for nutrients to grow crops, rain to water the earth to enable plant life to exist, carbon as a unique chemical necessary to produce life, chemicals necessary to provide us with the building blocks of biological life, the right amount of oxygen finely balanced to sustain life, and the necessary mechanisms of life producing excellence in the form of DNA to produce intelligent life on earth all of which and much more represent a vast kaleidoscope of order producing variables which go to make life on earth possible.

By the 1960s, physicists had discovered around 30 elementary different particles. As well as electrons, protons, neutrons and photons, there were dozens more exotic ones with names like pions, muons, kaons, sigma, quarks, up and down quarks, bottom top quarks, etc. etc. Even the humble atom is not so humble after all which has at its core protons and neutrons to form the nucleus of the atom to produce the strong force (one hundred billion, billion, billion, billion times stronger than gravity), encircled by electrons being driven by electromagnetic forces between them and the nucleus (or core) of the atom. Then we have different kinds of atoms made up of different chemical elements interacting with other atoms in a most complex and involved manner to produce molecules of many different kinds that produce chemical compounds as set out in the Periodic Table.

Then we have explain the vast complexity of a physical brain made up of some 100 billion or so neurons and one quadrillion synapses and then how a physical brain can generate conscious life endowed with elaborate attributes of understanding that sets it apart from inanimate matter that is bereft of all consciousness. But no matter how immensely complex, involved or ingeniously ordered everything is or becomes, it is just regarded by some as an endless stream of coincidences which is not science in any intelligently constituted sense and reads more like a book of fairy tales and just-so stories.

Nick Lane seems close to the mark when he declares that: "Few biologists are more than dimly aware of the black hole at the heart of their subject." (Lane 2015, p.2) Steven Pinker may well argue that "Michael Behe's theory of the irreducible complexity of life is nothing more than taking every phenomenon whose evolutionary history has not yet been figured out and chalks it up to design by default." (Pinker 2002, p.130) But how would knowing the entire history of evolutionary development in all its varied and inspiring order producing complexity mean that this is not a process of intelligent design? Just because we as intelligent beings can increasingly discover the ingenious order producing mechanisms behind an extremely complex and intelligently ordered world doesn't mean that these incredibly ingenious laws of order producing efficiency don't need to be explained. Michael Behe aptly argues that until all of the necessary elements that go to makeup intelligent life on earth are firmly in place and operating in conjunction with every other part we not have the ordered complexity of a living thing.

Moreover, this says nothing about how physics no matter how complexly arranged could produce a living self-conscious mind which is a different kind of reality altogether. As living entities endowed with different attributes of conscious being we need of logical necessity to trace our existence back to a cause that can explain how inanimate matter was brought to life and that our own attributes of being reflect the nature of the cause involved so that we are a finite reflection of that life producing cause from which we have come and can relate to that cause as a living effect to a living life producing cause the name to whom theists call God.

Ben Dupre seems right when he argues that: "There is one thing at once the most obvious and mysterious thing of all that has so far resisted the best efforts of scientist and philosopher alike … We are all immediately conscious of our own consciousness that we have thoughts, feelings, desires that are subjective and private to us; that we are actors at the centre of our world and have a unique and personal perspective on it." (Dupre2007, p.28)So the world of objective reality and the world of our subjective being represent two sides of the human experience and are intertwined and interdependent and represent the reality of the life world and the stage on which it is played out. As Albert Einstein has put it: "All means prove but a blunt instrument, if they have not behind them a living spirit:" while "Science without religion is lame, religion without science is blind."

Gareth Southwell argues that the medieval arguments of philosophers such as Aristotle were based on abstract "reasoning" which he describes as "a sterile philosophy" that is now replaced with, "experiment and observation." (Southwell 2013, p.24) However, how could experiment and observation mean that those things investigated and found to be both extremely complex and intelligently ordered do not need to be rationally assessed and apportioned to an appropriate cause? Some theorists seem so keen to dispense with the idea of God they are willing to forsake the ground of rational thinking which is the very ground of science based investigation. So abstract reason is not a sterile philosophy is the very ground of science itself.

We see something of the folly of things falling into place by chance when we know something of the fantastic nature of the odds involved. Something of a mere 200 parts falling into place by chance the odds work out at 1 with 375 zeros after it. The only way we can conceive something of the magnitude of these odds is to point out that the estimated number of *subatomic* particles in the entire universe is a mere I with 80 zeros after it in comparison. Atoms come out at 1 with 40 zeros after it. The nucleus of the atom is 10,000 times smaller the overall size of the atom. So if we have 200 hundred scrambled letters the odds of arranging them to produce an intelligible sentence the odds work out at the above odds of 1 with 375 zeros after it, odds that are inconceivably vast.

Therefore, in the light of this, what are the odds of a self-replicating bacterium *Mycoplasma genitalium* which has 482 genes with 580,000 letters coming into existence by chance when the odds of 200 things coming into existence by chance are so astronomically vast as that described above? As we have noted there are some 3.2 billion letters in the human genome which makes the odds of them coming into existence by chance so utterly vast it can it can be completely and emphatically discounted. What would the odds be to produce a human being with an estimated 50 to 60 or so trillion cells by chance – each cell being an exceedingly complex reality on its own right? All of a sudden the estimated length of the universe becomes an eye-blink compared to what is needed to produce a single living cell and as we shall see later in our study that Richard Dawkins is forced to admit this.

Dawkins not only accepts the magnitude of these odds but comes up with some figures of his own as to the enormity of the odds to produce something as small as haemoglobin cell, and fully accepts that chance alone could not possibly produce such a thing. This we will be examining more closely in a later chapter in which Dawkins is forced to come up with the idea of 'cumulative selection' with its 'replicator power' which turns evolution into a process of intelligent design. Matthew Cobb professor of Zoology at the University of Manchester readily accepts that what happened on earth to produce 'eukaryotes' which are small cellular structures with a nucleus that houses the chromosomes, organelles for synthesising proteins and mitochondria which are small energy-producing structures that enable eukaryotic cells to become up to a million times larger than cells without mitochondria and can also allow for cells to combine to form multi-cellular organisms.

In principle, adds Cobb, we could calculate the probability of the appearance of such eukaryotes, but alas: "we would soon run out of zeros, because the chances are so 'incredible improbable' because it requires some way of transporting matter, energy and information from the environment into its interior." (Aliens 2016, p.161) Cobb refers to this as a process of mind-boggling improbability and this only takes us as far as the level of the simplest living cells that combine to produce algae in which hundreds of thousands could "sit on the head of a pin." And to this adds Cobb: "makes it incredibly improbable that the kinds of organisms we see on Earth have their equivalents elsewhere" in the universe. (Aliens 2016, p.161) In the end Cobb concludes: "We are just very, very, lucky."

But how lucky can a process of blind randomness get operating blindly within what before was a state of primordial disorder when the odds are as vast as those described above even to produce the simplest living thing? There is a limit to what luck can do and the more luck we need the more likely it is that luck had nothing to do with it. It seems that every time scientists are faced with something that proves to be so massively improbable, even statistically impossible, it is just chalked up to luck making luck a convenient escape route for those who have no explanation for the order sum of anything. Such thinking reduces evolution to a weird form of cosmic magic minus a magician of course.

Similarly, Nick Lane argues that: "There is a black hole at the heart of biology. Bluntly put, we do not know why life is the way it is … We do know that this common ancestor was already a very complex cell." Moreover, ribosomes are orders of magnitude smaller still. You have 13 million of them in a single cell from your liver. But ribosomes are not only incomprehensibly small, on a scale of atoms they are massive, sophisticated super-structures. Therefore: "It has become starkly apparent in the past few years, and only to those who follow evolutionary biology, that there is a deep and disturbing discontinuity at the heart of biology." (Lane 2016, p.21) "So incorporating energy into evolution is long overdue and begins to lay a more predictive basis to natural selection." (Lane 2016, p.289) Therefore Lane concludes: "The internet swamps us with all manner of indiscriminate facts, mixed with varying degrees of nonsense. But it's not merely a case of information overload. Few biologists are more than dimly aware of the black hole at the heart of their subject." (Lane 2016, p.2)

In the book *Alas Poor Darwin*, Gabriel Dover likens evolution to an aeroplane described in the following way: "For example, we can envisage evolution having learned the trick of permitting ongoing changes in the design of an aeroplane, whilst the bloody thing is flying in the air! Biological evolution does not need to have the plane crash every time one of its thousands of its supposedly 'selfish' parts (genes) decides to mutate." (Cited in Alas Poor Darwin 2000, p.64) Well, praise the good Lord and pass the biscuits because that would be some aeroplane. An aeroplane that came into existence by chance, that can modify itself while flying in mid-air to become an ever-more sophisticated aeroplane by chance is not an aeroplane the writer would care to travel in. In fact, we could not travel in such an aeroplane because such an aeroplane could not possibly exist.

One feels like asking how utterly complex and sophisticated living things would have to be before some evolutionary theorists would even begin to consider the possibility that behind intelligent life on earth there is an order producing intelligence. For some, it seems there is no point they would begin to suspect that life on earth is so massively complex it needs to be explained in terms of a cause fit to explain it, and continue to believe that nothing of any order producing significance produced the ordered sum of everything.

Even Richard Dawkins admits that something like an eye or a haemoglobin cell coming into existence by chance is utterly impossible and with the chance of a single haemoglobin molecule coming into existence by luck is 'unthinkable'. But Dawkins doesn't explain that part of evolution other than luck that according to his own analysis is needed to produce intelligent life on earth. Dawkins goes on to work out the approximate odds of such a single haemoglobin molecule coming into existence by chance which is but an exceedingly small part of the body at 1 with 190 zeros after it. It is no wonder that Dawkins concludes that we need something more than luck to explain the vast complexity of living things, and goes on to introduce mechanisms of 'cumulative selection' into his evolutionary theory in which: "One sieving process is fed into a subsequent sieving process which is fed into … and so on and so forth." (Dawkins 1988, p.45)

These many processes all feeding into the evolutionary grid are meant to explain how evolution can work to do what a single process could not possibly do as of all these processes of ordered and integrated complexity did not need to be explained in terms of a most sophisticated process of order producing ingenuity imaginable. A multi-dimensional process with many different processes all feeding into the evolutionary grid to produce exceedingly complex living things. Dawkins within a different context explains that to produce a short phrase made up of a mere 28 steps such as "Me thinks it is like a weasel" which is a short phrase from Shakespeare which to produce by chance represent odds he works out are so vast it would take about a million, million, million times longer than the estimated age of the universe to come about. The age of the universe is estimated to be 13.7 billion years. (Dawkins 1988, p.49)

Then to continue with this analogy, this simple 28 letter phrase with its mind-boggling odds have to be joined to millions of other phrases, sentences, paragraphs, pages and chapters that would fill an inestimable multitude of books to hold those massive odds needed to bring into existence the human genome made up of some 3.2 billion letters. So if it would take a million, million, million years longer than the universe has existed to produce a 28-letter phrase by chance how long would it take to produce 3.2 million letters of genetic information falling into place by chance to produce a human being?

Dawkins asks to be allowed to introduce DNA to help explain how evolution works without explaining the origin of DNA of course. Evolutionists therefore, must face up to the fact that there comes a point when attributing the origin of exceedingly complex living things to a process of chance, luck and happenstance is not merely logically impossible but utterly ludicrous. And once scientists set out to show by means of intelligence how evolution operates they have lost the argument in terms of rational thinking because things must first be ordered intelligently before they can be investigated intelligently and understood intelligently.

We could not describe intelligently the results of the working of a process of blind randomness because within the context of primordial disorder would produce nothing but an endless stream of incomprehensible nonsense a perpetual morass of order-less entanglement. Therefore, there comes a point when things falling into place by chance to produce increasingly more complex living things move from being "a statistical improbability on a colossal scale," as Dawkins calls it, to an utter and complete impossibility on any scale. The fact is that it isn't natural to assume the selection into existence of complex living things where the means that make them selectable does not exist. The term 'natural' is added to 'selection' by evolutionists to make selection look natural and inevitable, when that which makes living things selectable is manifestly complex and singularly ingenious.

In fact, we find that the whole idea of natural selection has been shrouded in mystery and subsumed in obscurity and this has become an issue within an increasing number of evolutionary theorists themselves some calling the whole idea into question and having to resort to the genetic information within DNA to explain how natural selection actually works without explaining the origin of DNA of course. Richard Dawkins tries to qualify the term randomness by arguing that: "There is randomness and randomness, and many people confuse different meanings of the word. There are in truth, many respects in which **mutation is not random.** (Dawkins 1988, p.306) All I would insist is that these respects do not include anything equivalent to anticipation of what would make it better for the animal." But lack of anticipation and planning afore thought takes us back to a process of blind randomness which means that we are going round in circles and getting precisely nowhere.

It seems that some Darwinians have indeed dug themselves into an ideological hole with nothing to explain the ordered complexity of anything and the more they dig the deeper they get into what is a complete contradiction in terms. Even in the days subsequent to the publication of Darwin's *Origin of Species* the theory of 'natural selection' was not taken all that seriously with the focus being centred on the process of gradual change over time with the means by which this was accomplished was largely left unexplained. Some just assumed that order was somehow appearing out of chaos by means of natural selection without explaining how natural selection actually worked to accomplish this massive order-producing feat of biological engineering. Many of the early reviewers of his book were highly sceptical about the whole idea of 'natural selection' and its ability to do what Darwin thought it could do. This included some who were otherwise sympathetic to Darwin's theory and who gave good reviews of his book by way of technical merit.

John F.W. Herschel a philosopher whom Darwin admired, called it: 'the law of higgledy-piggledy', while Lyell an academic friend of Darwin never fully accepted it, arguing that the human mind at least required the services of a divine creator because it represented a living and spiritual dimension of conscious being that could not be explained in empirically based terms. Another referred to it as: "wasteful, blind and blundering." Darwin's old professor, Adam Sedgwick, was unsatisfied with Darwin's emphasis on materialism, argued that: "There is a moral and metaphysical part of nature as well as a physical. A man who denies this is deep in the mire of folly … and sinks the human race into a lower grade of degradation than any other into which it has fallen since its written records tell us of its history." (Cited in Spencer 2009, p.78) T.H. Huxley (Darwin's Bulldog) thought that the idea of natural selection could not be proved and Darwin himself was never completely happy with this element of his thesis knowing that natural selection was an inference as opposed to a proven fact.

Huxley defended Darwin's theory of evolution, but believed that it did not amount to much scientifically and was of the opinion that evolution did not disprove the existence of God, merely that his existence could not be established scientifically. (Cited in Watson 2005, p.871) Richard Owen accepted evolution but insisted that its course was predetermined by a divine plan. Huxley would not fully accept evolution preferring to believe that "variation was directed instead of being random as Darwin supposed." (Cited in Making Modern Science 2005, p.150)

The fact remains that living things had first to be ordered intelligently before they could be selected as viable living things and had to be increasingly ordered to have any life enhancing direction. But even with this, Watson rightly concedes that there was a major weakness in the theory of evolution, there was no explanation of how inherited characteristics were passed on to subsequent generations. (Watson 2005, p.872ff) Henry Plotkin rightly observes: "Cause and effect are correlative terms… Causation implies action, agency and, perhaps, motive." (Plotkin 1997, p.177) In the final analysis it is evolutionary theorists themselves who have sabotaged their own theory by refusing to allow the idea of intelligent design or an intelligent and a sufficient cause of any kind over the threshold of their theory of evolution.

This is why as alluded to earlier that, Michael Behe after reading Michael Denton's well-researched book, *Evolution, A Theory in Crisis,* was surprised that a theory he believed in was seriously called into question. This caused him to do some research for himself and after careful examination of the relevant evolutionary literature he discovered that while evolutionists would argue how natural selection could produce the ordered complexity of living things, *"the how was always missing."* (Behe 1996) Thus, natural selection is really an unproven assumption, and what many neo-Darwinians now do is to introduce mechanisms of DNA and RNA to explain how natural selection actually works without explaining the origin of these mechanisms of life generating genius.

Others slip intelligent design in by the back door under the guise of other names such as Richard Dawkins theory of 'cumulative selection' with theorists like Dean Keith Simonton arguing that with evolution: "The elements themselves contain properties that will determine how well they fit together" to produce complex life-forms without giving due credit to those order producing elements. (Simonton 1988, p.9) Even with this we still need the much-needed energy to bring all these means together and the intelligence to fit them into their right place before we have the ordered complexity of anything.

If the carbon atom alone had been not existed, life on the earth would have been rendered impossible. The odds of the carbon atom coming into existence by chance, such are the delicate and utterly complex variables that are needed to produce it, Sir Fred Hoyle, as we have already mentioned, admits that it shook his atheism to the very foundation.

And yet we have to explain how the vast complexity of a physical brain made up of some 100 to 120 billion neurons and one quadrillion synapses fell into place by a process that wasn't trying to do anything, and in the end can produce more by way of conscious mind than a physical brain could conceivably explain. Mel Thompson points out in his book *Religion and Science* that: "Religion and moral aspects of humankind require a holistic rather than a reductionist approach." (Thompson 2000, p.88) In the final analysis, what is the point in doing science if nothing of any order producing significance produced the manifest sum of everything? It could be said of those who believe that life on earth could come into existence by an never ending process of luck, happenstance, or a random configuration of chemicals could fall into place to produce the ordered sum of living things could be likened to what Shakespeare described as: "A tale told by an idiot, full of sound and fury signifying nothing?"

Chapter 5
Seeking the Living Among the Dead

Theology could be regarded as a language game forced upon us by means of reason. That is to explain an intelligently ordered world full of intelligently ordered things in terms an intelligent and sufficient cause and to explain living things in terms of a living life producing cause. That cause takes us by logical necessity into the realm of theology which centres on the idea of a wise creator whose existence we believe to be rationally compelling and as conscious beings of life-defining and substance and significance that cause is and must be a living life producing cause commensurate with all that we experience ourselves to be. Theology could be regarded as the working of a rational mind endeavouring to come to terms with themselves as human beings biologically complex, consciously alive, qualitatively profound. We can existentially connect as sentient beings with other human beings and different animals in the kingdom by means of attributes we possess as a species such a sense of presence, emotionally charged feelings of psychological connectedness such as love, fascination, excitement, love and mutual respect. So also, we would argue, we can connect with our maker who had endowed us with these attributes of being having stamped his image upon us and with whom we can relate to as spirit with spirit and mind with mind.

We also have also a sense of awe and wonder, a sense of moral purpose, an appreciation and excitement of being alive, with the capacity to love and a sense of being loved hopes and aspirations to which the human heart aspires. We can therefore relate to God as our Father and creator and to our fellowmen with whom we share these different attributes of being. We are endowed with a conscience and a sense of good and evil. As Peter concluded in the book of Acts, "Of a truth I perceive that God is no respecter of persons: But in every nation he who fears him and does that which is right is accepted by him." But if we are nothing of any order producing significance and just tumbled into existence by some freak accident to live our lives as oddball freaks in a purposeless world then everything changes.

But that is not how we perceive ourselves, we can glory in our intelligence as human beings, delight ourselves in the beauty of the earth, proceed to investigate all that exists in terms of intelligence and be inspired at the wondrous complexity of it all, award ourselves degrees and accolades for our academic ability to understand some particular aspect of it, see life as precious and mourn over the death of a loved one, look up to the heavens and stand in awe and wonder at it and then in one enormous cowardly cop-out some attribute it all to nothing and that it all ultimately means nothing. But these are those who defy reason and deny the evidence not theists who take the evidence as meaning something profound and that the sum of the evidence points to an origin of enormous and ineffable significance.

It is true that we don't know our creator as He knows us that is a given, but we can know Him as God has ordained it to be in spirit and in truth and according to our own powers of reason as we reflect on ordered and living sum of the effects produced and thereby get some clear approximation of the cause involved in relation to the ordered and living sum of the effects produced. When we lose that logical connection between effects in relation to their causes we lose all sense of reality are can believe almost anything. John Polkinghorne captures the holistic vision emerging from the religion-science dialogue with his thesis being essentially that: "We live in one world and science and theology are exploring different aspects of it." (Hodgson 1994, p.87) One is operating to an empirically based reality of what is a highly ordered physical world and the other to evidence of the life world and putting the two together we get a clear approximation of the nature of the origin of all thing. The rational mind naturally comes up with the idea of a wise creator, so if the idea of such a creator had hitherto never been conceived we would need to forthwith postulate it and begin to engage that supreme being both in terms of reason as well as in spirit and in truth.

But it seems that some are moving in the opposite direction so that the more incredibly ordered and immensely complex they find the universe and everything in it to be the more they are determined to apportion all to nothing of any order producing significance. In this the evidence is not on their side and that in spite of their so much of boasted intelligence defy the logic of rational thinking and apportion the ordered sum of all that exists to nothing of any order producing significance or to an endless stream chanced upon occurrences. Mark Henderson argues in the publication *50 genetics ideas you really need to know* that: "Natural Selection is a powerful engine fuelled by genetics." (Henderson 2008, p.18) But this mechanism of life producing genius does not merely result in a biological body, but a biological body that comes to life within us, even though we cannot understand or explain how a physical brain can of itself generate all that we experience ourselves to be as sentient beings and the different attributes of understanding we possess as a species.

Henderson goes on to argue that: "For all Darwin's brilliance, his theory still lacked something critical at its core because it had no way of accounting for the variations that were passed on from one generation to the next." (Henderson 2008, p.8) However, the problem is even greater than this because the life producing information within evolution has first to be explained before that information could be passed on to subsequent generations. Information that can explain not only the biological complexity of a physical body, but an intrinsic world of inner being that constitutes the life world.

Darwin's finches, for instance, had first to have a desire procreate and the necessary biological equipment with which to do so before they could produce posterity to perpetuate their species. Richard Dawkins asks to be allowed to introduce DNA to explain how natural selection works to produce intelligently ordered living things. (Dawkins 1988, p.141)But when Dawkins asks to be allowed to use the order producing genius of DNA to explain intelligent life on earth he is asking to use something he cannot explain, either in terms of a complex biological body or a conscious living mind that determines who we are living in a complex physical world. This leaves the "Blind Watchmaker" theory in tatters failing miserably to explain how a blind and brain-dead watchmaker could perform such a feat life generating creativity. Either that or the Blind Watchmaker is not so blind and gormless after all.

Daniel Dennett readily affirms in his book *Darwin's Dangerous Idea* that: "Even the simplest replicating macro is far from simple, however, a composition with thousands or millions of parts depending on how we count the raw materials that go to make it." (Dennett 1995, p.157) While Erwin Schrodinger suggests that: "living creatures drink orderliness from the environment." (Cited in Ridley 199, p.12) But we cannot by definition get living things out of dead and inanimate matter no matter how ingeniously it is arranged, something else is needed to bring matter to life and scientists have not yet discovered it because they are looking in all the wrong places to find it. It is our inner reality of being that determines who we are and what life is really all about, the body being the physiological reality within which life is played out within a physical world. Therefore, the body is the object while the mind is the subject within which we live and move and have our being.

For Plato it was the mind and soul, the essence and attributes of moral being and intellectual truth that was the bases on which the purpose of life has been established and revealed. Reason was the divinely inspired faculty by which the human soul could discover its own essence and the world's meaning. The mind therefore reveals within itself knowledge of its own nature of being which sets out the agenda of how life is played out in the physical world. The inner world of being, the spiritual world, for Socrates and Plato was regarded as forever superior to the temporal world of physics. This is why Socrates urged his hearers to *"know thyself"* lest in living they missed or misunderstood what life was really all about. What does it really matter if we had all knowledge of the physical world, could solve the mysteries about the mundane world of matter if we don't really know who we are or why we are on this earth? As Richard Tarnas writes with respect to the philosopher Emanuel Kant:

The human spirit does not merely prescribe nature's phenomenal order; rather, the spirit of nature, brings forth its own order through the human mind when that mind is employing its full complement of faculties. Then human language itself can be recognised as rooted in a deeper reality, as reflecting the universe's unfolding meaning.

While "Hegel emphasised, the evolution of human knowledge is the evolution of the world's self-revelation." (Cited in Tarnas 1996, p.435) It is not physics that makes the man it is the world of the spirit that is different in character and more profoundly real than the unconscious external world of physics but in both we have a true and holistic science of life. We need a science of the existence of man, and it seems to the writer that the modern scientific worldview failed to engage the larger intellectual challenge of being and that science's mechanistic and objective conception of reality was not merely limited but fundamentally flawed. As Richard Tarnas writes: "The natural world was not just an opaque material stage upon which men briefly resided as a foreigner to work out his spiritual destiny … Rather, nature and spirit were intimately bound up with each other, and the history of one touched the history of the other." (Cited in Tarnas 1996, p.180) For many early scientists from Copernicus to Newton and from Boyle to Locke, science they believed confirmed the existence of God as a necessary cause to explain the ever increasing complexity that science was revealing the world to be. As Paul Johnston points out: All agreed that scientific knowledge was a powerful agent against atheism while Locke argued that: "The visible marks of extraordinary wisdom and power appear plainly in all the works of creation that a rational creature who seriously reflects on them cannot miss the discovery of a deity." This is undoubtedly why even Huxley refused to accept natural selection as the sole mechanism of evolution and that it was not random as Darwin supposed. So as Richard Tarnas aptly perceives:

In this perspective, nature pervades everything, and the human mind in all its fullness is itself is a living expression of nature's essential being. And it is only when the human mind actively brings forth from within itself the full powers of a disciplined imagination and saturates its empirical observation with archetypal insight that a deeper reality of the world emerges. [Tarnas 1991, p.434]

Augusta Comte coined the term 'sociology' and insisted that it signified an area of science that would have laws of its own, laws that were metaphysical in nature as opposed to that of the physical senses, thus we have social Darwinism that takes us into the world of the spirit that determines how we react with and engage with other living things. Just as reason is the cement of the physical universe so love in all its forms is the glue of human relationships. Even David Hume the eighteenth century philosopher and sceptic accepted that the power of human nature breaks the force of sceptical arguments and completely destroys what he believed was the weakness of human reason. Therefore, David Hume ends up arguing in his dialogue concerning Natural Religion that: "To a philosophical sceptic is, in a man of letters, the first and most essential step towards being a sound believing Christian." In other words, the limited powers of human reason eventually runs into infinity in a world of vast complexity beyond our finite mind to fully comprehend so that we should trust our own nature which has stamped upon it the idea of a wise creator. So both nature and reason based science are telling the same story and are each reinforcing the other.

Matthew Alper talks about how chemistry diverges into a whole new science, namely bio-chemistry by which the raw and inanimate chemicals of the earth are turned into all manner of living things as if this was all so natural and inevitable needing no intelligent explanation over and above that which we apportion to physics. Alper goes on to add that: Miller had simulated the earth's evolution. He had synthesized amino acids the building blocks of all organic matter, the essence of all life. In doing so, Miller had accomplished what was formally believed to be the exclusive privilege of Gods. "And yet, here it was organic evolution without gods." (Alper 2006, p.32)

But Alper is confusing organic matter and organic compounds with the reality of conscious life which is a different thing altogether. Moreover, even organic compounds as the basic ingredients of life are so utterly complex they could not be explained by blind chance. Moreover, just because science has discovered something of the vast complexity of life at the level of biochemistry does mean this doesn't need to be explained in terms of sufficient cause. And if it took intelligent minds, even the best brains in the scientific world, to discover this complex world of organic matter it would surely take an intelligent mind to order it so. How did Miller achieve this synthesis of chemicals to produce a few amino acids? Was it not by using his intelligence? And as we know it was, what measure of intelligence would it take to produce a complete living cell and even more to produce an exceeding more complex multi-cellular organism? Its intelligence all the way, so that scientists are only discovering a process of intelligent ordering which had nothing to do with them and that was operating long before they arrived on the scene to investigate such things and that by means of their God-given intelligence. Miller did not set up his experiment by having a brainstorm or with no thought or intelligence.

Brian Silver argues that even if heat, radiation, and lightning, on the young earth had produced the amino acids and nucleotides needed for present forms of life, the gap between an aqueous solution of these molecules and a living cell are stupendous. It is a question of organisation in the absence of a guiding intelligence. (Silver 1998, p.345) To this day no one has been able to produce an actual living cell out of lifeless chemicals in a laboratory so the debate about the first moment of life's incarnation still rages. So when some apparently self-assured scientist points to a piece rock that fell from the sky and claims that inside it they have found a few amino-acids as if they were halfway to explaining intelligent life on earth they are being both singularly naive and highly misleading. It is a bit like saying that because we have the necessary chemicals to produce a bulldozer we are well on our way to having a bulldozer. Or because we have the necessary bricks to build a house, and that just appeared by blind chance, we are well on our way to having a well-build house when even the bricks need to be explained.

It is worth remembering that in thousands of experiments scientists have never got any farther in producing better results than the few amino acids of Miller and Urey experiments of 1953. The reason, of course, was as Professor Brian Silver points out that: "the gap between an aqueous solution of these molecules and a living cell is stupendous." We should also remember that the Miller and Uray experiment produced only two simple molecules when we need forty or so to produce a simple primitive cell. While Arthur Schopenhauer could rightly affirm that: "To believe that physical and chemical forces could of themselves bring about an organism is not merely mistaken but, already remarkably stupid." (Cited in Silver, 1998, p.339) "We are…" adds Silver:

"…intelligent beings who can purposively bring together chemicals under carefully controlled conditions. This is very different from accounting for the spontaneous formation of living systems in an inanimate world empty of intelligence. And we have come nowhere near creating life in a laboratory." [Silver 1998, p.339]

The Haldane-Opera-Miller experiment is out of date and scientists have generally given up on repeating this experiment because many repeated failures to get anywhere, and it is a fact that in spite of their exceedingly small size. Moreover it is not enough that extremely simple cells could come into existence by chance, those cells needed to be able to replicate or they existence would have led nowhere. The problem is the lack of what are called nucleotides (DMA and RNA) as independent systems capable of replication of which it can be said:

There are no systems more ordered than the living cell and its components. … It stretches the credibility of a materialistic abiogenesis fanatic to believe that protons and nucleotides persistently emerged simultaneously, and at the same point in space, from the primordial soup. We are in trouble enough without adding events of an astronomical improbability… [Silver 1998, p. 347]

Of the forty or so simple molecules that would be needed to form a simple primitive cell, the experiment produces two, and as Silver observes, in the Millar experiment deliberately handpicked particular chemicals with malice aforethought to help enable their experiment to bring about the desired effects formaldehyde and cyanide ion because they are highly reactive to help and was chosen because contains carbon and nitrogen. Moreover, we have no reason to suppose that cyanide and formaldehyde was to be found anywhere in primitive earth or in nature, only in manmade chemical factories, adds Silver. (Silver 1998, p.245–6) It is little wonder that physicist Paul Davies should remark that: "It seems bizarre, but in my opinion science offers a surer path to God than religion." (Cited in Strobell, p.286)

Julian Huxley imagined that something like a horse could have evolved into existence by something like a million mutational steps, and this is to assume that we already have the necessary complex molecules and living cells to produce more complex living things like a horse. Moreover, this number of steps seem extremely small from such small beginnings as molecules to produce a horse be chance, but even on these terms a thousand mutations represent odds that are so staggering immense they are unthinkable working out at $2^{1,000,000}$, or one out of $10^{3000,000}$, which represent odds so utterly vast they are effectively incomprehensible.

When we understand that there are reckoned to be only some 10^{80} electron sized subatomic particles in the entire universe, and 10^{18} seconds in 30 billion years do we get some idea of the incomprehensible nature of these massive odds. So, within a subtle, and one might say misleading, form of reductive absurdity the complex reality of life is explained away leaving us with a totally false impression of the origin of life on earth with the origin of life on earth being passed off as a veritable host of lucky flukes from the beginning of time to the present day. We also must remember that these million or so steps need to produce a horse by means of a slow but steady progression towards the evolution of the horse, but a sequence of events operating randomly within primordial chaos would never ever produce a horse. We now know that this is so because of the discovery of DNA, the order producing origin of which is as great a mystery today as it ever was, and not merely set up to produce horses but a veritable multitude of different living things.

Rupert Sheldrake argues that even the most ardent defenders of the mechanistic theory of evolution smuggle purposive organising principles into living organisms in the form of selfish genes or genetic programs of immense order producing profundity. In the light of the big bang theory, the entire universe is more like a growing, developing organism than a machine running out of steam. (Sheldrake 2013, p.55)But when we ask evolutionists to explain the origin and nature of this exploitative force operating within evolution, they then inform us that it is only a figure of speech and should not be taken literally. Thus we have a massive cosmic game of *who done it?* Evolution was blind and couldn't do it, the physical environment devoid of intelligence couldn't do it, and if God is dead he wasn't there to do it, then in a flash of inspiration it was decided that nothing did it.

Matthew Alper can also recognise that man is a spiritual animal, a musical animal and a cultural animal due to the fact that we possess a neurophysiologically based spiritual functions which he refers to as the God part of the brain. This all sounds all so sophisticated, but Alper does not explain how all that we know about the working of the brain can generate that which is spiritual in nature, sacred in form and qualitative in character. This is a different kind of reality altogether to the working of a physiological organ we call the brain. Moreover, if we are neurophysiologically wired up to think God-like thoughts then this is part of who we experience ourselves to be, and are surely as genuine and authentic as any other thoughts and ideas we possess as human beings.

But alas just when one thinks we are getting somewhere we have a qualification in which it is argued that this doesn't mean that God is: "… a transcendental force or entity that actually exists 'out there', beyond and independent of us." (Alper 1996, p.130) It is in fact a copying mechanism that compels us to believe in an illusionary reality so as to help us survive our unique awareness of death. But why should meaningless *dorks* whose origin is as meaningless as it is futile fear death and seek repose in an imaginary deity. Who or what could engineer this feat of biological engineering as a corrective to our fear of death? Or perhaps it's not a case of corrective surgery at all to correct a previous fault, but the subtle ploy by Alper to avoid the idea of a wise creator to whom he might be answerable as a moral being. And seeing that the idea of a wise creator is both a logical and compelling we had surely be best to stick to the original plan in the idea of a wise creator than modifying his thinking that runs against the whole course of rational thinking.

And if belief in God is a means to ally our fear of death why doesn't Alper keep his mouth shut and his pen try because he is only resurrecting our fear of death thus defeating the whole exercise. And seeing that he an atheist is not afraid of death this must mean that the whole exercise is a utter waste of time so that one doesn't need to invent God to alleviate one's fear of death because some can reverse the whole course of rational thinking and deceive themselves into thinking that they don't need the services of a wise creator to explain the ordered complexity of life on earth. And yet if the same people were to invent something of some useful purpose they would be of the parent office to record their invention, laugh at those who would suggest that it didn't need to be ordered at all and it fell into existence by blind chance, and to sue those who dared copy it.

Nietzsche may have hypothesized that God was dead, but now science has proved it argues Alper. But not, we would argue, unless Nietzsche is God and Alper his sidekick. But finite men should be extremely careful about playing around with life as though it was something to be kicked carelessly around leaving our children having no ultimate purpose in life turning to drink, drugs and anything else they can dream up to satisfy an otherwise empty and meaningless existence. It seems that there is no lengths to which some will some will go to keep their prejudiced soul their own. Nietzsche denied the existence of God and this did not turn so well for him in the end: but perhaps we should pity Nietzsche because no one knows what inner struggles led to his hapless condition and theists generally believe is a God of love and mercy that always leaves room for hope. But those who refuse to take life seriously and think they can explain it away within a vacuum of causeless irrelevance are surely skating on very thin ice.

Darwin thought he could do away with the cause and effect logic of rational thinking and considered that evolution seemed to explain intelligent life on earth without reference to an intelligent and sufficient cause in the form of a wise creator, But he was wrong, because unknown to him God had in place the necessary means within evolution in the form of DNA and RNA to bring into being intelligent life on earth. Darwin may well have described what he believed was happening with birds with different beaks on the different Galapagos Islands, but he was completely unaware of the existence of DNA which we now know are needed before any such birds could come into existence in the first place. Darwin did not therefore explain how the finches in all their ordered and integrated complexity came into existence in the first place, or how evolution knew that such creatures needed beaks to survive within any island when evolution as a process of blind randomness could not possibly have known or foreseen what was available to eat on any island and that could be foraged by means of a beak.

Such ordering undoubtedly represents an ingenious process of planning-afore-thought by a mind that must have known what food was available to eat on a particular island and equipped its prodigy to come into existence and to survive within the resources available within a particular environment. Life had first to exist before any form of selection could take place, and it is obvious that one cannot select what isn't there and for intelligent life to exist it had first had to ordered so. We now know the ingenious means by which life on earth was ordered into existence but these ingenious order producing means still need to be explained or selection could not have taken place. Such birds must first exist before they could be fine-tuned to a particular or changing environment.

There is nothing natural about exceedingly complex living things coming into existence by means of blind randomness ready and equipped to live within a particular environment which before their existence they knew absolutely nothing about. Natural selection, therefore, strictly speaking only applies to fine-tuning, not to the order complexity of the bird, beast or living thing which had first to exist by means so ingenious that this could not possibly have fallen into place by a process of blind and blundering randomness. This is the fatal flaw that lies at the heart of the theory of Darwinian evolution because if the means were not available to produce the ordered complexity of the living bird there would be no bird no ordered sum of anything in a universe devoid of intelligence. Richard Dawkins admits that: "To try to make a man, you were to shake your biochemical cocktail-shaker for a period of time so long that the entire age of the universe would be an eye-blink, and even then you would not succeed."

But then Dawkins does a peculiar thing to try to get himself out of this most embarrassing conundrum, he introduces evolution as the solution. But if evolution is a process of blind randomness and nothing to do with a process of intelligent ordering sufficient to bring into existence the immense complexity of life on earth this does this solve his problem? Unless evolution is operating to an order producing intelligence sufficient produce intelligent life on earth he has explained nothing so we are back to square one. He can't use DNA to explain intelligent life on earth because DNA is as difficult to explain as life is to explain without it. So to argue that the existence of DNA and RNA can explain intelligent life on earth we are back to a process of intelligent design behind which there is, and indeed must be, an most ingeniously creative designer at work in the universe to do what Dawkins admits a process of blind randomness could not possibly explain.

And this designer has many other ingenious designs up his sleeve which he wants to use to produce all kinds of intelligently ordered living things until the whole earth is full of all manner living things, and then proceeds to beautify the whole earth with many forms of flowers and plant live which also serves to help sustain life on earth. Without such an ingenious order producing cause operating in the universe to produce the resplendent and inspiring complexity of intelligent life on earth we have nothing to explain the ordered complexity of anything. The standard theory of evolution is a dead end until like theists we introduce the idea of wise creator.

Richard Gregory, a notable Darwinian, has the integrity to admit this gross inconsistency that lies at the heart of the standard theory of evolution when he writes: "The question of 'success', and 'progress', and 'fittest' biologically and socially, has never been satisfactorily answered. As a result there is an essential circularity in Darwin's theory of evolution." (Gregory 1993, p.172) Mary Midgley has aptly argued that: "Genes cannot be selfish or unselfish, any more than atoms can be jealous, elephants abstract, or biscuits teleological." Mark Henderson may well argue in reply to this that Dawkins only said that genes give the impression that they are acting selfishly when they really aren't. (Cited in Henderson 2008, p.62) Moreover, it seems utterly futile to refer to something as being selfish when according to empirically based science there is no verifiable self to act selfishly operating within the bog-standard theory of evolution. There is nothing but a process of blind dumb luck operating aimlessly within the context of primordial chaos.

In fact, DNA puts a process of intelligent design at the very heart of evolution, and for Dawkins to apportion intelligent life to DNA is like apportioning the existence of a bulldozer to the factory in which it was produced without recognising the need to explain the order producing efficiency of the factory. Certainly, once we have a baler we can bale hay, once we have a combine harvester we can thresh corn, once we have a factory we can produce many wonderfully designed things, and once we have a most ingenious chemical factory in the form of DNA/RNA we can produce intelligent life on earth. But it is one thing to lay claim to DNA but it is quite another thing to explain it, especially when the impossibility of it coming into existence in a universe we are informed is empty of intelligence. But Darwinians want to introduce mechanisms of massive order producing significance into the evolutionary equation without acknowledging that this turns evolution into a process of intelligent design – in other words they want to have his cake and eat it.

Dawkins in his book the *Selfish Gene* is forced to admit that even if we were to shake our biological cocktail shaker about for the entire age of the universe it is "but an eye blink" compared to what we need to produce the biological complexity of a single person and even then "you would not succeed." (Dawkins 1989, p.16)We simply cannot get intelligently ordered things by randomly moving disordered chemicals about even if we were to shake thus for all eternity. The question here is not necessarily whether life evolved or not, but the kind of process evolution is as an order producing phenomenon of immense order producing significance and life generating profundity.

In the final analysis, it seems that we have a multitude of scientists of many different kinds who think they are explaining the universe and everything in it, when all they are really doing is describing how they find it but not how it was ordered into existence for them to admire it and for scientists to intelligently investigate it. Richard Dawkins in his book *The Blind Watchmaker,* endeavouring to show how evolution can explain intelligent life on earth outside of a process of intelligent design argues:

That by gradual step by step transformations from simple beginnings, from primordial entities sufficiently simple to come into existence by chance. Each successful change in the gradual evolutionary process was simple enough, relative to its predecessor, to have arisen by chance. But the whole sequence of cumulative steps constitutes anything but a chance process, when you consider the complexity of the final end product relative to the original starting point. [Dawkins 1986, p.43]

It is not hard to see there is a serious problem with Dawkins analogy, because how could a process in which each and every step in a process is of no order producing significance whatsoever, yet the sum of these causally inconsequential steps when added together constitute a process of order producing creativity? In other words, each step and all the steps when added together mean nothing in terms of adequate cause which means nothing is explained. Steps in an order producing process never get so small and insignificant that they do not mean anything in terms of cause and a cause sufficient to explain that which is being produced or coming into existence. One doesn't have to be a philosopher or the son of a philosopher to see that this claim simply doesn't add up. Nothing plus nothing is nothing no matter what school we go to, how often we add it up or whatever planet you are on.

Dawkins goes on to liken evolution to a long line of stones lined neatly along a beach placed there by chance. But of course this not the result of pure chance, because it is the waves of the sea pushing the stones to the edge of the beach into neat lines. But there in a huge explanatory gap between stones strewn in neat lines along a beach to the simplest microscopic living things millions of which Dawkins informs could sit on a pinhead. (Dawkins 1988, p.120) Dawkins imaginary beach would only become significant as an order producing force if stones arranged themselves to produce a house with appropriate walls, spaces for windows, doors and a chimney. And then drift wood from the sea was arranged to produce doors and window frames, and then windows appeared within the window frames to keep the wind out and light in, and then smoke rose upward from the chimney, and vegetable patches with all manner of plants appeared, and then animals of different kinds appeared in the fields around the house and people appeared to work the fields and light the fire and gather the eggs, to care for the chickens and love their children, after which we might well have reason to consider that all this was not due to a process of blind chance.

In the end, Dawkins is forced to admit that evolution is not a process of blind randomness and that to suppose that evolution is operating to blind randomness in which all changes are: "held to be possible and all equally likely. Far from holding this belief, I don't see how you would begin to set about making such a belief meaningful." (Dawkins 1986, p.307) Dawkins goes on to qualify the blind watchmaker out of existence in which he is forced to admit that there are at least five different ways in which evolution is not blind so the Blind Watchmaker in not really so blind after all. (Dawkins 1986, p.306–312) Darwin argues that there is: "randomness and randomness and many people confuse different meanings of the word. There are, in truth many respects in which mutation is not random." (Dawkins 1986, p.306)

Darwin explains his theory: "As the origin of species by natural selection or the preservation of favoured races in the struggle for survival." But Darwin fails to explain how living things were so highly favoured as to be ordered sufficiently to come alive and survive and in many different forms on planet earth. Furthermore, how could inanimate matter struggle to produce intelligent life on earth and how could a process of blind randomness produce the ordered complexity of anything? It is abundantly self-evident that behind evolution there is an order producing intelligence of spectacular life producing significance. As Professor Brian Silver points out: "The basic problem facing anyone who is looking for the origin of life is to give an account for the formations of a complex, highly organised, self-sustaining and self-replicating system out of a mixture of chemicals that certainly in the early days the soup, displayed none of these characteristics." (Silver 1998, p.350)

Frances Crick, co-discoverer of DNA, described the existence of DNA as "almost a miracle," and one suspects that the "almost" is added to save face and avoid having to concede the principle of sufficient cause. Crick spent much of the rest of his life trying to find a way to explain the existence of DNA away so that it had nothing to do with a process of intelligent design and it is not surprising that he failed. The best he could do was to come up with the theory of *panspermia* (emanating from another planet in the universe) which needs to be explained no matter from whence it originated. But to suggest that God as a wise creator produced it and sent it to earth to seed the earth with living things would be regarded as anathema, when no matter who produced it or sent, it needs to be explained in terms of a life producing intelligence.

Crick's son explained that his father's desire was not to make himself wealthy, popular, or famous: "But to knock the final nail in the coffin of vitalism." (Cited on Sheldrake 2011, p.9) But if Crick as a human being has nothing to do with this vital living life-producing cause how could he ever have deemed himself wise enough to solve what is the most vexing problem in the known universe. Crick thinks of himself as being so vitally relevant and intellectually endowed so that the cause that brought him into existence must by wiser than he thinks.

What was Crick's problem with vitalism when that which is vital is that which has to do with life and the joy of living that takes us to the heart of our existence as human beings. It seems that some are willing to sacrifice their very humanity on the altar of a mundane materialism to avoid coming face to face with a vital and living cause that would hold sovereignty over them in the form of a wise creator. Crick in his passionate and fervent determination of mind to deny vitalism is proving the very thing he was trying to deny because this is not a case of disproving vitalism, but a form of human vitalism in rebellion against that vitalism to which he owes his very existence. The truth is that: "No effect can be qualitatively superior or quantitatively greater than the cause that brought it into existence. This could be regarded as a human being trying to make themselves more vital and qualitatively superior to that cause that brought them into existence: – and this simply cannot be. Crick by denying God is playing God, him who is no god at all which is a very dangerous game for finite man to play in which there can be only one winner.

"So, even if the origin of life arrived on the earth by two little green men on a bicycle built for two, or by a parcel delivered by Postman Pat marked urgent, it still needs to be explained. But for some it could not possibly have anything to do with a wise creator who seems to the writer to be the only one up to the job. But such an idea is not allowed to surface out of what seems to be nothing but blind prejudice and an inherent fear of being confronted with the logic of a wise creator to whom we owe everything and in the end be answerable to Him as moral beings.

"Daniel Dennett in his book *Darwin's Dangerous Idea* gives us an example of how algorithms could arise so creating design out of chaos without the aid of an intelligent mind. This is brought about by changes so small they do not need to be explained in term of an intelligent cause of any kind. Add these inconsequential steps up and they represent nothing in terms of sufficient cause. Although the steps yield brilliant results, each constituent step, as well as the transition between steps, is so utterly simple the whole process is causally inconsequential. How simple asks Dennett? Giving an example of the process he is suggesting in the baking of a cake he affirms. Simple enough for a dutiful idiot to perform – or for a straightforward mechanical device to perform. The standard textbook analogy notes that algorithms are recipes of sorts designed to be followed by *novice* cooks. A recipe book written for great chiefs might include the phrase 'poach the fish in a suitable wine until almost done,' but an algorithm for the same process might begin choose a white wine that says 'dry' on the label; take a corkscrew and open the bottle; pour an inch of wine in the bottle of a pan; turn on the burner under the pan on high." In other words we have: "a tedious breakdown of the process into dead simple steps requiring no wise decisions or delicate judgments or intuitions on the part of the recipe reader." (Dennett 1995, p.51)

Such recipes, therefore, could be written down in steps so small and simple (algorithms) they could be written by an 'idiot' and read by 'novice cooks' requiring "no wise decisions or delicate judgments or intuitions" on the part of the recipe reader, to understand them or carry them out. Those who write books of recipes on how to bake many different culinary delights and those who follow the instructions to create such culinary delights will be flattered to know that this can be done by idiots requiring no intelligence, delicate judgements or purposeful thinking or wise decisions. Thus, they be regarded as simpletons and something akin to idiots "requiring no wise decisions or delicate judgments." The whole idea, of course, is absurd and is a futile attempt to avoid the obvious in the form of a wise creator and it simply doesn't work.

The fact is that to produce a recipe, or to follow the necessary instructions of a recipe to bring intro existence a cake, requires an intelligent mind operating to a realisable purpose, motivation of mind to carry simple and clear instructions, competence in the use of at least one language to write down the recipe or read the recipe and to understand what it us saying in intelligible terms and for others to read and understand those instructions and the ability to faithfully carry them out, and this applies no matter how simply you break the process down or how small the steps to complete the process. Such instructions expressed in capsules of intelligent information intelligently linked together in which each letter, word, phrase and sentence when joined together with other sentences mean something in intelligently constituted terms. We simply cannot get something like a cookbook full of recipes to produce many different culinary delights by writing gobbledygook in small syllables or by blindly pressing the keys of our typewriter in the hope that if we type long enough the instructions to produce some culinary delights will eventually appear.

The above description is not a random process at all, it is one in which a rational mind is being informed down to the last detail how to produce a recipe to bake a cake on how to carry out those instruction by which to do so. To be completely random the instructor or the reader would have to suspend their rational judgment and say the first thing that comes into their head and repeat this process and see how long it would take to get coherent instructions on how to bake a cake. To fulfil a particular task, or set of tasks, the steps never get so small and utterly insignificant that they don't require to be joined by means of intelligence operating to an intelligent and coherent purpose. Each step in the

125

above instructions is directed toward a particular purpose and someone who understands each step with ability to carry them out.

Algorithms it just another failed attempt to explain how evolution works to bring into existence massively complex living things by means that have nothing to do with an order producing intelligence and it simply doesn't work. A chicken is not an altogether stupid creature, after all it can cross the road to get to the other side. But read to it the instructions to bake a cake and you will wait a long time before you get your cake, because although the chicken has instincts it is not endowed with the attribute of abstract rational thinking to think logically and reason causally.

Richard Dawkins in his book *The Blind Watchmaker* goes on to illustrate how his form of evolution works by liking it to a marble statue of the Virgin Mary. He suggests that such a statue that appeared to wave at us might first appear like a miracle: "But on closer inspection we may find that it came about by chance if by some sheer coincidence all the molecules just happened to move in the same direction at the same moment causing the hand to move." (Dawkins 1986, p.159) Well ten out of ten for trying Mr Dawkins, but such illustrations show signs of desperation and it must encourage theists to no end to see evolutionary theorists clutch so pathetically at such imaginary straws and then refer to themselves as "intellectually fulfilled atheists."

Moreover, in the case of evolution we are not asked to believe in one such event that is so profoundly unlikely but an endless and ongoing sequence of such events that are so spectacularly unlikely until the marble statue becomes a living person with blood coursing through its veins and that can see, walk, talk, think, feel, procreate, plan, reason and wave their arms about at the excitement of being alive. Such an utterly remarkable sequence of events would take some explaining and that sequence of events actually took place as evidenced in the ordered and living sum of ourselves who appeared from disordered chemicals of the earth by a multitude of order producing events of life producing ingenuity both marvellous and awe-inspiringly wonderful. In fact, Dawkins has still to explain the statue to which he refers and which cannot be explained by blindly wielding a mallet and chisel about.

There can be no means, mechanisms, motivation or order-producing necessity taking place within a world of inanimate matter that is dead to itself, and void of meaning, purpose or sentient significance. A process that operates to a random accumulation of events will not lead to the ordered sum of anything and be nothing but a heterogeneous confabulation of mindless confusion. There is no design space, no design process, no design-producing mind in such events to explain the intelligently ordered complexity of anything and what we end up with is an elaborate form of fairy-tale physics for grown-ups. Denying the idea of intelligent design may seem to some like a good way of getting away without paying their dues to their maker, but it is a very poor excuse for so big a debtor. It is little wonder then that evolutionist Franklin M. Harold admits that: "we must concede that there are presently no detailed Darwinian accounts of evolution or any biochemical system only a variety of wishful speculation." (Cited in Strobel 2004, p.193)

Dennett in his book, *Darwin's Dangerous Idea*, goes on to talk about evolutionary cranes that build from the bottom up, as opposed to what he refers to as the skyhooks of theists who ultimately apportion living things to a sufficient cause in the form of a wise creator. (Dennett 2000, P.75) But unfortunately for Dennett it is his cranes that are the skyhooks that appear from nowhere and originate from a process of blind randomness to do what a process of blind and blundering randomness could not conceivably do.

Take for instance, the well-known mountain illustration of Richard Dawkins in which he argues that the mountain of living things which cannot be scaled by one giant leap up the face of the mountain can be ascended in simple steps up the gradual slope at the back of the mountain. But this illustration is nothing but so much hot air because the fact remains that evolutionists, cannot explain, and admit that they cannot explain, the coming into existence of a single replicating cell let alone the whole mountain of living things. Therefore, this mountain of ordered complexity needs to be explained whether it came about gradually over a long period of time or appeared more suddenly from within a world of disordered matter.

Dawkins readily admits that: "coincidences means multiplied improbability." (Dawkins 1986, p.159) In other words, the more coincidences we need to produce something the more we are constrained to conclude that coincidences has nothing to do with it and consider that we need a better explanation like that of as intelligent and sufficient cause operating through the necessary means to produce that which a stream of coincidences could never explain. There comes a point in which the existence of life on earth defined by Dawkins: "as a statistical improbability on a colossal scale" must come to a point in which the improbability becomes so utterly vast it becomes strategically and utterly impossible.

Living things are said to adapt to the environment in the interests of survival just like Darwin's finches on the Galapagos Islands. In other words, those birds with beaks that were unsuited to live on the resources of that environment died out while those with more appropriate beaks survived, prospered and successfully reproduced. But this does not explain the ordered sum the bird so postulated already equipped and appropriately prepared to live on the resources of a particular environment which evolution as a process of blind randomness could not possibly have known what any environment was like let alone to produce birds fully equipped to live on the resources of that environment. We now know this was brought about by means of bird producing information contained within DNA and the ability of RNA to carry out those bird-producing instructions with great precision to produce the ordered sum of the bird. So we have to explain the origin of DNA and RNA to explain the ordered sum of the bird suitably equipped to live within a particular environment which a process of blind randomness could not have known anything about let alone produce the ordered sum of a bird suitably equipped to live, survive and thrive within a particular environment.

Moreover, evolution would have to produce two complementary birds, one male and the other female each suitably equipped with the necessary means to come together with impeccable precision in order to procreate and thereby perpetuate their species: and all this outside of a process of intelligent design which would represent two miracles in one day of massive order and complementary complexity with no one and nothing to explain it. So how could the ordered sum of the birds referred to by Darwin come into existence in the first place by a process of blind randomness. It is not enough to say that those best adapted to the environment were able to survive while those that were not died out by virtue of the fact that this does not explain how the birds were ordered into existence in the first place and fully equipped and appropriately suited to live within a particular environment when evolution as an unconscious process of mindless randomness without sight or foresight plan or purpose could not have performed any such feat of biological engineering. Or why fish changed to live in a completely different environment when they were ordered and equipped and happily adapted to live in water and then why for some reason changed direction and decided to live on dry land when there was no evolutionary pressure for them to do so.

Moreover, how did the beak of a bird come into existence before the idea of a bird or potential bird existed when everything was operating to a process of incoherent randomness within a sea of seething chaos, when there was no way to explain the idea of a bird, the ordered sum of a bird, or knowing there was food that could be foraged by any bird on any island and that by means of a beak? Whatever the island or whatever the environment, a bird had first to exist fully equipped to survive within a particular environment and fully equipped to live on the food available in that particular island.

Moreover, the bird had to have eyes to see the food, the insight to identify it as food, the will to eat it for nourishment to survive, the right digestive system in place to digest that particular food, a circularity system to carry the proteins around its body to provide for it the energy to survive, neck muscles to move the beak to appropriate the food, a bird brain to act as a bird should act and give it the appetite to eat that particular food, a central nervous system to carry messages from the eyes of the bird to its brain and from its brain to its beak to appropriate the food, a suitable digestive system in place to digest the food, a heart to drive the circulatory system to take the nutrients around its body to give it energy to survive, the ability to excrete the waste, wings complete with the necessary bone structure, sinews, muscles, nerves and feathers to fly along to find the food, the desire to procreate and a suitable partner with which to procreate, an instinct to care for its young, the thankfulness of mind to sing its lilting song as a happy and fulfilled species.

If all these things and much more were not first ordered into place and operating effectively within the ordered and integrated sum of the bird, there would be no bird, no beak no ordered sum of anything. So, we first need to have the ordered sum of the bird before it could thrive and survive in a particular environment. Therefore, the means of its coming into existence and its ability to adapt is altogether a most wonderfully ingenious thing and to explain all this we need an immense amount of bird producing intelligence.

Therefore, in any of these descriptions and explanations of evolution we have not got from the disordered nature of disparate chemicals to the ordered sum of anything; unless as we have noted, by an intelligent and sufficient cause operating to the specific purpose and equipped with the necessary means to bring into being intelligent life on earth. While Gerald Schroeder MIT trained scientist and writer quite rightly asks: "life seems to be inevitable. The question is – what made it inevitable?" (Schroeder 2001, p.212)

It is naïve to suppose that we just have to: "strip away the complexity and uncover the underlying simplicity" as some argue: because no matter how simple the steps are we need a multitude of them arranged appropriately and sufficiently formed to produce the viable complexity of even the simplest living things. So while something like a helicopter could be reduced to the sum of its many parts, even to the atoms that make up the existence of those parts we would never dream of apportioning the ordered sum of the helicopter to a process of no order producing significance. Nor would we ever dream of saying that a factory that makes helicopters could be reduced to steps so simple and insignificant the helicopters don't need to be explained in terms of an intelligent and efficient helicopter producing cause.

We have noted that to order something so simple having but 100 pieces the odds of falling into place by chance are 100^{159} which is equivalent to 1 followed by 258 zeros after it which is estimated to be more the subatomic particles in the entire universe. We might build a house out of bricks and mortar that will eventually crumble to dust but it will never rebuild itself back into another house by randomly moving the dust about. It is the ordered sum of the whole that needs to be explained and we need to understand the incalculable multitude of small things that have to be ordered meticulously into place before we have the simplest viable living things.

In the light of this, how long might it take for 580,000 parts to fall into place by chance to produce the simplest living cell (*Mycoplasma genitalium*); or to order some one hundred thousand million axons of the human brain with its million billion (1,000,000,000,000,000) dendrites to produce an intelligent functioning brain? The mind boggles and is lost within an utter infinity of odds that can scarcely be conceived. So the idea of an underlying simplicity is but a myth because even the simplest living thing is anything but simple. We would never dream of arguing that a building could be reduced to dust and that the dust is so small and simple in its composition that by randomly moving the dust about a new house could appear.

Colin Tudge likes to describe how Gregor Mendel and his experiments with pea plants unwittingly discovered what modern scientists now refer to as *genes* that explain the existence of intelligently ordered things like plants and other living things. But what he seems to forget, or conveniently ignore, is that

Mendel did not bring into existence these ingenious mechanisms of order producing efficiency. Mendel merely chanced upon one of life's great secrets without realising the full significance of what he discovered. So the truth is that, neither Mendel, Darwin or Tudge had anything to do with those ingenious order-producing laws of nature or the ingenious mechanisms by which nature operates to bring about her wonderful designs.

If nature can do it, then we don't need God to explain it some argue. But at the risk of spoiling the party, we feel compelled to ask, what is 'Nature' that it can do what only a process of intelligent ordering could possibly do and a most creatively ingenious mind explain? It seems that nature is making an exceedingly good job of mimicking the order producing genius of a wise creator, or acting as the ingenious order-producing agent thereof.

We were born into this territory and there is no escape from it except by going irrational to avoid the idea of an intelligent and sufficient cause which is like denying the existence of fish while fishing off the back of a whale. Moreover, the mind brings forth its own truth totally different in nature and character to all that we predicate of corporeal substance. A qualitative reality of being, consciously alive, qualitatively profound, spiritually sublime, sacred in nature, endowed with different hopes and aspirations and within this context we as human beings build a life for ourselves for good or ill.

Some wonder how if life is so utterly complex it only takes twenty or so different genetic letters to produce a human being. But this is explained by the fact the English alphabet has only 26 letters but these letters have produced all the books in all the world written in English including Encyclopaedia Britannica and the writers had to arrange every letter very precisely and in the right order to produce books that make sense and are intelligible to the reader. What are the odds of getting two letters into their right place to produce a simple intelligible word by chance the odds are of course 50/50.

To get 4 letters into the right order by chance is 1 in 24.
To get 6 letters ordered into the right place by chance is 1 in 720.
To get 8 letters ordered into the right place by chance is 1 in 40,320.
To get 10 letters ordered into the right place by chance is 1 in 3,628,800.
To get 100 letters ordered into the right place by chance is 1 in 100^{158}.
To get 200 letters ordered into the right place by chance is 1 in 200^{376}.

The last number represents 200 multiplied by 1 with 376 noughts after it that is estimated to be more that the entire subatomic particles in the entire universe. This is referred to as the combinational explosion problem and the mind boggles as to the odds of ordering some 40 or 50 or so billion living cells into their right place to produce a human being with each cell representing an extremely complex entity in their own right. The only way to beat these odds is by an intelligent mind operating to a specific purpose and adopting the right and appropriate means to accomplish a realisable purpose.

We would remind the reader that by typing randomly the best we can do by way of intelligible information is about half a line until the process reverts back to unintelligible nonsense, and moreover those few randomly chanced upon words would not necessarily represent what we wanted or need to say or even make a complete sentence. The fact is that we would never get an intelligible book by pressing randomly on the keys of our typewriter or word processer.

As Henry Morris points out: "A growth process which proceeds by random accumulations will not lead to an ordered structure but merely to a heterogeneous blob." So it seems that with evolution as commonly understood by many Darwinians, when we separate the ordered wheat from the evolutionary chaff we have an awful lot of chaff and very little wheat. And with respect to living things, it seems perfectly obvious that empirically based science fails miserably to account for the phenomenology of human consciousness and man's sense of being as a personal volitional entity different in character from the unconscious impersonal world of physics. It all seems like trying to find the living among the dead.

Chapter 6
Following Reason to Where It Leads

If we want to remain within the realm of rational thinking we have to accept that that which we have been ordered to be gives us a clear indication of the kind of cause from which we have come, the kind of being our creator is and the overall purpose for which we were created. We not only need to explain the vast complexity of a physical brain but the experiential reality of a living self-conscious mind that determines who we are and how we relate to the world of other people and things. Our origin cannot be less than that which we experience ourselves to be, body, mind and spirit. In other words, the origin of all things cannot be less than the sum of the all effects produced, while the origin of conscious life cannot be less than all that we experience ourselves to be as living beings in an ordered world.

Moreover, all that we know and experience ourselves to be goes beyond our finite minds to fully understand, so what we are faced with living life producing effects we cannot deny but which goes beyond our finite minds to fully explain. So what we are confronted with is a living life producing cause, that takes us beyond our human comprehension to fully understand and in this we are logically confronted with the one theists call God. So the kind of beings that we are reflects something of that living life-producing cause from which we have come, both biologically in relation to an extremely complex physical body, and ontologically in relation the attributes of a living self-conscious mind. Therefore, the ordered sum of who we are and experience ourselves to be obviously reflects something of the nature of our creator who brought us into existence and the purpose for which we were created. This forces us to stand in awe at out creator and seek to honour, respect and fear him in the same way that we fear an earthly father. It calls us to relate to Him in spirit and in truth as our faculties of understanding allow and with all our attributes of being of which love is the crowning glory and therein a relationship with Him is established not only in theory but in practice.

Love is something that comes into our relationship with our maker because we have been created with the capacity to love so we must love him who endowed us with the gift of life and the capacity to love which is a natural and compelling response to our creator. It is perfectly logical and appropriate to love the cause from which we have come because the capacity to love is a gift bestowed on us by Him and should be returned in kind. And as other people of like image and nature to ourselves we are naturally called to honour and mutually respect and to love and care for the world in which we live. All of creation is a gift from God and we are honour-bound to care for it and God after the act of creation in Genesis committed Adam and Eve to care for the garden he had created for then, to enjoy, to manage, care for and protect.

We are moral beings, which means that our maker must be a moral being and has shared this attribute of being with us and to learn to use it in a way that pleases him both in relation to him and other human beings and life forms with who we share this earth. Therefore, we are honour-bound to relate to our creator in terms of all that he has created us to be and the world into which he has placed us. As finite beings we are honour bound to respond in awe and wonder at our maker even though we do not understand all that our creator is or how he made us moral beings with many different attributes of being whereby we live life and relate to him and our fellow human beings. Therefore, as finite beings we live by faith, not faith in a vacuum, but faith within the contest of all that we have been ordered to be operating within an ordered world.

Therefore Plato argued that the highest philosophical vision is possible only to one with the temperament of a lover. The philosopher must permit himself to be inwardly grasped by the most sublime form of Eros – that universal passion from which all things have come, to restore a former unity, to overcome the separation from the divine and to become one with it, believing that knowledge of the divine was implicit in ever soul but forgotten or displaced by being taken up with and preoccupied with a temporal and mundane existence. The goal of the true philosopher was to recover a direct knowledge of the true causes and source of all things. Therefore, for Plato the challenge facing mankind was to turn from cave of ephemeral shadows into the archetypal light which was the true source of being. Aristotle believed that the mind's greatest power of cognition derived from something beyond empiricism and the rational elaboration of sensory experience. Only a society founded on divine principles and governed divinely informed philosophers could save mankind from its destructive irrationality to the changeless spiritual realm superior to whatever human beings tried to accomplish in the temporal world.

As the saying goes – *I Think Therefore I am.* But it is not just that we think; it is how we think as human beings with our different qualitative attributes of being that together go to makeup the sum of how we think and as rational beings to draw the necessary conclusions within life and all that this implies by way of effect in relation to the cause involved. Fraud identified within us what he called the self-seeking and rebellious *id* doing battle with *superego* (our moral being) with the *ego* (or arbitrating will) called to make decisions within the vicissitudes of life. It seems that our maker wants us to learn by personal experience how to choose good over evil so that we become competent and trustworthy agents of moral integrity. In fact, this could be the very raison d'être of our very existence. God doesn't want puppets on a string, he wants human beings mature in truth and goodness he can trust and have fellowship with in truth and goodness. If this is the case, men and women would need to take care to which voice they ate listening to when they are making their choices and decisions whether the *superego* calling us to life up to our full potential as human beings or the rebellious self-seeking *id* tempting us kick over the traces to indulge ourselves in all manner of excesses and selfish indulgences forgetting, or even denying, that we has a creator or that there is no any real purpose in life.

James Rachels seems to think he is making a very profound statement when he writes a book entitled *Created from Animals.* But the difference between us and other animals is determined not only by our physical form but attributes of understanding not least of which is our capacity to reason which allows us to reflect on the origin of our existence, and the origin of all things, in the light of the effects produced. Even if we did evolve from animals in the lower kingdom these need to be explained in terms of sufficient cause as do we who have been endowed with reason and intelligence to understand that all that exists needs to be explained in terms of an intelligent and sufficient cause. Our mind takes us beyond the world of sense impressions to attributes of understanding that need to be used if we are to live up to our full potential as human beings.

Rather, nature's unfolding truth emerges only with the active participation of the human mind. Nature's reality is not merely phenomenal, nor is it independent and objective; rather it is something that comes into being through the very act of human cognition. Nature becomes intelligible to itself through the human mind. In this perspective, nature pervades everything, and the human mind in all its fullness is itself an expression of nature's essential being. And it is only when the human mind actively brings forth from within itself the full powers of disciplined imagination and saturates its empirical observation with archetypal insight that that the deeper reality of the world emerges. … Hence this human intuition is not a subjective distortion but is the human fulfilment of that reality's essential wholeness … the human imagination is itself part of the world's intrinsic truth; without which the world is in some sense incomplete [Tarnas 1991, p. 434]

Moreover this view of life is fully consistent with rational thinking in which we need to explain the origin of life in terms that are consistent with the ordered and living sum of all that we experience ourselves to be. To deny the rational implications of who we are and reduce ourselves to a chanced upon arrangement of corporeal substance represents a form of self-denial and twisted logic that debases us and insults that cause from which we have come. This could be regarded as a base form of ontological suicide to avoid taking full responsibility for our lives as human beings.

Moreover, when we mourn for the death of a loved one we are not mourning because a biological body and physical brain ceases to function but because of all that that person meant to us as a human being and the attachments of loyalty, love and affection that bound us to them. These attributes of being affect us more profoundly than knowledge of the physical world. Therefore, we cannot claim that life equates with all we understand the working of a physical brain and that death is of no more significance than the passing of a biological body. The inner world of being, sometimes referred to as the soul, is that which makes life qualitatively rich, existentially profound, precious, sacred and utterly sublime. We should not merely judge life by the significance of the body or the complexity of the brain but by the experiential reality of a living mind. Some may even have a vested interest in denying the reality of the inner world of being to call their prejudiced soul their own. So when we deny that which we cannot explain when it comes to the reality of conscious life is like someone cutting off their nose to spite their face.

As intelligent but finite beings the logical and reasonable thing to do is to conclude that there is a wise creator who can do things we as human beings cannot deny even though we cannot always explain or understand the means of their deliverance to our consciousness. We have heard of those who confess to having out of body experiences when they are seriously ill and near death and this gives us some indication that the spirit is different from the body. One such person had such an experience but by modern means of resuscitation were brought back to life and afterwards testified that it was a life changing experience. One such person who had such an experience could testify that they rose above their own body out of the room and above the hospital in which she was being treated and saw an old wellington boot lying on the flat roof of the hospital. When the roof was later examined, an old wellington boot was found lying where she said it was.

Matthew Alper argues that by injecting 50–50 mg of ketamine into the body reproduces the symptoms of near-death experience, but how does knowing what triggers it negate the experience of it? John Polkinghorne argues that: "Our knowledge of entities must be allowed to conform to the way in which they actually can be known. If we are to meet reality at all, we must meet it on its own terms." (Polkinghorne 2000, p.7) Life is more than physics and the body more than clothes and this is why different words are needed to explain life in all its emotive and spiritual reality of being different in nature and substance to the world of empirically based things.

This is why the Scriptures declare that: "The just shall live by faith." Why is this? Because these are those who are willing to accept that there are things they cannot fully understand and yet there are things such as life which they cannot possibly deny. Aldous Huxley referring to his belief that there is no meaning to life because it was "… an instrument of liberation" to him and he wasn't ashamed to admit it. But liberation from what? Such a belief only delivers him into a world of meaningless irrelevance in which we can: "abandon the presumption and life is nothing but a wearisome vexation of spirit."

Daniel Dennett, trying desperately to explain away the significance of the origin of life refers to Darwin whom he believes inverted the whole course of rational thinking so that we can abandon the presumption of sufficient cause argues:

Why couldn't the most important thing of all be something that that arose from unimportant things? Why should the importance or excellence of anything have to rain down on us from on high, from something more important, a gift from God? Darwin's inversion suggests that that we abandon that presumption and look for sorts of excellence, of worth and purpose, that can emerge, bubbling up out of 'mindless, purposeless forces…. [Dennett, 1095, p.66]

But of course Darwin did no such thing, he was but ignorant of the ingenious mechanisms DNA and RNA that lay at the heart of evolution which were endowed with the necessary means to produce all manner of intelligently ordered living things, and these are as hard to explain as evolution is to explain without them. Unfortunately Dennett has not updated his theory of evolution to take account of this fact. One should be very careful about going against the whole course of rational thinking which when we do so we can believe anything, and this has disastrous consequences when it has something to do with the origin of life on earth and our significance as human beings. When we do so, we can apportion everything to anything or nothing at all.

Just to highlight the contradictory nature of Dennett's thinking we again quote from his argument: "Let me start with regularity, the mere purposeless, mindless, pointless regularity of physics – and I will show you a process that eventually will yield products that exhibit not just regularity but purposive design." (Dennett 1996, p.65) But how could a process described as purposeless, mindless, and pointless operating within the context of primordial disorder exhibit not just regularity but purposive design? It seems that Dennett wants to have it both ways, to have his cake and eat it. The idea that evolution is operating to some form of order producing regularity that could exhibit purposive design yet is described as a purposeless, mindless and pointless is really a manifest contradiction in terms and the whole idea shows sign of desperation. To put it the other way round, if physics was somehow producing things that showed clear signs of purposive design we would have to conclude that it was a process of intelligent ordering whether we understood how it operating to do this or not.

Paul Davies in his book seems right when he argues that when it comes to minds these can be: "no trivial detail, no minor by-duct of mindless purposeful forces." (Davies 1992, p.232) It is reasonable to suppose and logically compellingly to conclude that the wellspring of being emanates from a higher source cosmic creativity so as Tarnas argues:

> In this view, the theory of a Copernicus, a Newton, or an Einstein is not simply due to the luck of a stranger; rather it reflects the human mind's radical kinship with the cosmos. It reflects the human mind's pivotal role as a vehicle of the universe's unfolding meaning. [Tarnas 1991, p.436]

But the modern world of scientific empiricism and the technology that bombards us with new ideas to kill the boredom of a restless world so that things are the saddle and ride mankind. But as Socrates has said: 'Happiness' can only be achieved: "through living the life that best serves the nature of the soul." This is why Socrates urged his pupils to search their own inner world of being to understand the kind of beings that they are, that reality that takes us to the centre and soul of our existence and reveals something profound about the origin and the purpose of our existence. The unexamined life, he argued, is not worth living. Thus argued Socrates:

> Only a society founded on divine principles and governed by divinely informed philosophers could save mankind its destructive irrationality; and that the best life was one directed away from mundane life and toward the world of eternal ideas. The changeless spiritual realm preceded and was forever superior to whatever human beings tried to accomplish in the temporal world. [Cited in Tarnas 1996, p.44]

There are those who seem to believe that it is beneath them to even consider the idea of a wise creator or to keep an open mind on the subject which itself is highly suspicious in the light of the evidence around us and the evidence that is us. Moheb Costandi writes:

> Some say that we have learned more about the brain in the past decade than we did in the hundred years preceding it. Even so, we are only beginning to scratch the surface, and a huge amount remains to be discovered … Some believe that gaining a better understanding of how the brain works will provide answers to life's big questions. It will not: brain research cannot tell

us everything about ourselves, or what it means to be a human. [Costandi 2013, p.3]

The mind and the brain relate but they do not equate because there is more to the mind than all that we can predicate of a physical brain no matter how complex it is or we imagine it to be. Just as no matter how much water we might add to water it will produce wine because something else is needed to turn water into wine than endless streams of water. At the marriage feast of Cana in Galilee it took a miracle to turn water into wine. Emanuel Kant has rightly argued that: "morals are just as absolute and unalterable as the law of causality", and this applies even though morality cannot be quantified or verified in empirically based scientific terms. This shows us that there are things intrinsic to our existence as human beings that pertain to the life world that are existential imperatives that take us beyond the world of physics.

Kevin Nelson writes: "Many volumes have been written about the self, and many more are waiting in the wings, it is mysterious and elusive hotly debated, and now awesomely arcane." (Nelson 2012, p.59) The mind has be likened to the ghost in the biological machine, but is more than a mysterious and ill-defined ghost rattling around in the caverns of the brain, it a veritable reality of conscious being that constitutes the living essence of who we are operating to clearly defined categories of understanding. It is in fact us, the jewel in the crown of our existence, something ineffable, precious, sacred and sublime, more that words can adequately describe. What shall a man give in exchange for his own soul asked the One who came to redeem the soul of fallen humanity that always thinks it knows better than their creator. We do not have to explain ourselves to understand that which we have been created to be and live as we were meant to live.

Thomas Nagel published a paper asking the question as to what it is like to be a bat. Nagel succinctly captures the essence of the discontent that many feel with current attempts to analyse consciousness in purely physical terms. (Dupre 2007, p.32–33) But the just must live by faith, knowing that there is more to their existence than the working of a physical brain, something deeply mysterious, but yet something sublimely spiritual that calls us forth from within ourselves to listen to the voice of reason.

It is true to some extent the driving force behind liberal democracy, human equality and the caring nature of a social welfare society was driven by Christian norms and values, but this reformist worldview is threatened by the danger of taking it all for granted, a hedonistic world-view that needs a constant supply alcohol and drugs to sustain its underlying spiritual emptiness, a rampant materialism, and a devaluing of the intrinsic nature of life itself in which the origin of life was increasingly regarded as an oddball rarity that had its origin in nothing but blind chance leaving mankind on an a meaningless journey from nothing to nowhere.

The earth seems to be heading into serious cosmic crises of epic proportions by global warming and the question is, does mankind have the courage and moral fibre to make the necessary steps to save us? Or will we languish in a hedonist mindset and fatalistic stupor with the rich getting richer and the poor getting poorer in a world of the survival of the fittest? Mr Putin reminds us of the inherent corruption of the human heart that can justify a merciless attack on its neighbour Ukraine and for no other reason than its ill-motivated expansionist purposes. The rich must play their part by being willing put more into the public purse to better balance a world of increasing inequality and the dangers of global warming. Richard Tarnas reminds us that: "Plato's implication seemed to be that Socrates (his mentor) resolute attention to his mind and soul, to moral virtue as well as intellectual truth on which world order itself has been contracted and revealed."

As moral beings we have choices within the realm of our own understanding, one of which is that effects have causes, causes commensurate with all that we understand ourselves to be as well as the world we live in, and decisions made with regard to the world we live in and how we share it with fellow human beings and other living things. Life regarded as something precious, even sacred that goes beyond how we perceive and understand material things is the ultimate cause. To fail to live up to our full potential as human beings, both rational, moral and existential is to become not only a failure as a human being, but morally culpable and end up in a kind of baseless nihilism on our way from nowhere to obliteration Therefore:

The human spirit does not merely prescribe natures phenomenal order: rather, the spirit of nature brings forth its own order through the human mind when the mind is employing its full complement of faculties – intellectual, volitional, emotional, sensory, moral, imaginative, aesthetic, epiphanic. In such knowledge, the human mind lives into the creative activity of nature.

141

Then the world speaks forth its meaning through human consciousness and life is seen to be rooted in a deeper reality reflecting the origin from which we have come and life's unfolding meaning. [Adapted from Tarnas 1001, p.435]

Our maker wants a free and willing response from us, to enter into a meaningful relationship with him and He with us. Earlier we referred to the son of Francis Crick Michael who explained at his father's funeral that his father had no desire to be famous, wealthy or popular, but to knock the final nail into the coffin of vitalism. Who or what was he trying to kill, and what are we left with when we suppress, deny or obliterate the vital and consummate sum of our existence as human beings? These are the very things that make life worth living, precious and worth preserving, and points us to immortality which is something to which human beings have aspired from time immemorial. Plato came up with his idea of vitalism in which:

The philosopher must permit himself to be inwardly grasped by the most sublime force form of Eros – that universal passion to restore a former unity, to overcome the separation from the divine and become one with it. Plato described knowledge of the divine as implicit in every soul, but forgotten. The goal of philosophy is to free the soul of this deluded condition in which it is deceived by finite imitation and veiling of the eternal. The goal of the philosophy is to free the soul from this deluded condition in which it is deceived by finite imitation and veiling of the eternal. The philosopher's task is to bring to recollection the transcendent ideas, to recover a direct knowledge of true cause and source of all things.
[Adapted from Tarnas 1996, p.41]

The world in which man lives today is as the cosmos of his science with its pervasive austerity of concrete reality, an environment determined by technology and soul-less materialism in which the capacity of man to retain his humanity seemed increasingly in doubt. Modern communication via the internet has proved to be a vehicle as much for evil as for good, and one wonders if mankind will have the moral courage to face up to the impending doom of global warming and do what has to be done. The optimistic belief that the world's dilemmas could be solved by scientific advance and social engineering has been confounded with technology taking over and dehumanising mankind with an empirical austerity and sense of inner emptiness. The death of God brought the shadow of death to fall over the shallow horizons of mankind who could not see where it all was leading – namely to a hapless nihilism and a self-fulfilling prophecy of fatalism. So it is not just the world that needs saving but mankind itself, lost within its own self-righteousness that dares to defy its creator and live as though they were an end in themselves.

Heidegger at the end of his life for all his faults could say: "Only God can save us", and argued that "*being* in itself was a reality in its own right and not only needed to be accounted for and explained, but set the boundaries of our knowing and understanding. Who are we and what kind of beings are we, was for him a crucial and decisive question that needed urgent investigation! Therefore, being itself needed accounting for as a reality in its own right. But as Kierkegaard pointed out, such forgetfulness – particularly when one's topic is what it is to be human – is liable, were it not so comic, to be tragic in its consequences." (Mulhall 2000, p.33) In his book *Being and Time*, Heidegger attempts to trace out the tragic-comic effects of this repression in which we are the most important reality that needs to recognised and explained, and the power that is realised when this repression is lifted.

Therefore, the most important question a person is to ask is who we are as human being in the world of other beings. Hegel's challenge is similar which was to move beyond objectivity and develop a philosophical system which claims to be an ontology – a science of the existence of man – a study of living experience and what it is to be human. This takes us back to Socrates and Plato whose clarion call was "Know thyself": who are we among the world of things and what kind of an effect do we represent and what kind of a cause does this imply. If we abstract ourselves from the world of objective reality we will neither understand ourselves nor the world, both are intertwined within the world of our experience and both combined determine how we understand the world and our place within it. The way to truth is the study of living experience so that knowledge gets subsumed within the larger context of living.

For Kant knowledge is involves two separate mental faculties, that of things perceived by our senses and the faculty of understanding through we perceive and experience them. Our own conscious faculty of being determines that we perceive them, and our different categories of understanding determine how we perceive, something we can see to be highly ordered needs to be explained in terms of sufficient cause, some act of violence perceived as evil, something like a flower as beautiful, some act of kindness as morally commendable, the life that is within us as precious, the death of a loved one as sad and the desire for immortality and to be reunited with them. This and much more is all part of who we are.

So, just as we can benefit from a computer even though we may not know in technical terms how a computer works, but if we use it as it was meant to be used it can be a mine of information and an aid to knowledge and understanding. So it is with our mind, we cannot understand how it generates the ineffable reality of being we experience ourselves to be, but it does and this is the programme to which it operates through different faculties of understanding, hopes and aspirations. One description of brain activity goes:

> Neurons are specialised to produce electrical signals that travel along their fibres. These signals, called nervous impulses or 'action potentials' are generated by the flow of tiny electrical currents across the nerve cell membrane. Neurons can produce up to a thousand action potentials per second, and information is encoded in a pattern of impulses produced.
> [Costandi 2013, p.16]

But there is nothing in this description of brain function that explains consciousness and who we are as human beings with different attributes of being consciously operating within the world of physics. Kevin Nelson refers to Sherrington who changed our thinking about how the brain works, but the problem which remains vexing for us today: "Is how is it that these individual nerves of the brain, communicating one way across a gap and acting reflexively, transforms to that energy which is the mind." (Nelson 2012, p.46) The inner world of being is more than energy, it signifies something existentially profound and reason if we want to use it forces us to face up to the fact that life needs to be explained in terms that are able to explain the profound significance of it in existential terms, a world of inner being that we experience ourselves to be as an indubitable reality life-defining truth. We might reduce life to the working of a physical brain to make life easier to explain, but we only end up with a grossly distorted view of life that could well one day rise up to haunt us.

Nelson again argues that: "spiritual experiences should be judged by the profundity of their effects upon us and not by what seems to us to be causing them." (Nelson 2012, p.32) The brain seems to be a conduit through which conscious life flows as opposed to being the intrinsic nature of it and acting to mobilise the body in response to things perceived and act upon inner needs and desires. As one brain surgeon has put it: "I've operated on many clever brains but I have never seen a single thought." Consciousness is always accompanied by a distinct sense of selfhood spiritually profound and qualitatively rich beyond all that we presently understand the working of a physical brain to be.

Costandi brings us down to earth by affirming: "That despite centuries of speculation by philosophers and, more recently, neuroscientists, we still have little idea of what consciousness actually is, or how the brain generates it." (Costandi 2013, p.78) But this should not stop us using it to good effect to live life, which forms the bases whereby we relate to our fellow human beings as well as other living things, and to our maker who has endowed us with these rich and ennobling attributes of being – in which a 'thank-you' now and again would not be out of place. Therefore, Plato's advice is not as farfetched as some in the modern world of materialism might suppose when he argued: "The philosopher must permit him or herself to be inwardly grasped by the most sublime form of Eros – that universal passion to restore a former unity, to overcome the separation from the divine." That knowledge: "of the divine implicit in every soul" that is a precious thing we call life but which is smothered by the world of sensual sensations, the temporal world of physics, and the temptation to indulge our baser nature.

It is also worth reflecting, by way of illustration, on the fact that we might meticulously investigate the workings of a television and describe in down to the last detail and then concluding that this is all there is to a television that somehow the mechanisms within the television its transistors, diodes, wires etc., are all there is to a television and explains all that we see on the screen. But in this we would be completely wrong. As we well know, the secret behind the working of a television is to be found through signals we cannot see carrying information to the television which the television deciphers and turns them into live pictures on the screen. Therefore, we need to get beyond physics and develop a philosophy of the existence of man and the study of living experience that determines who we are as human beings.

A rat, a fox, a bird and a lion have different understanding of the world and live according to their own peculiar nature of being even though their sense based attributes are essentially the same as our own. What is it that makes an animal

145

brain so different that its responses to things perceived are so very different? In this the subject of knowledge is as important, and even more profoundly important, than objects of knowledge in a physical world.

But some would reduce a living mind to the working of a physical brain and a physical brain to an accidental conglomeration of inanimate matter and matter to the chanced upon Big Bang some eight billion or so years ago so that life is explained away by a process of *re-duc-tio–adab-sur-dum* until we have a totally distorted sense of reality. We know that some 95 percent or so of the universe is made up of dark matter and dark energy which we cannot see or explain, but this doesn't stop scientists believing in these things. And while consciousness will possibly be forever be a kind of dark matter to us, we would be foolish in the extreme to suppose that there is nothing more sublimely real going on within our own heads, turning matter into mind that drives and controls us within the world of physics. Martin Heidegger has argued speaking of the mind: "Nor does this most universal and hence indefinable concept require any definition, for everyone uses it constantly already and understands what he means by it." (Heidegger 1962, p.2)

The truth is that our physical senses are but the handmaid of a living mind operating existentially in a physical world, while Kant believed that there was a transcendental realm: "a part of total reality that is not of the empirical world," and that this "is rationally demonstrable, and therefore known by us with certainty." (Magee 2000, p.195) In other words, our reality of conscious being is known to us because in the experiential sense it is in fact us! Therefore, what we need is an all-inclusive epistemology, a holistic science of life that does justice to life as we know and experience it to be.

We would argue, therefore, that the position of the *National Academy Of Sciences* that denies the reality of that which cannot be verified in empirically based scientific terms to be completely erroneous and leads to a pernicious form of dehumanisation in which life is reduced to a complex assemblage of inanimate matter that chanced its way into existence for no good purpose. Human reason which is the servant of being is not the ultimate definer of being and represents that which we can reason about within the larger context of living and that takes us beyond empirically based reality to understand and explain. Moreover, the brain with between 80 to 120 billion neurons and its quadrillion synapses could not possibly with any stretch of the imagination be wired up randomly to operate intelligently. Scientists need to explain the origin of the intelligence by which

146

they do science and why it is that they have so many intelligently ordered things to investigate and reason intelligently about.

Life cannot be reduced to empirically based reality which is an insult to our humanity, part of which is reason which in itself informs us that intelligently ordered things must of logical necessity be explained in terms of an intelligent and sufficient cause, and living things in terms of a living life producing cause. So to reduce reality to empirically based criteria is a totally flawed methodology both in method and in substance when what we need is an all-inclusive and authentic science of life. Bryan Magee rightly points out that logical positivism (the theory that limits reality to empirically based criteria) not only negates the world of inner being but: "wiped out the whole of science, and this criticism, if clinched and few people today would deny that Popper pretty well clinched it and it spelt total shipwreck for logical positivism." (Magee 2000, p.57)

John Heil rightly argues that a neuroscientist observing your brain while all this is occurring would observe nothing but veritable panoply of neural activity. But you can rest assured that the neuroscientist will not observe anything resembling the qualities that represent who you experience yourself to be. (Heil 1998, p.4) Therefore, it is only when we put a comprehensive science of being together with the world of empirically based reality that we get something approaching a holistic and inclusive science of life. Until science as a discipline adjusts its methodology to include every aspect of reality both physical and metaphysical it will continue to be a deeply flawed and seriously deficient truth gathering exercise that not only distorts reality but perverts or negates the most vital and important part of it.

If we were to continually stir a saucepan full of what we believed to be ordinary soup and ever so gradually a bird appeared and was eventually ordered sufficiently to spread its wings and fly away, we are not as rational beings going to conclude that this does not need to be explained and superstitiously attribute it to some form of magic. Rather, we are going to say to ourselves, *what wonderful soup* and ask what was within the soup to produce the ordered and living sum of the bird and wonder how it is that all the means got into the soup to perform such an order-producing feat of bird producing excellence. It makes no difference if we need to stir the soup for hundreds, thousands or even millions of years before the bird appeared, the means must be within the soup or gradually added to the soup to explain the ordered sum of the bird with the ability to come to life and fly away.

How long might it take before the raw chemicals of the earth outside of an intelligent agent of ordering to produce a physical bird that comes alive and flaps its wings to fly away and goes looking for another bird with which to mate to bring forth replicas of its living self in order to perpetuate its species? How long might we wait before the chemicals of the earth would come together by chance to produce something as simple as a safety pin, a, sweet mouse, or pencil sharpener? The answer to this question is seen in the fact that in some four or so billion years of the earth's existence such things have never appeared simply because the means were not available within the soup to produce such things. God left such things for us as intelligent beings to produce from the intelligence with which he has so richly endowed us as a species, but to him belongs the credit for the existence of intelligent life itself of which we are a living microcosm. Evolution is merely a blind but brain-dead watchmaker according to Richard Dawkins, but as Moheb Costandi writes: "We experience ourselves and the world as a constant flow of thoughts and sensations. But how the brain generates this stream of consciousness is a mystery." (Costandi 2013, p.76)

By referring to Fraud's idea of the word *ego* Hundert points out that it is a word that in better translated from the German word '*Geistesenchafen*' as 'science of the spirit' or 'my soul' as opposed to the cold and distant Anglicised translation *ego*. (Hundert 1990, p.135) This concurs favourably with Kant's model of the mind and even Hegel's perspective for the need for a science of living experience which takes us into the affective side of life where the secrets of life are revealed. Therefore, at the heart of our knowing is a living spirit within which God who is Spirit can be known and experienced by us his creations. Here, in fact, is the perfect place for God and man to meet, that place that determines who we are and that affects us so profoundly as mind meets Mind and being engages that life generating Being from which we have come and with whom we have an existential connection. The Scriptures inform us that God has declared: "My Spirit will no always strive with man", but for those who say they have no soul, this may well be already true for them, but it is by choice and not by nature.

Human reason can only take us so far and point to the existence of a wise creator, but we can only know Him when we exercise those attributes of being with which we have been so richly endowed as a species, So as the Apostle Paul affirms that, "We are without excuse", if we fail to use them as they were meant to be used. (Romans Cp.1) But to know God we must not merely see the need to postulate the idea of such a Being but to engage Him as he was meant to be engaged. So as Mill the philosopher concluded: "Socrates dissatisfied is better that a fool satisfied."

In the final analysis, God doesn't argue toe to toe with finite men or with the warped prejudices of mankind, he presents us with truth we cannot deny as human beings with spiritual attributes of understanding which when engaged can relate to Him. While Goethe, Shiller, Coleridge and Emerson that enlarged Kant's dualistic approach to what has been referred to as a participatory definition of understanding in which the minds own principles of understanding was itself an expression of the world's own being the outworking of which was a process of Nature's self-revelation. While Augustine argued that the mind was forever superior to the world of finite human reason with reason being the means by which we activate the world of being as the servant of being and not the judge of being. But for those who questioned the reality of God in creation Augustine could write: "Fool! By operations of the body I know thee to be living, canst thou not by the works of creation know the creator?"

Thus as Tarnas again writes: "In this perspective, nature pervades everything, and the human mind in all its fullness is itself an expression of nature's own being ... The human imagination is itself part of the world's intrinsic truth." (Tarnas 1991, p.434) So we need to see as Kant could see that we need to start from within ourselves to realise that fundamental truths are apprehended from within our inmost nature of being as the greatest truths in the universe that are existentially revealing, spiritually enlightening, meaningfully powerful and logically compelling. So if we see two lovers walking down the street hand and hand they are not merely connected by means of their hands but by means of their mind. Or if we look at a bouquet of flowers we are not just looking at rich variety of different colours but a thing of beauty. If we witness an act of gratuitous violence, we are not just witnessing a range of bodily movements but unacceptable behaviour that disgusts and repels us. Or if we see something that we can clearly understand is extremely complex and intelligently ordered we are constrained to conclude that it owes its existence to an intelligent and sufficient cause. If we see worshippers going into a church, we should consider that they are not just going to admire the building or pass their time but the give praise and glory to the one to whom their they owe everything. If we see paramedics giving medical assistance to an injured person on the side of the road, we can reasonably conclude that this is not just done out of mere duty but driven by a sense of pity, compassion and love for one's fellowman.

So, life is a dynamic balance between physics and metaphysics, mind and matter, sense and sensibility. So as Einstein once remarked: "Concern for man himself and his fate must always be the chief interest of all technical endeavours … in order that the creations of our mind should be a blessing and not a curse to mankind." And when we love our neighbour we are in a real sense loving God because He loves all mankind and wants us to share in this most resplendent attribute of His being.

Chapter 7
The Ongoing Search for a Holistic Science of Life

The theory of behaviourism which was prevalent in the early part of the twentieth century argued that behaviour is essentially learned behaviour, but we can only learn that which we are programmed to know and capable of experiencing as the different behaviour of different animals aptly show. We couldn't teach a lion of its own volition not to hunt and eat meat because it against its very nature. Therefore, cognitivism argued that behaviour was related to an innate endowment of being that allowed us to understand that which we perceive under many different categories of understanding so that we come primed to learn and equipped with the necessary mental tools to understand and make sense of the world we live in. This Noam Chomsky refers to as general-purpose learning machinery by which to learn such things as language and to engage and interact with the world and everything in it in many different ways.

Henry Plotkin affirms that cognitivism recued psychology from the cripplingly narrow vision of behaviourism and liberated psychologists conceptually and allowed causal powers to be relocated in the mind and brain. In other words, that which constitutes the reality of who we are as conscious beings while essentially invisible to us: "enabled psychology to mature into a science that is in important ways now compatible with physics or genetics." (Plotkin 1997, p.33) Therefore, the causes of behaviour can be related mechanisms of the mind in which there was a cause and effect relationship between nature and behaviour. But nature of being that determines behaviour takes us beyond the realm of physics into the world of mind where different desires, feelings, hopes and aspirations come powerfully into play. Religion is obviously a natural part of human beings nature of being because of its universal practice from time immemorial.

The attribute of rational thinking which is an intrinsic part of our nature as human beings forces us as conclude that effects have causes commensurate with the nature of the effects produced. So as the effect, or effects, prove to be – so the cause will be. Not only will this mean that the vast complexity of a physical brain needs to explained in terms of an extremely intelligent and sufficient cause, but who we are as sentient beings with different feelings, hopes and aspirations need to be explained in terms of a living life producing cause capable of producing in us these highly evocative life producing effects within us. This makes the cause from which we have come, a living entity of vast order producing power and life generating efficiency. This brings us face to face, both logically and existentially, with the idea of a wise creator, so that if the idea of God did not exist scientists worthy of the name would in all good conscience have to invent Him, or more appropriately to believe in His existence.

Therefore, naturalists and creationists are essentially singing from the same hymn-sheet and it must be a song worthy of that order producing and life generating cause from which we, and all things, have come – it is just that some carnal ill-motivated theorists haven't recognised this fact yet and are determined to be beholding to no one, not even their creator. Some such theorists end up attributing all that exists to the order-producing sum of nothing, which to realists like theists is anything but consistent with the ordered and living sum of the effects produced.

Moreover, just because we as finite beings cannot explain all that is involved in relation to that first cause, is no reason to go irrational and plump for no intelligent or sufficient cause at all. In an essay in 1982, Richard Dawkins wrote that: "all adaptations are for the preservation of DNA *and DNA just is.*" (Cited in Plotkin 1997, p.93–94) However, it seems to the writer that the 'just is' of DNA as Dawkins calls it, seems very like and indistinguishable from the 'just is' that theists call God who having seeded the earth with all manner of living things both biologically complex and ontologically rich making DNA the work of a wise creator who set the working of the universe up not merely to be life permitting and life producing with a veritable host of interacting variables in a way that blind chance could not by any stretch of imagination explain.

Bryan Magee for instance, doubts the existence of the soul and thinks that it might just be something he wanted to believe but which had nothing to do with the truth. But does his very idea of having a soul (a reality of conscious mind within which he lives and moves and has his being) nothing to do with who he is as a human being. Does it not, in fact, take him to the centre and source of who he is as a human being that determine who he is and aspires to be as a human being? So the question much be asked as to why he even wants to have an immortal soul and why the idea on not having an immortal soul terrifies him. The fact of having an immortal soul must be possible because the life producing cause that endowed him with it in the first place must have within their power to generate such a living life producing effect and as part of the package of the gift of life.

But does Magee as a human being the most profound compendium of ordered complexity in the known universe nothing to do with the truth of an intelligent and sufficient cause at work on the earth? Moreover from where did his fervent desire that he had an immortal soul originate? Such longings cannot be explained within a vacuum of mindless irrationality but from a cause that has these hopes and aspirations inculcated into fabric of their being. But it seems that for some that empirically based reality has so taken over their thinking of the modern world of reductive materialism some don't really know who they are and see themselves as nothing more than a chanced upon arrangement of corporeal substance of no ultimate order producing significance.

In this a monkey is a more happy, fulfilled and privileged species than some human beings because it faithfully follows the natural instincts of its own being and never questions it and behold it works and in this they are a happy and fulfilled species. But we humans have extracurricular attributes of being that inform us that effects have causes and that all that we experience ourselves to be emanates from a sufficient cause that created us to be human beings who can make good and fulfil for us to all we aspire to be as a species. Our psychology of being is as a crucial part of who we are as human being as is our physiology and both combine to constitute who we are as human beings. Thus Socrates postulated a transcendent primordial mind (*Nous*) which set the material universe into motion to give it form and order. In this way, the human soul is assimilated to the world soul and thence to the divine creative mind of the universe.

When Mr Magee feels hungry or thirsty does he question such feelings because he cannot explain how his mind produces them, when he feels angry at seeing as act of cruelty does he question because he cannot work out how his mind works to give him such a feeling, if he has the desire to male love with a wife or partner does he hold back and resist because he cannot explain the nature of love that draws him to that partner and the desire to make love with – me thinks not. Or if his conscience bothers him does he pass it off as mere imagination or seek to address the problem and endeavour to put it right. So when the idea of God enters his head and the idea of having an immortal soul why does he question it, especially when the idea of such a creator is logically consistent with an ordered world full of lively human beings who depend on these instincts and desires to live and survive, and human beings who regard life as sacred and exciting who have this insatiable desire for immortality?

Richard Tarnas aptly puts it with regard to an empirically based world view: "The new universe was a machine, a self-contained mechanism of force and matter, devoid of goals or purpose, bereft of intelligence or consciousness, its character fundamentally alien to that of man … This was accompanied by a new sense of alienation from a world that no longer responded to human values, nor offered a redeeming context within which to understand the larger issues of human existence." (Tarnas 1996, p.326) How could things that we humans create be of such great significance by way of cause and purpose that we heap great praise and shower with accolades those who are so creative in human terms, and yet the cause that brought them and all things into existence to be of so little relevance by way of cause it can be referred to as no cause at all. How could we possibly outsmart our creator to be smarter and be more creatively ingenious that that cause that created us?

As Gerald Schroeder aptly points out with regard to hearing: "…I don't hear biochemistry I hear sound," and we can obviously make sense of sound in the form of language as giving expression to many different categories of understanding and personal experiences. But: "In that passage between brain and mind we are looking for a physical link that does not exist," writes Schroeder. (Schroeder 2002, p.6) What we have is an existential link that unites us to other people with bonds of love and affection and to that living life producing cause from which we have come. We do not know how a physical brain operates to being living things to conscious life endowed with many different attributes of being, hopes, feelings and aspirations – but it does. There is something ineffably mysterious and awe-inspiringly enchanting about life that cannot be explained by all that we experience a physical brain to be.

Even when we describe a physical brain with all the modern sophisticated technology scientists cannot identify or define anything that remotely resembles life as we experience it to be. Thus as Moheb Costandi explains: "And yet, despite centuries of speculation by philosophers and more recently,

154

neuroscientists, we have little idea of what consciousness is, or how the brain generates it", so that consciousness, "is a mystery." (Costandi 2013, p. 76)

But what kind of a mystery is it the mind, it is we would argue exactly what it reveals itself to be, a dimension of conscious being that it operates as living oracle of being sensibly perceiving the world of physics in a way that the physical world of things no matter how empirically complex cannot perceive and experience us. So we can two one of two things, we can explain our unique qualitative reality of being away because we cannot understand its form of working and how a physical brain can generate its unique qualities of profound life-defining significance. Or is this a subtle way to avoid the idea of God, who we as moral being are ultimately answerable. The neuron theory of consciousness is a deeply flawed theory of consciousness, As Moreb Costandi explains: "Some believe that gaining a better understanding of how the brain works will provide answers to life's big questions. It will not: brain research cannot tell us everything about ourselves, or what makes us human." (Costandi 2013, p.3)

Information somehow gets entangled between particles, raising the possibility that everything is connected by invisible threads. The mind so real and yet its reality so unique and illusive some scientists have wondered if there could possibly be a link between the phenomenon of quantum physics and consciousness. As Joanne Baker writes: "Speculation is rife about whether we might experience consciousness due to a quantum tickling of the microscope structure in the brain, collapsing wave wave-functions and entanglement." (Cited in Joanne Baker 2013, p.200) In other words there could possibly be a connection between quantum physics and the mind, a spooky action at a distance as it has been called, somehow generating consciousness. A quantum signal speaking into the deep working of the brain bringing it to conscious life similar in principle though different in nature to the way a signal entering a television brings the television to life in a way the inner workings of the television cannot of itself explain. Signals that cannot be seen with the naked eye, but nevertheless are transmitting information that brings the brain to life by receptors deep within the brain or operating in conjunction with it, that can decode that information which in turn uses the brain to activate the body into response to that life information.

This opens up a whole new world of wave-particle duality described by Richard Feynman as the: "only mystery from which all others flow. You can't explain it in the sense of saying how it works you can only say how it appears to

155

work." Some have wondered if quantum physics could possibly play a part in producing consciousness or information the brain can interpret and act within the brain to produce consciousness, remembering that electromagnetic waves extend beyond the familiar spectrum of visible light which cannot be seen with the naked eye, but nevertheless operating to bring the physical brain to conscious life and which in turn activates the body to respond to things consciously perceived.

Tarnas affirms this deep interconnectedness of phenomena encouraged a new and holistic thinking about the world with respect to social, moral and religious implications. (Tarnas 1991, p.357) Others talk about microtubules that have been discovered deep within the neurons of the brain that might be acting as receptors to bring the brain consciously to life and operating with different categories of qualitative being and understanding that move and motivate us in the world we live in. Searching for such means is not mere speculation, scientists know there is something going on deep within matter they just haven't worked how it operates yet. Erwin Schrodinger argues that: "From all we have learnt about the structure of living matter, we must be prepared to find it working in a manner that cannot be reduced to the ordinary laws of physics." Cited in Baker 2013, p.199) As Baker again writes: "The more we have learned, the stranger the quantum universe has become. Information can be entangled between particles raising the possibility that everything is connected to everything else in the universe by invisible threads of organic connectedness." (Cited in Baker 2013, p.3)

It is little wonder that Thomas Lewton suggests that: "There may be life in the idea of a quantum brain yet." (Cited in New Scientist Magazine August 2021) While Max Plank explains: "I regard consciousness as fundamental, I regard matter as derivative from consciousness. We cannot get behind consciousness. Everything that we talk about postulates consciousness." (Cited in Baker 2013, p.292) While Niels Bohr and Edwin Schrodinger have thought that: "biological systems, including brains, might behave in ways that are indescribable using classical physics." (Cited in Baker 2013, p.201) While Anil Seth explains: "Somehow, somewhere inscribed in the brain is what makes you – you. But how do our brains turn electrical impulses into the vast range of perceptions, thoughts and emotions we feel from moment to moment?" (New Scientist Magazine August 2021)

So: "as photons are waves and particles and we observe one from the other under different circumstances, so mind and matter are projections onto the world of a deeper level of ordered connectedness. They are separate aspects of life: being complementary, looking at matter tells us nothing about consciousness, and vice versa." (Cited in Baker 2013, p.202) Therefore, speculation is rife about whether we might experience consciousness due to quantum tickling of the microscopic structures in the brain, collapsing wave functions or entanglement so that it is wondered if quantum theory could explain some of the brains unique qualities. (Cited in Baker 2013, p.201) What we can be fairly sure is that particles and waves are closely intertwined that are performing two different functions in the formation of life and that Gamma waves operating at 40 Hz frequency could be important in producing consciousness.

Therefore, the quantum world runs according the working of the exceedingly small deep within the atom, behaving like waves in one sense and a stream of bullets in the form of exceedingly small particles of matter that when joined produce cells that go make up the biological complexity of physical world. Therefore, as Baker writes: "The more we learn, the stranger the quantum universe has become. Information can be 'entangled' between particles, raising the possibility that everything is connected by invisible threads. Quantum messages are transmitted and received instantaneously, breaking a taboo that no signal can travel faster than the speed of life." (Baker 2013, Introduction)

So we seem to have a web of quantum connections. But that is how it is, the universe is a big quantum system some suppose. Behind this cosmic interconnectedness it is not too presumptuous to suppose that behind it is the mind of a wise creator God. So as the Scriptures' declare: "In Him we live and move and have our being," and the means by which this achieved is what theorists now describe as quantum physics. One thing we know is that science has not explained how the rich qualitative reality of a living self-conscious mind is generated by all that we know and understand a physical brain to be and which is calling out for an adequate explanation. As Fritj of Capra has said: "Quantum theory thus reveals a basic oneness of the universe": while Max Born has concluded that: "I am convinced that theoretical physics is actual philosophy," Philosophy, which is the act of thinking the art of reasoning which underlies the working of the universe. While we do not yet have all the answers but quantum physics may or may not be the answer, but we know for certain that all we understand a physical brain to be does not explain either in substance or nature all that we experience ourselves to be as living entities of profound ontological substance and qualitative significance.

As Richard Tarnas argues, belief that the empirically based scientific method had unique access to the truth was seen as not only epistemologically naïve but within the larger context of life such a limited perspective of reality that could be a very dangerous thing. As we have already noted the modern world with its rampant materialism and preoccupation with things of the senses rang hollow in which man's capacity to retain his humanity seemed increasingly to be in doubt. (Tarnas 1996, p.364–365)

Mel Thompson reminds us, it would be utterly pointless examining the working of a physical brain to see how the mind works as it would taking a Stradivarius apart in order to discover why a violin concerto can be so moving. (Thompson 2000, p.92) Monkeys, though intelligent in their own way, do not sit down and think about their origins, carry out experiments to discover the nature and functioning of different things, or ponder the significance of life in general and what its existence mean in terms of sufficient cause. So we must decide whether to go with the monkey and take everything for granted, or take up the cause as rational beings that after examining different things to see how they were ordered into existence making sure to attribute empirically based things to an intelligent and sufficient cause and living things to a living life producing cause.

Henry Plotkin points out that psychology of being needs to be explained within the evolutionary context but great tracts on this subject have been left on one side and is now ripe for the picking and this crucially subject should be given the attention it deserves. Tarnas aptly points out: "In this perspective, nature pervades everything, and the human mind in all its fullness is itself an expression of nature's essential being. And it is only when the human mind actively brings forth from within itself the full powers of its disciplined imagination and saturates its empirical observation with archetypical insight that the deeper reality of the world emerges." (Tarnas 1998, p.434–135)

While Schroeder rightly points out: "We talk about missing links. We have a missing link right in our heads at the brain/mind connection." (Schroeder 2002, p.157) But for some if it can't be measured it isn't real, if it can't be examined under a microscope it has nothing to do with the truth. But the human subject: "Can never presume to transcend the manifold predispositions of his or her subjectivity." But by means of intelligence we human beings operating to the logic of cause and effect thinking can draw some serious conclusions about the origin of our existence by virtue of the fact that the cause must be able to explain all that we predicate of ourselves as human beings both mentally and physically.

Fred Heeren is surely right when he argues: "Thus the first cause must be greater in power than anything in the universe; in fact must be greater than the sum of all the powers of the universe." (Heeren 2000, p.90) While Mel Thompson points out that: "Random perception would make nonsense of all human thought: hence the importance of Einstein's point that ultimately you cannot think and encounter the world on the basis of randomness. For science to make sense there has to be the presupposition that the world itself makes sense." (Thompson 2000, p.89)

Mel Thompson sums it up: "If things behaved in random fashion, no science or technology would be possible, for it works by predicting and examining the results of predictions." (Thompson 2000, p.88) Therefore, for the world to make sense it has to be ordered intelligently in a way conformable to human intelligence and human intelligence operates to the principle of sufficient cause both in theory and in practice in which the cause must be able to explain all that we know and experience the effects to be both physical or metaphysical. As Einstein insisted: "The harmony of natural law ... reveals an intelligence of such superiority that compared with it all the systematic thinking and acting of human beings is an utterly insignificant reflection." (Cited in Einstein 1974, p.40) Therefore, it seems obvious that we are microcosms of that life producing intelligence that ordered us into existence and this is why we can go on to produce intelligently ordered things in our own right.

Science has for so long focused primarily on the cognitive side of life the thinking subject in general terms, but the cognitive side does not operate in a vacuum bur with rich and varied categories of understanding, part of which is our capacity to reason which constrains us to relate effects to necessary causes and ultimately to the idea of a wise creator. Moreover, causes do not operate within the constraints of a mindless empiricism but within a world of conscious being and a qualitative reality of being that bind us to those with whom we relate and variously interact and that combine to make life worth living.

And when the origin of life is denuded of a cause fit to explain it the mind is free to believe anything. But as Margaret Maher aptly observes: As we begin to enter the storms of emotional strain and conflict that characterises the human condition, we may well have to give up some of this neat (and we would add simplistic empirically based) 'precision' in exchange for a richer, deeper understanding of the verities of human experience. (Mahler 1965a, 1965b, 1974) While the universal threat of global warming that threatens civilisation we will need every ounce of moral integrity, grit and determination to avert a looming disaster. Is our existence worth preserving is the question, those who think of the origin of life on earth to be so little significance in the first place are going to struggle to accept the sacrifices that need to be made to preserve it.

Richard Dawkins describes evolution as *The Blind Watchmaker,* an unconscious process of mindless change devoid of purpose and denuded of ultimate meaning such a process by definition could produce nothing worth preserving, nothing but a never-ending round of randomly rearranged chaos operating to no real purpose. And if science is not based on intelligence and life on earth is not ordered intelligently we would have a world of utter confusion and everyone running about like headless chickens trying to make sense of that which by its very nature makes no sense. Call it 'Mother Nature' if you will but it makes no difference, because Mother Nature needs to be explained how out of primordial chaos the vast complexity of intelligent life appeared in all its ordered glory. As Tarnas discerns: "That human language itself can be recognised as rooted in a deeper reality, as reflecting the universes unfolding meaning." (Tarnas 1996, p.435)

Johnjoe McFadden Professor of Molecular Genetics at the Universe of Surrey points out: "It has been estimated that the chances of generating a self-replicating molecule by a random process alone is so exceedingly small it can be discounted." (Cited in Aliens 2016, p.141) When DNA was discovered in 1953 by Crick and Watson it was said by evolutionists that at last they had the means to explain how natural selection actually worked. But evolutionists had for some hundred years or so argued that 'natural selection' had nothing to do with an order producing intelligence of any kind, but now that this mechanism of order producing genius has been discovered in the form of DNA proves that Darwin was wrong all along but all those who naively followed him were essentially mislead.

Even when evolution is likened as a sifting process in that natural selection: "sifts the ordered wheat from the disordered chaff," with the chaff being that which is not ordered sufficiently to be selected into existence while the ordered wheat is gathered into the environmental barn to be used as it was meant to be used. But how could there be anything of any ordered significance to sift in a process of mindless shuffling through chaos? We cannot get ordered complexity by randomly moving chaos about: a combine harvester has wheat to sift from the chaff, but evolution outside the working of an intelligent and sufficient cause has no way to explain the wheat of ordered complexity that needs to exist before it can be successfully sifted from the chaff of unadulterated chaos.

Even Richard Dawkins accepts that something as basic as blue-green algae could not come into existence by means of "higgledy-piggledy luck", but what he puts in place of higgledy-piggledy luck are mechanisms of life producing genius of DNA which he fails to explain or granting to it the order producing credence it deserves. So while Crick and Watson declared in 1953 that they had discovered the secret of life on earth, the fact is that they had ultimately explained nothing leaving this life-producing power of DNA unexplained and with its origin being just as much a mystery today as it ever was. But even with this, it doesn't explain how life on earth became consciously alive which is a different thing altogether and with Jim Baggott concluding such reality is a metaphysical concept that takes us beyond the capacity of empirically based of science to deal with or explain. (Baggott 2013, p.8) As a result he concludes: "we have to content ourselves with knowledge of empirical based reality" because empirically based science cannot deal with or explain metaphysical concepts.

But the fact is that science itself is a metaphysical research programme carried out at many different levels of investigation to better understand ourselves and the world we live in and the information gained by such investigations and decisions made as a result of such investigations in many different fields of investigation are by definition metaphysical which we refer to as science. Even when we are investigating physical things to better understand them we are using the metaphysical reality of mind guided by our intelligence to better understand that subject matter and draw appropriate conclusions accordingly we up to our necks in metaphysics. That which is beyond the physical and material realm of empirically based reality as intelligent minds drawing the appropriate conclusions with respect to information is gained.

So as a result if we study something like a subatomic particle or a living cell or a bicycle well can conclude that these things are extremely complex, finely tuned and well ordered, with the implication being that they came into existence by means that are both intelligent and ingenious. But Baggott doesn't want us to draw any such conclusions because such conclusions take us beyond the world of empirically based science. This is of course an intellectual cop-out and a deceitful ploy to avoid drawing the necessary logical conclusions with respect to the nature and functioning of different subject matter how it functions and how it was ordered to function so effectively as it does. In other words, explaining things of whatever nature in terms of a suitable and sufficient cause. This of course science rigged in such a way that effects are of whatever nature and no matter how complex and well ordered don't need to be attributed to an intelligent and sufficient cause. And moreover, scientists engaged in science operating in their many different fields of study are themselves entities of immense complexity and intelligence whose existence also needs to be understood and explained in terms of sufficient cause.

But Baggott is determined not to go down this road lest he is confronted with the compelling logic of a necessary and sufficient cause in the form of a wise creator. So while our metaphysical reality of being may indeed be beyond the reach of empirically based science to quantify and explain, nevertheless, it is who we experience ourselves to be and without which there would be no one to do science and to draw the necessary conclusions with respect to intelligently ordered things perceived and investigated in a world of vast complexity. Thus Baggott argues that we must be content with empirically based explanations, the bald physical facts without considering the implications of what scientists are doing when they engage in science. (Baggott 2013, p.8)

Brian Silver reminds us that in most of the eighteenth century, due in great measure to Newton, the highest quality of man was seen in his ability to use reason to get to the truth about the origin and existence of different things, but for some the highest ability of man seems to be to avoid using their intelligence and end up in a world of causal absurdity in which the cause can be the very antithesis of the ordered sum of the effects produced. Plato believed that intelligence was a divine attribute passed on to us by our creator to regulate our thinking and to know as surely as reason can teach it to us that we owe our existence to an intelligent and sufficient cause sufficient to produce all that we predicate of the effects produced in a world of massive complexity. While Edmund Husserl reminds us that the primary reality of being through which we live life and do science is indubitably real in a way that empirically based things are not, so if we want to build a conception of reality on a rock-solid foundation the inner world of being is the place to start.

Mel Thompson points out that: "Random perception would make nonsense out of all human thought and cause us to come to all the wrong conclusions about intelligently ordered things perceived." Hence the validity of Einstein's point: "that ultimately you cannot think and encounter the world on the basis of randomness. For science to make sense there has to be the presumption that the world itself makes sense." (Thompson 2000, p.89) And for the world to make sense it must be ordered intelligently in a way that conforms to human intelligence.

As Einstein has again remarked: "The eternal mystery of the world is its comprehensibility", but to be comprehended intelligently it must be ordered intelligently. So what we need is a holistic science of life which not only logically ties us to that cause from which we have come but existentially unites us to that cause as living effects to a living life producing cause. It is only when the human mind actively brings forth from within itself the full powers of its developed imagination and saturates empirical observation with archetypal insight that the deeper reality of the world emerges. But when verifiable reality is reduced to empirical based scientific terms as *The National Academy of Sciences* does they are rigging the scientific playing field so that theists cannot win, because no matter how marvellously ordered, immensely complex, exquisitely designed it all comes to nothing in terms of sufficient cause. So the mind by which we humans intelligently engage in science also needs to be explained as much as intelligently ordered things perceived even though intelligence as a metaphysical reality of conscious being cannot be defined in empirically based scientific terms.

In fact, the metaphysical reality of the mind needs to explained on two counts: firstly, how it was ordered intelligently to reason intelligently and then how the mind as a metaphysical reality of being different in nature and substance to inanimate matter came into existence endowing us as human beings with intelligent minds to think intelligently and ontologically sophisticated operating within different attributes of understanding. And as we pointed earlier, *The National Academy of Sciences* do exactly the same thing so that no matter how intelligently ordered or inspiringly complex something is it cannot be ascribed to a process of intelligent design because intelligent design as a concept cannot be validated in empirically based terms. We would suggest that this is because this would immediately bring them face to face with the logic of sufficient cause in the form of a wise creator which seems to be something some are determined to avoid. The motives for such thinking could possibly be found in the words of Bertrand Russell who, after rejecting the existence of God, could explain, *I revelled in my newly achieved freedom from God's moral strictures. For me, living without God meant living one hundred present for myself, Freed from someday being held accountable for my actions, I felt unleashed to pursue personal happiness and pleasures at all costs.* (Cited in Strobel 2004, P.25)

This is hardly the worthy motives of one in an honest search for the truth, but rather one who is willing to distort much of reality to avoid facing up to things that lie closest to the human heart and the wellspring of being within which we are confronted with something truly ineffable. The world in which modern man lived was becoming as impersonal as his science, with man's capacity to retain his humanity increasingly in doubt in an environment subsumed in technology and the mundane world time and sense.

Chapter 8
Evolution – A Theory in Crisis

Michael Denton in 1986 wrote a book entitled *Evolution – A Theory in Crisis* because in spite of much geological investigation in every corner of the earth, Darwinians failed to discover the different connecting links of steady progression in the fossil record which showed that evolution in all its intermediate stages actually took place. In other words, there were huge gaps in the fossil record. But even if theorists were to find all the connecting links throughout all evolutionary time these order producing links in the evolutionary process need to be explained and why there is such a long line of order producing means and mechanisms available and operating effectively to produce the vast and varied complexity of life on earth.

To try and make evolution seem simple and inevitable Andrea Sella affirms: "… that chemistry tends towards complexity and order in a way that shines light on both our own origins and the possibility of life on other planets." (Cited in Aliens 2016, p.117) But the question remains as to what is it about chemicals that enables them to tend towards complexity? Even the simplest things made up of many different chemical elements is massively complex it their own right. So the Periodic Table represents a massively rich complex mix of chemicals which are elements that are needed to produce the immense biological complexity of life on earth which in themselves represent a more than a happy coincidence. What are the chances of an accidental big bang occurring in the vacuum of space and by shear chance producing all the right mix of chemical ingredients to bring existence a life permitting planet earth, and then the right mix of chemicals ordered sufficiently to produce the first basic living cells so small we a microscope to see them? The mind boggles, and we still haven't got to the first simple multicellular living things which we now know to be extremely complex in their own right? And then for the right order producing mechanisms to appear with all the necessary means to order those chemicals into the first simple micro-organisms into existence which are incredibly complex in their own right for which we need energy, order and massive of complexity.

Life right down to the simplest single living cells are anything but simple and are so complex in themselves scientists accept that they could not have fallen into place by chance or by spontaneous generation or by some freak accident or a long series of accidents. Even spontaneous generation is only spontaneous if the right means are available within a given mix of chemicals to make it spontaneous. Louis Pasteur firmly established in his many experiments the fact that life can only come from that which was itself alive. While Thomas Henry Huxley could affirm that: "I intend to suggest that no such thing as abiogenesis. (That life could spontaneously generate itself) has ever taken place in the past, or ever will in the future." (DK Books 2014, p.156–159) Then how multi-cellular life forms appeared made up of billions and even trillions of ordered and integrated living cells. Then how conscious life was imputed into that complex mix of chemicals is still a complete mystery.

Johnjoe McFadden in the same book *Aliens* writes: "It has been estimated that the chances of generating a self-replicating molecule by random processes alone are so exceedingly small they can be discounted." Cited in Aliens 2016, p.142) While Matthew Cobb argues that if we want try to work out the odds of a single eukaryote (a complex cellular structure) coming into existence by chance you would soon run out of zeros. Moreover, Strikingly we have no evidence from earth that evolution by natural selection is able to find such a solution – in the nearly 4 billion years life has not come up with an answer, natural selection failed. Instead there appears to have been a single event of mind-boggling improbability, for it involved two life forms interacting in the most unusual way. (Cited in Aliens 2016, p.159) That is, to explain how living cells exceedingly complex in their own right came into existence in the first place and then had within them the means to replicate and later as with multicellular organisms to reproduce in kind.

We have seen how Richard Dawkins and others make the same point about how exceedingly lucky it is that even the simplest living things came into existence at all, but in spite of this everything just goes into the lucky bucket until it is running over with things that nothing created. Therefore, Andrea Sella's assumption shows a lot of wishful thinking and a certain naivety with regard to biogenesis in which chemistry tends towards complexity and order, and even if it did there must be a reason of immense order producing ingenuity to explain this feat of chemical engineering.

However, if living things can only arise from what before were living things as scientists inform us, how did life arise before the first life forms existed? We now know that we need nucleotides (DNA and RNA) to produce biological complexity of living cells and to infuse more complex things with conscious life which is a different thing altogether and warrants as infusion of qualitative being from a cause that is able to explain it. And even with this we still need to explain different attributes of being that we associate with more complex animal life. The theory of endosymbiosis (complex cells with internal structures called organelles) argues that complex living things emerge from simpler living systems merging to produce ever-more complex living things. But these means still need to be explained and how they all combined so ingeniously to produce ever-more complex living things some of which like ourselves are made up of trillions of even more complex living cells.

This is a process that cooperates together so expeditiously they are sometimes referred to as self-organising systems. But nothing is self-organising unless and until there is the necessary means within it driving it towards ever-greater order and complexity. A Factory is a complex self-organising system operating effectively and efficiently to produce something like motor cars, which are a lot less complex than single living cells. But if we were to suggest that such a factor fell into place by some freak accident, or by a long series of freak order producing accidents, we would be considered inept and even a fool. So it seems that evolution is operating to a form of endosymbiosis in which simpler life forms become part of more complex life forms with each one needing to be explained and then how they came together to cooperate in the most ingenious way to form evermore complex living things.

But who set up the whole universe to operate in such a stupendous order producing fashion to produce such the vast array of massively complex living things? As one theorist has put it: "Symbiosis is everywhere", and it is obvious that these inter-related systems drive evolution and join together to increasing produce ever more complex living things from very simple beginnings. Life on earth seems to originate from an exceedingly long of cosmic creativity but was happening so slowly some haven't noticed this yet, and haven't used their God given intelligence to add it all up and recognise that what we have is a utterly massive process of order producing ingenuity and life generating creativity that can bring something out of nothing, order out of chaos, exceedingly complex living cells out of the raw chemicals of the earth, and animal life in all its rich and varied complexity of which human beings are the highest form endowed with many different attributes of being one of which is rational thinking whereby they can reflect on the wonder and ingenuity of it all and give thanks to the creator of all things.

What we seem to have is a world subsumed in a subtle and dangerous form of cosmic superstition in which everything is apportioned to a never-ending sequence of luck in which there is no end to what luck can do that insults our intelligence and makes a mockery of our claim to be rational beings in which effects have causes, causes sufficient to explain the ordered and integrated sum of the effects produced, things both animate and inanimate so that the ordered sum of effects produced reflect something of the nature of the cause involved. But for some, from the starry hosts above us to the moral being within us represents nothing of any order producing significance, so we can make of it what we will or nothing at all which for effects so ineffably vast and life generatingly profound is surely not merely a huge risk but to fly in the face of reason itself.

As we have already noted, the late Professor Brian Silver points out that: "the gap between an aqueous solution of these molecules and a living cell is stupendous ... It stretches even the credulity of a materialistic abiogenesis fanatic to believe that that proteins (the stuff of life) and nucleotides (the order producing genius of DNA/RNA) emerged simultaneously and at the same point in space, from the primordial soup." (Silver 1998, p.245–349) The simplest living cells millions of which could sit on a pinhead are held together by electro-magnetic forces referred to as Covalent Bonds, Hydrogen Bonds, Ionic Bonds, Metallic Bonds and Van der Waals Forces that are awe-inspiringly complex. It is little wonder that Silver goes on to say that: "The finger of God is certainly a tempting way out." (Silver 1989, p.349) But it is not just a tempting way out, it is the only conceivable solution to our problem, namely that there's a God in heaven and we are not Him.

While John Lennox points out: "Even the tiniest bacterial cells, weighing less than a trillionth of a gram are 'veritable microminiaturised factories containing thousands of exquisitely designed pieces of intricate molecular machinery made up altogether of 100 thousand million atoms, far more complicated than any machine built by man and absolutely without parallel in the non-living world." (Lennox 2007, p.116) Moreover, all these processes of biogenesis need massive amounts of energy to bring everything together into an ordered and integrated whole just as a man-made factory needs massive amounts of order producing energy to bring together all the necessary means to produce intelligently ordered things. In fact, Richard Dawkins makes the same point when he writes: "Every living cell, even a single bacterial cell, can be thought of as a gigantic chemical factory ... The word gigantic may seem surprising for a cell, especially when you remember that 10 billion bacterial cells could sit on the surface of a pin head ... There are about a million, million, of these large pieces of apparatus in a cell, and 2,000 different kinds of them." (Dawkins 1988, p.120–121) Therefore, Natural selection is not some simple process of never-ending luck it encompasses a group of processes embodied in a very complex set of mechanisms.

Recognising the problem with evolution by natural selection some one hundred leading American scientists in response to a television series extolling the virtues of evolution took out an advert in a national magazine entitled: "*A Scientific Dissent From Darwinism*" in which they stated: "We are sceptical of claims for the ability of random mutations and natural selection to account for the complexity of life." (Cited in Strobel 2004, P.100) Richard Dawkins accepts that something as simple as blue-green algae could not come into existence by "higgledy-piggledy luck." So the crucial question therefore, is what kind of process evolution is that it can bring order out of disorder, living things out of inanimate matter in ever-increasing degrees of ordered sophistication? If it's not down to luck then it must inevitably be some form of order producing cause sufficient to explain all that we predicate of the effects produced. But Dawkins doesn't follow the logic of his own argument and refuses to apportion the vast complexity of intelligent life on earth to a cause that is able to explain it. The fact is that that which is supposed to have created us could not possibly confer on us that which it did not itself possess. So life must emanate from a life producing cause in the form of an intelligent and sufficient cause synonymous with the one theists refer to as a wise creator.

Some, however, argue that the design argument is vulnerable to the idea of infinite regress because we then have to explain the designer. But we do not have to explain our maker to know that we as rational beings need such a maker, a maker who can explain not merely all that which we perceive in the world external to us, but the ordered and living world that is us. Why should the thing created need to explain that which created them before they can accept the existence of such a creator? We don't need to go to a factory where something like aeroplanes are being produced to know that we need a wise manufacturer operating to the necessary means to produce the ordered complexity of aeroplanes. We judge the ordered sum of the effects produced in the light of the effects produced even if we may not understand all the necessary complex means involved.

And when it comes to life on earth, we cannot reason back into a causeless vacuum of nothingness, we must reckon up the cause involved in the light of the effects produced and we cannot avoid such a conclusion just because we don't want to be morally obliged to the life producing cause involved. Thus the cause comes alive within us to reflect something of the power, nature and purpose of that cause in the light of all we have been created to be as conscious beings endowed with many different attributes of being and understanding. It is only when: "the human mind brings forth from within ourselves the full powers of a disciplined imagination that saturates its empirical observation with an archetypal insight that a deeper reality of the world emerges." (Cited in Tarnas 1996, p.434) We are spiritually connected to one another with life-defining bonds of love, affection and moral obligation, and so we can connect with that life generating cause from which we have come by the same means if we have a mind to do so and a will to cultivate a relationship with them as creature to creator.

We do not experience from within ourselves the working of a physical brain, we experience ourselves as conscious beings looking out into the world of other beings and things, and these do not merely have a profound effect upon us, we respond to them according to different categories of understanding with which we have been so generously endowed. So who are we looking out from within a world of being and interacting with the world and everything it in psycho-dynamic terms? All that we understand our physical brain to be doesn't explain who we are and how we perceive and understand the world around us and interact with it in psychodynamic terms. We need to identify who it is who is looking out from with us into the world of different beings and things and how it affects us in the way it does who we are as ordered and integrated beings responding and interacting with that world.

The world of being holds the secret as to who we are and that cause from which we have come and is different in form and substance to all we understand

170

a physical brain to be. We rise above the limitations of our own body, even the workings of our own brain as conscious living entities and move around the world as a free spirits bringing our physical body with us. Who are we talking too when we are conversing with a friend, it is not with a physical brain but a living embodied spirit connected to a physical body and engaging them as one being with another. Therefore, the mind creates a world of conscious reality of being that opens up into world of spiritual understanding beyond the world of physics to explain and all that we understand a physical brain to be.

This means that there is a real and dynamic relationship between a working brain and a living self-conscious mind that we simply do not understand. This is why it is perfectly understandable why people have out of body experiences especially when they are seriously ill and near death so that the physical body including the working a physical brain are moving apart because they are two separate aspects of life enabling the dying person to be able to look down upon their physical form as life slips away. As we have already noted, scientists do not know how consciousness is generated by the physical brain, it is 'a mystery' and its vast complexity alone cannot explain all we predicate of ourselves as conscious beings operating within the world of physics any more than electricity could generate love, oxygen explain the art of rational thinking, or water equate with wine no matter how much water we might add to water. As the saying goes, "The humble knowledge of thyself is a surer way to God than endless speculation and biased academia." The mind represents embodied reality of conscious being, it is the most precious thing we possess, it is master controller in the act living and the greatest challenge in life is to know *thyself*.

Thus, the brain is the extremely complex organ of the body that operates to the promptings of a living self-conscious mind as needs, feeling, hopes and aspirations determine to execute its will in the world of other beings and things. As Moheb Costandi explains: "… thoughts and behaviour are not determined by the brain alone" making life a combination of mind ant matter, but how these combine to produce life as we experience it to be is still a mystery – the mystery of life. Nancy Frankenberry, however, regards the concept of the religious experience as slippery, unreal and elusive like a ghostly shadow haunting the premises. But this is because she is trying to understand it in empirically based scientific terms which is trying to find the passion of love, a guilty conscience inside the working of the physical brain, or many other categories of understanding peculiar to life in which we a serious case of slip-sliding away into a mindless obscurantism. We are not referring to a physical heart as a blood pump when we say to a lover "I love you with all my heart", we are transposed into different world more profoundly real and pertinent to life than anything physics of itself can explain.

As Hundert reminds us: "The senses, after all, can only supply the intellect with bunches of raw data ('intuitions' in Kant's jargon) it then remains for the 'understanding' to make sense of that data by organising it into a coherent experience of the world." (Hundert 1990, p.21) Moreover, Kant defined understanding in terms of twelve different categories of understanding while Hegel emphasised the rational part of being so that he argued that what is rational is real and what is real is rational because if it wasn't we could not understand or make sense of it. As Hundert observes:

> It is actually almost surprising how far we have been able to come while focusing only on the 'cognitive' side of life. There comes a time, however – and that time has come – when we finally break out of this limited view and begin to consider the 'affective' side as well: all the love, hopes, fears, wishes, frustrations, and dreams that many people would say make life worth living in the first place. … As we begin to enter the storms of emotional strain and conflict that characterise the human condition, we may well have to give up this neat 'precision' in exchange for a richer, deeper understanding of the *varieties* of the human experience. [Mahler 1965a, 1965b, 1974]

Wittgenstein argued that such descriptions as beauty, goodness and religion were beyond explanation and referred to those who tried to explain such things as a form of 'shallow patted rationalism', obviously because such ideas were self-evident to us as human beings who knows exactly what they mean by the use of them. (Cited in Ben-Ami Scharfstein, p.155) As John Heil aptly puts it:

> I believe we have a right to be suspicious of anyone who embraces the formal apparatus of possible worlds while rejecting the ontology. Indeed, I think we might be more suspicious of formal techniques generally, when these are deployed to answer substantive questions in metaphysics and the philosophy of mind. [Heil 1998, Preface p.x.]

It seems that some who claim to know so much about so many different things in the world of physics haven't the foggiest idea who they are as living entities of life-defining substance and significance which shows just how intellectually confused and spiritually bankrupt they really are, and then they call it science and we are meant to be impressed. We are often asked for proof of God, but we ourselves are the proof of God's existence both as rational brings in an ordered and complex world and as conscious beings with a living conscious mind endowed with different attributes of understanding whereby we can experience Him. Such regard their coming into existence as so natural and inevitable, but it is natural for birds to fly but this doesn't negate the fact that they have to be ordered intelligently with the necessary means by which to do so both physically and mentally. It is natural for a piano factory to produce pianos, but we still need a manufacturing process that was set up intelligently with the clear purpose to produce pianos where before no pianos existed.

Therefore: The eternal laws governing Creation, the divine handiwork itself, now stood unveiled by science. Through science man had served God's greater glory, demonstrating the mathematical beauty and complex precision, the stupendous order reigning over the heavens and the earth. The luminous perfection of the discoverer's new universe compelled their awe before the tremendous intelligence which they attributed to the Creator of such a cosmos.

The only people who didn't seem to be getting it seemed to be those who didn't want to get it and went on to write books on how creatively ingenious nothing is. Shaun Carroll claims that Darwin upended our view of life. This means that: "the world as a single, unified reality is not caused or sustained or influenced by anything outside of itself." (Carroll 2017, p.10) But alas, what kind of a process does this single unified reality of the vast complexity in the form of an ordered world full of extremely complex and intelligently ordered living things represent within itself and how do we explain it? Is it magic, is it a mirage, is it all down to the tooth fairy, or attributable to nothing whatsoever at all? If you don't have to explain it in terms of sufficient cause you can attribute it anything or nothing at all – but this not a true science of life or a true science of everything.

While Darwin did not upend our view of the origin of life, he just failed to see it for what it really was and did not live to see the marvellous order producing mechanisms of DNA and RNA that were operating effectively within the evolutionary process that enabled it to be such ingenious process of order producing profundity. Moreover, a factory constitutes an ingenious order producing process that doesn't need anything outside itself to produce that which it was set up to produce, but it still needs to be set up with order producing precision to produce the ordered and integrated sum of what it produces which could not possibly have fallen into place by chance or a process of mindless randomness.

Carroll goes on to argue that: "Purpose and meaning in life arise through fundamentally human acts of creation rather than derived from anything outside ourselves." (Carol 2016, p.11) How could we as human beings through human acts of order producing creativity produce many different intelligently ordered things if we ourselves were not ordered intelligently to act creatively in this way? It seems that some theorists are all too keen to take the glory for their own acts of creation and charge plenty for it, but are unwilling to give any credit to that cause that brought them and all things into existence so that they seem to be the uncaused cause who of Course is God and not them. In fact, science has revealed to us something if the utterly ingenious means by which life on earth came into existence which means that some theorists are willing to deny the very thing they are describing to avoid coming face to face with logic of a wise creator.

Albert Einstein once remarked that: "The eternal mystery of the world was its comprehensibility." In other words, if the world and everything in it can be comprehended by us by means of intelligence then the origin of that world must have something to do with an order producing intelligence. The old argument that we cannot apportion everything to God because we can't explain God is just another one of those red herrings in a frantic effort to be beholding to no one and to whom we as moral beings we would be accountable. Something like a bulldozer doesn't have to know how it was ordered into existence to be an effective functioning bulldozer but we as rational beings know that it was. But human understanding runs into a veritable infinity of wisdom beyond our finite understanding to fully comprehend and that is why it is an awe-inspiring mystery which theists refer to as God.

Carroll goes on to argue that: "Life and consciousness do not denote essences distinct from matter; they are ways of talking about phenomena that emerges from the interplay of extraordinarily complex systems." (Carroll 2017, p.11) But consciousness is something that in nature and substance is wholly distinct and completely different from inanimate matter regardless of how much of it we have or how it is arranged. No scientist has ever produced something

174

that came alive and rose up to confront them with attributes of qualitative being charged with emotions and a will of their own. There is a quality of mind with attributes of being that cannot be explained by all that we understand matter to be and anyone who could bring mind out of matter could rightly be called God.

Even a most sophisticated computer in not consciously alive and if it was and endowed with attributes of being it would be wrong to hurt its feelings and a serious crime to pull the plug and kill it off to replace it with a newer and more powerful computer. Even a computer no matter how ingeniously complex is conscious of nothing, has no feelings, has no conscience and did not order itself into existence, does not fall in love with a fellow computer, or mourn if one of its fellow computers crashes even though it might be programmed to use such words referring to feelings it feels nothing. And if it did, to throw it in the dustbin and crushed to be recycled because we want a more powerful computed should be regarded as a crime punishable by law.

Scientists cannot explain, and admit that they cannot explain, how a physical brain can generate sentience and many different attributes of understanding together with affective feelings of many different kinds that constitute who we are as human beings. It seems obvious that there is another dimension to the brain we haven't yet discovered or something over and above the brain that explains consciousness and who we experience ourselves to be as conscious beings.

So, just as water of itself cannot be rearranged to produce whisky, so matter of itself by definition cannot be arranged to produce a conscious mind irrespective of how much matter we might have or how it is arranged. The human brain is not just a matter of having lots of neurons affirms Anil Seth: "In fact, consciousness cannot be traced to any single region of the brain. It's true that some regions that if damaged will abolish consciousness forever, but these are better understood as on/off switches than actual generators of conscious experience." (Cited in Aliens 2016, p.49) No matter how large and powerful the engine of a motor car might be this it is never going to produce the means to produce light that would enable the driver to see at night. This requires a totally different kind of means altogether in the form of alternator that can generate electricity that is able to produce light. So with conscious life we have a double truth of ineffable proportions, an immensely complex working brain and the conscious reality of living mind.

We now accept the reality of quantum physics and dark matter even though we cannot explain these forces, scientists do not reject these forces because they cannot understand or explain them. So perhaps it is time to admit that there is something about the mind that we cannot explain by means of a physical brain or something over and about a physical brain we have not yet discovered that explains how a working brain can transmute into a living self-conscious mind. Moreover, scientists cannot even explain how a process of blind randomness could produce the vast complexity of a working brain let alone the conscious reality of a living mind. But some undoubtedly for their own reasons want to reduce the mind to a complex physical organ we call the brain that fell into place by an extremely long line of happy coincidences or freak accidents which is scarcely a scientific statement consistent with the principle of sufficient cause.

Two things are certain to us as rational being – something cannot proceed from nothing, order cannot be accounted for by a process of mindless randomness rummaging randomly through inanimate matter, and there no way known to man that can turn matter into mind except a mind-producing intelligence. So with respect to all that exists and who we experience ourselves to we are confronted with something we cannot deny yet something truly ineffable that takes into God territory because it has all the hallmarks of a wise creator written all over it. The Apostle Paul in the New Testament writes: "For since the creation of the world God's invisible qualities, his eternal power and divine nature have been clearly seen, being understood by what has been made so that we are without excuse." While Francis Collins head of the Human Genome Project that successfully mapped the human genome in 2000/1 has argued in his book *The Language of God* that: "… belief in God can be an entirely rational choice, and that the principles of faith are, in fact, complementary with the principles of science." (Collins 2007, p.3)In the same book, Collins asks: "Why couldn't God have used the mechanism of evolution to create?"

Collins also points out that B.B. Warfield, the highly acclaimed Theologian of Princeton accepted evolution as a theory that could be the method of the divine providence and argued that evolution itself must have had a supernatural author. (Collins 2007, p.98) While the eminent theologian Charles Hodge insisted that the Scriptures should be interpreted in the light of firmly established scientific facts and gives an example of this in the fact that it was once believed that the sun circled the earth when we now know that it is the earth that circles around the sun, we should accept the scientific proof of this knowing that the scriptures were given at a time when this was the way it appeared to be from an earth-bound human perspective and these were those to whom the Scripture were then directed.

And when it is argued by that we can never get beyond our own human way of seeing things, when the fact is that reason in which we humans like to boast points us beyond our own finite limitations to the fact that there is a cause that can explain the ordered complexity of all things even though these go beyond our own finite mind to fully understand. We do not reason within a vacuum or within the context of a mindless obscurantism but from within a world we as rational beings can clearly see is extremely complex and intelligently ordered.

In the end, we come to know the truth about the origin and significance of many different things, not merely by means of reason operating within a physical world, but also by our own constituted nature of being that takes us to the soul and centre of who we are as sentient beings both of which needs to be explained by a cause that is able to explain the ordered and coordinated sum of them. As Richard Tarnas has stated: "Materialism failed to account for the subjective phenomenology of human consciousness and man's sense of being a volitional entity different in character from the unconscious impersonal world." (Tarnas 1991, p.352) But some firmly cloistered in their ivory towers of empirically based science are so detached from the real world they scarcely know who they are and either apportion life to a cause that cannot explain it or to no cause at all. These are they who are willing to deny much of reality to call their prejudiced soul their own.

As reason is so fundamental to ascertaining the truth about anything in which effects are commensurate with the effects produced, so we must follow where reason leads lest it become a case of the blind leading the blind in which both are destined to fall into the ditch a mindless obscurantism. And when reality goes beyond what we cannot explain we must have the humility to accept it as proceeding from someone much wiser than ourselves. Evolution could be likened to a factory in which different components are joined to other components in an order producing fashion to produce exceedingly complex and intelligently ordered things. But the evolutionary process operating so slowly over an exceedingly long period of time some people have lost the logical interconnectedness of all that is going on and never seem to think to trace the order producing genius of it all back to an intelligent and sufficient cause in which they would be confronted with the inescapably logic of a wise creator.

But rather those who claim that nothing produced the ordered complexity of all things haven't even the sense to be embarrassed and the best they can do is to attribute it to 'blind dumb luck'. We cannot go on in an infinite regress of reductio-ad-absurdum; we must find a place on which to build that which can bear the weight of all that needs to be explained. While another argues that many scientists: "fail to grasp the true nature of science and produce theories of science which have ontological implications of which they seem to be blissfully unaware."

Therefore, we as human beings can only find the true explanation of it all by facing up to evidence from within a unity of consciousness both existentially rich and rationally compelling that a wise creator was at work in the universe. So when God calls us to the bar of our own soul to listen to the evidence, but those who have convinced themselves that they have no soul are as a distinct disadvantage and have sold themselves short both in terms of instinct and intellect and find themselves worshipping at a man-made shrine of hedonism and materialism of one form or another. So evolution outside of an intelligent and sufficient cause is a theory in crisis because it hasn't the wherewithal to explain itself or sustain itself rationally, morally or spiritually in a world of causeless irrelevance so that those who adhere to this world view become just another materially object moving within a causeless vacuum of mindless irrelevance.

Chapter 9
The Confused Out-Working
of a Contradictory Paradigm

The human brain is made up of some 80 to 120 billion neurons which are something equivalent to all the trees in the 2,700 square miles of Amazon Rain Forest, while dendrites operating between those neurons are equivalent to the leaves on those trees. It is inconceivable how such a massively complex organ could be wired up appropriately to produce an intelligent functioning brain by means of blind randomness or by a process of luck operating within what was originally in a state of primordial disorder. When Stephen J Gould argues that science and religion represent non overlapping magisteria that cannot be reconciled, he seems to befailing to see the connection between an ordered world full of extremely complex living things and the need for a cause sufficient to explain the ordered and living sum of it all.

As Plato has said: "To discover *Kosmos* in the world is to reveal *Kosmos* in one's own soul. In the thought life of man, the world spirit revealed itself." (Tarnas 1991, p.47) But then, one has to be in tune to their own soul both rationally and ontologically to know what the world sprit by means of reason is trying to teach us. Richard Dawkins in his book *The Blind Watchmaker* states that: "The present lack of a definitely accepted account of the origin of life should certainly not be taken as a stumbling block for the whole Darwinian world view. " (Dawkins 1988, p.166) But why would Dawkins see the need to make such a statement if he really believes that evolution by natural selection can explain the existence of life on earth? When Dawkins asks to be allowed to introduce DNA to explain how evolution works we, of course, can grant it to him, but it's the origin of it which is the problem in a universe absent of intelligence. Moreover, another problem arises as to how an ordered compendium of inanimate matter in the form of a physical brain could explain the conscious reality of life which is different qualitative attributes of being different in nature and substance to all that we understand a physical brain to be? The combined sum of which represents a reality of God-like creativity.

If we have a car-producing factory we can explain the existence of motor cars, and if we have the life-producing factory of DNA and RNA we can explain intelligent life on earth. But we still have to explain the origin of DNA and working partner RNA that carries out the instructions contained within DNA to produce intelligent life on earth – biologically speaking at least. In this, we see that the blind watchmaker is not so blind after all and has at its disposal an order producing mechanism of vast life producing efficiency.

Dawkins admits that, "simple sieving on its own is not enough," and as we have seen introduces what he calls "cumulative selection" which he admits, "is quintessentially non-random." But if cumulative selection is quintessentially non-random then surely this means that it must be a process of intelligent ordering because that is precisely what non-random means. (Dawkins 1988, p.49) Dawkins in the last page of the same book declares: "And provided we postulate a sufficiently large series of sufficiently finely graded intermediates, we shall be able to derive anything from anything else … And also only if there are mechanisms for guiding each step in a particular direction, otherwise the sequence of steps will career off in an endless random walk." (Dawkins 1988, p.318)

But what exactly are 'finely graded intermediates', and 'mechanisms for guiding each step in a particular direction' away from an 'endless random walk' if it is not a process of intelligent design? It seems to be a rare kind of delusion when a person denies the very thing they are describing. The above description is a far cry from Dawkins' original definition of evolution which earlier in the same book he writes that evolution: "… has no purpose in mind. It has no mind and no mind's eye. It does not plan for the future. It has no vision, no foresight, no sight at all. If it can be said to play the role of watchmaker in nature, it is a blind watchmaker." (Dawkins 1988, p.5) At least here we here have a watchmaker of sorts which takes us beyond a world random producing chaos but one who is said to be blind.

But someone who is blind is still alive and isn't obviously brain-dead and has at his disposal all his or her mental faculties including reason, being, and in the case of the blind watchmaker a most ingeniously creative mind. And with the meticulous skill and precision with which he operates it is highly questionable that he is blind. So either the blind watchmaker has been miraculously healed of his blindness or was never really blind in the first place, and seems now to be operating with the order producing wisdom of a wise creator endowed with a whole series of "finely graded intermediates" and using "mechanisms to guide each step in a particular direction" to produce intelligent life on earth. It is little wonder that Dawkins in the same book ends up qualifying the term *blind* in at least 5 different ways until the Blind Watchmaker appears to be not blind at all and Paley's God of intelligent design would seem to be back in business. (Dawkins 1986, p.312) So Dawkins is all the time qualifying the blind Watchmaker out of existence and slipping mechanisms of intelligent ordering in by the back door in the guise of other names in a frantic attempt to avoid make evolution work without giving the game away.

In the same book, Dawkins is forced to concede that: "There are many respects in which evolution is 'not random'." (Dawkins 1986, P.306) In fact, Dawkins has declared that: "Natural selection is about as non-random a force as you can imagine." Dawkins makes this crystal clear when he writes: "This belief that Darwinian evolution is random is not merely false. It is the exact opposite of the truth. Chance is a minor ingredient in the Darwinian recipe, but the most important ingredient is cumulative selection which is quintessentially non-random." (Dawkins 1988, p.49)

But if the coming into existence of life on earth is quintessentially non-random this of logical necessity means that it must be a process of intelligent ordering of the most ingenious and sophisticated kind. While his theory of cumulative selection represents many different processes all feeding into the evolutionary grid specifically set up to bring into existence intelligent life on earth, what is the origin of this multi-dimensional operation of vast order producing of profundity. These represent a highly sophisticated and coordinated process of intelligent design which Dawkins goes on to deny. But with all the necessary means and mechanisms strategically in place and operating toward the specific purpose of producing intelligent life on earth we have a process of the most ingenious order producing and life-defining kind imaginable. So evolution is nothing like the working of a blind watchmaker blundering aimlessly about within primordial chaos.

As we have seen, Dawkins argues that evolution is a process of steps so exceedingly small when you add them up are so causally inconsequential they don't represent a process of intelligently ordering at all. However, this convoluted way of thinking shows signs of intellectual blindness, because it is perfectly obvious that these order producing steps that produce extremely complex and intelligently ordered living things never get so small and causally insignificant that they do not add up to be a process of intelligent ordering with each part playing its own part to produce intelligent life on earth. So what kind of philosophical schizophrenia does this represent, it seems on the one hand that the blind watchmaker hasn't the faintest idea what he is doing and on the other hand is operating to a process of exquisite design with all the necessary means in place to produce intelligent life on earth.

As we have seen, Dawkins accepts that: "we can accept a little bit of luck, but not too much." (Dawkins 1988, p.139) But it seems that here we have a world crammed full of luck piled upon luck producing intelligent life on earth so that we end up with process of base superstition operating outside the parameters of rational thinking. But to avoid the cause and effect logic of rational thinking Dawkins must live within what is a monumental contradiction in terms overlaid with fine sounding words that when carefully examined don't logically stack up. So we need to ask as to the origin of that dimension which is other than luck which Dawkins admits we need to bring into existence intelligent life on earth?

In the final analysis, Dawkins unabashedly declares that natural selection is about as non-random a force as you can imagine and admits that to think that a haemoglobin cell could come into existence by sheer luck 'is unthinkable.' (Dawkins 1988, p.44) Bill Bryson writes: "The simple amoeba is just one cell big and without any ambitions to exist needs 400 million bits of genetic information in its DNA – enough, as Carl Sagan notes, to fill 80 books of 500 pages each." (Bryson 2003, p.166) But the problem of arranging that amount of genetic information into the right formation to produce a living cell is not seriously considered or reckoned up so that the origin of such causes are dumped into the nothing box to mean nothing of any order producing significance. But this is quite ridiculous and utterly deceitful because the possibility of such a vast amount of genetic letters, 400 million of them, falling into place by luck to produce a simple amoeba cell it is utterly and completely impossible.

Dawkins goes on to work out how long it might take to produce a simple phrase made up of a mere twenty eight characters to produce. The phrase he chooses, though it could be any phrase, is taken from Shakespeare is: 'Methinks it is like a weasel.' The odds of it falling into place by chance Dawkins works out to be 1 in 10,000 million, million, million, million million. "To put it mildly" adds Dawkins – "the phrase we seek would take a long time coming, to say nothing of the complete works of Shakespeare." The chances, Dawkins adds, to produce this simple phrase by chance with the odds just described above he estimates would take about a million, million, million, million, million years to produce which is more than a million, million, million times longer than the universe has so far existed, and this to produce a simple four-word phrase. When there are estimated to be some forth to fifty trillion cells in the human body each one made up of millions of parts so that the odds run into infinity beyond the capacity of the human mind to conceive – so that we are well and truly in God territory.

But to help solve the problem Dawkins brings his trusty computer into play and sets it up to find the target phrase by informing it of the phrase it needs to find, so all it has to do is run through the English alphabet unit it comes to the appropriate letter which only takes a few seconds and then it goes on to the next letter until it gets to the end of the simple target phrase. But this is not a process of luck at all because the computer knows the phrase it needs to find and quickly running through the alphabet letter by letter can quickly finds the phrase it is set up to find.

So if luck has anything to do with evolution it is that we are lucky that we have an intelligent and sufficient cause in the form of a wise creator who knows how to bring into existence intelligent life on earth and sets the whole earth up with the necessary means and mechanisms by which to do so. After all, how lucky could a process of blind randomness get when it comes to producing intelligent life on earth, even to produce the simplest living things out of primordial chaos in the light of the odds as those described above by Dawkins himself?

But for Dawkins this non-random process as he describes it, has nothing whatsoever to do with a process of intelligent design, and if you don't find this as bewildering as it is illogical then you haven't really grasped what Dawkins is really saying. Dawkins writes in his book *The Selfish Gene*: "… a man consists of over a thousand million, million, million, million, atoms. To try to make a man, you would have to work your biological cocktail-shaker for a period so long that the entire age of the universe would seem like an eye-blink, and even then you would not succeed." (Dawkins 1976, p.14)

Dawkins also argues that: "It follows that design comes late in the universe, after a period of Darwinian evolution." But design does not come late in the

183

universe because intelligent design is, and must be, built into the very nature of the universe or intelligently ordered living things of exquisite design and of vast complexity would never have come into existence at all. But Dawkins goes on to insist that: "Design cannot precede evolution and therefore cannot underlie evolution." (Cited in Brockman 2005, p.9) This means that Dawkins believes that evolution can produce intelligent life on earth outside a process of intelligent design which contradicts what he says when he argues that evolution by natural selection is about as non-random a force as you can imagine and openly affirms that to think a haemoglobin cell could come into existence by sheer luck "is unthinkable." So it seems that Dawkins is somewhat confused about his own theory of evolution. What Dawkins is desperately trying to do is avoid the idea of intelligent design but then introduces mechanisms that reek of intelligent design. In this, we can see what an intellectually 'fulfilled atheist' looks like as many evolutionists like to think of themselves. To put it in metaphorical terms, the problem for evolutionists like Dawkins is to explain how Jacobs got figs into Jacobs fig rolls before Jacobs existed.

Dawkins goes on to describe the odds of a simple haemoglobin molecule coming into existence by chance, which is an exceedingly small part of the human body, at 1 with 190 noughts after it. "The amount of luck that would be required for this order producing feat is unthinkable" concludes Dawkins. (Dawkins 1988, p.44) Dawkins argues that: "The belief that Darwinian evolution is random is not merely false it is the exact opposite of the truth. Chance is but a minor ingredient in the Darwinian recipe, but the most important part is: 'cumulative selection' which is 'quintessentially *non-random*'." (Dawkins 1988, p.47) But by what means has Richard Dawkins Blind Watchmaker been so wondrously healed of his blindness and has become such a clear-sighted watchmaker with 20/20 vision and a mind so creatively ingenious so as to inculcate into his cosmic watch so stupendously complex means so excellent as to bring into existence intelligent life on earth? But alas, these means he refers to as *cumulative selection* are never really explained in any intelligently constituted sense in which the mechanisms become as impossible to explain as that which he is trying to explain without them. Dawkins desperately trying explain these means without giving the game away writes:

Cumulative selection is the key to all our modern explanations of life. It strings a series of acceptably lucky events together in a non-random sequence so that, in the end of the sequence, the finished product carries the illusion of being very lucky indeed, far too improbable to have come about by chance alone.[Dawkins 1988, p.139–140]

In other words, we have a veritable multitude lucky order producing events which are then arranged in a non-random (order producing) fashion to produce the ordered complexity of life on earth. But how could an endless stream of luck operating to nothing but blind chance within a scene of primordial disorder get so lucky to produce the massive complexity of life on earth even in its most simple form? In other words, how could a process of luck arrange things in a non-random (order producing) fashion to produce the vast complexity of intelligent life on earth? In other words, nothing is explained in any intelligently constituted sense.

We have seen even with Dawkins own calculations the chance of a very short phrase with 28 letters coming into existence to be so astronomically vast, what are the chances of getting 3.2 billion letters of order producing information in DNA to produce a human being falling into existence by chance, and then RNA that knows how to interpret that information and operate to execute those instructions turn the raw chemicals of the earth into the biological complexity of a human being? And even with this we haven't explained how the vast complexity of a biological body was endued with conscious life operating to many different attributes of being. And we need to include in this explanation all manner of living things that fill the whole earth with a rich variety of living things. Even all vegetation owes its existence to other kinds of ingenious order producing gene machines.

Another way Dawkins tries to explain cumulative selection is: "The essential difference between single step selection and cumulative selection is this. In single step selection, the entities selected or sorted, pebbles or whatever they are, are sorted once and for all. In cumulative selection, on the other hand they 'reproduce': or in some other way the results of one sieving process are fed into a subsequent sieving (processes), which is fed into and so on. The entities are subjected to selection of sorting over many 'generations' in succession. The end product of one generation of selection is the starting point for the next generation of selection, and so on for many generations. Each generation would need to have a ready supply of components and materials and to continue from where the previous generation ended and the ability to take over from where the previous generating process left of which represents a seamless order producing precision of the most sophisticated kind."

Moreover, a sifting process cannot sift into existence intelligently ordered things if the means are not within the sifting process to explain each stage of order producing development, let alone explain all these stages of order producing development that join seamlessly together so expeditiously to produce the vast complexity of intelligent life on earth, and that in ever increasing degrees of the ordered sophistication. Therefore Dawkins concludes that: "This belief that Darwinian evolution is 'random' is not merely false, it is the very opposite to the truth." (Dawkins 1988, p.49) So even Dawkins seems confused about his own theory of evolution, and if you think that Dawkins has explained evolution outside of an intelligent and sufficient cause of any kind, you don't really understand what Dawkins is saying and mistaking a plethora of fine sounding words and highflying ides that ultimately lead nowhere.

Dawkins knows that he has boxed himself into a corner and ends up arguing that: "that discriminating minds see this as the fundamental flaw in the theory of Darwinian evolution. They see it as the ultimate proof that there originally must have been a far-sighted watchmaker that requires, not a blind watchmaker, but a far-sighted supernatural watchmaker." Having nowhere else to turn Dawkins then argues that the design argument leads nowhere, because we then need to explain the origin of the supernatural designer. But the living things like ourselves ordered into existence as living self-conscious beings endowed themselves with intelligence do not need to explain their creator but can clearly discern as rational beings that the ordered complexity of all things goes beyond their capacity to understand or explain points convincingly to a wise creator infinitely wiser than themselves.

Moreover, why should that which is so obviously created by means so ingeniously complex have to explain their creator when the all the evidence is there within the ordered and living complexity of themselves that such a creator exists? We must trace the existence of all things back to a first and sufficient cause that is able to explain the ordered and living sum of all things and we are not that cause, and a blind and brain-dead watchmaker cannot conceivably be that cause. That order producing excellence of that cause goes beyond what our own intelligent but finite minds can fully comprehend and into an infinity of order producing wisdom that can only be defined as the one theists call God.

As we have noted, Dawkins himself has argued that to produce something like a single haemoglobin cell the odds are exceedingly massive as to be altogether impossible. And to arrange 28 letters together to produce a coherent sentence the odds are as Dawkins himself explains are about 1 in 10,000 million. Million, million, million, million, and we know that the human genome has some 3.2 billion letters of life producing information. Dawkins acknowledges that discriminating minds see this as the fundamental flaw in the theory of Darwinian evolution. They see it as the ultimate proof that there originally must have been a far-sighted watchmaker that requires, not a blind watchmaker, but a far-sighted supernatural watchmaker.

But Dawkins totally rejects the very idea and goes back to his self-defeating circular argument declaring that: "Once we are allowed simply to postulate organised complexity, if only the organised complexity of DNA protein replicating engine, it is relatively easy to invoke it as a generator of yet more organised complexity." (Dawkins 1988, p.141) But these are the very mechanisms that need to be explained and when their order producing significance is seen for what they really are they represent a process of the most exquisite design.

Eventually Dawkins is forced to go back to the old worn out argument, namely that we then need to explain the origin of the supernatural designer. But that which has been ordered into existence don't have to explain what, or who, ordered them into existence to be what they were ordered to be, but as conscious beings endowed with the attribute of intelligence we can clearly deduce that we owe our existence to a living life producing cause capable of creating all that we are and ordered to be and whose existence goes beyond our own finite understanding to fully comprehend – and that is why we call that cause God.

Dawkins affirms that: "… a miraculous theory is exactly the kind of theory we should be looking for in this particular matter of the origin of life." (Dawkins 1988, p.159) However, the ideas of the 'miraculous' takes us into God territory beyond human comprehension, and this being theists call God which Dawkins cannot in all good conscience rule out seeing that he also is looking for a miraculous explanation. But when the idea of God arises we find that Dawkins miraculous theory reverts back to blind and brain dead watchmaker without sight or foresight plan or purpose and devoid of the wherewithal to explain the ordered complexity of anything. This is all the more bewildering when Dawkins affirms that to the hold to a theory of blind chance: "Far from holding this belief, I don't see how you would begin to set about making such a belief even meaningful." (Dawkins 1988, p.307)

Another variant of Dawkins evolutionary critique is that he argues that: "the great majority of mutations do make things worse. It is true that a small minority of mutations may make things better and this is ultimately why evolution by natural selection is possible at all." (Dawkins 1988, p.305) But if the majority of changes make things worse and only a few makes things better how are we ever going to get anything of any ordered significance? In a factory we know that only one mistake or malfunction in the order producing process can bring the whole process to a grinding halt – a spanner in the works as the saying goes. But can we imagine that if the vast number of changes in factory made things worse and only a few made things better how we would ever get the ordered complexity of anything? Thomas Heinze in his book *Creation Vs Evolution* writes: "Actually a living being is such a delicately balanced instrument, with everything having to function almost perfectly for it to remain alive, that the possibility of a really accidental change making it better is much less than the possibility of dropping your watch on concrete will make it run better." (Heinze 1973, p.70)

This is how Dawkins explains how the mechanism by which evolution operates: "Every living cell, even a single bacteria cell, can be thought of as a gigantic chemical factory...The word gigantic may seem surprising for a cell, especially when you remember that 10 million bacterial cells could sit on the surface of a pin's head. But you will also remember that each of these cells is capable of holding the whole text of the New Testament and moreover, it is gigantic when measured by the number of sophisticated machines that it contains ... Each kind of protein machine churns out its own peculiar chemical product." (Dawkins the Blind Watchmaker.) He adds: "To get an idea of the size of these protein machines, each one is made of 6,000 atoms, which is very large by molecular standards. There are about a million of these large pieces of apparatus in a cell, and there are more than 2,000 different kinds of them, each kind specialised to do a particular operation in the chemical factory the cell." (Dawkins 1998, p.121)

It is little wonder that Arthur Koestler refers to evolution outside of an intelligent and sufficient cause: "as a labyrinth of tautologies." (Koestler 1978, p.171) And again he writes: "But holism never got a grip on academic science." (Koestler 1979, p.26) While as we have seen how Daniel Dennett argues that Darwin tried to show us that life on earth does not need a mind first explanation because natural selection can do the job without such a mind. But Darwin did no such thing and as we have seen his confusion was based on the fact that he was totally unaware of the life producing genius of the genome which was operating effectively to produce intelligent life on earth and which is a mechanism of exquisite design the origin of which has yet to be explained.

To try and get round this problem Dennett argues that if we need a mind first explanation to explain intelligently ordered things robots that do not such mind could not act intelligently or operate creatively as we know they do. (Dennett 1995, p.27) But this is somewhat pitiful because while robots and computers may not have conscious minds as we human beings do, the person or persons who ordered them intelligently into existence most certainly had? Robots did not come into existence by means of blind randomness but by the intelligent minds of human beings who produced the necessary electronic parts, ordered them intelligently together, wired them up and programmed them to operate as they were ordered and programmed to do.

This means that they have a mechanical kind of mind in the form of artificial intelligence that was ordered into existence by means of human intelligence so that we have a mind first means of ordering – thus if we have no intelligent human mind, we would have no artificial intelligence. Robots are, therefore, a reflection of human intelligence just as we are a reflection of that life producing intelligence that ordered us into existence. Things produced by robots or computers have their origin into the intelligent minds of human beings who ordered them into existence to simulate human intelligence so ultimately things made by computers have their origin in a mind first way of thinking, so no intelligent human mind – no intelligent functioning computers.

Of course artificial intelligence has no conscious thoughts, free will, feelings, hopes and aspirations in the same way as we humans have. They operate intelligently in an electronic and mechanical fashion because they were programmed to do so. Thus, a robot may indeed be programmed to say 'I love you', but as a piece of electronic circuitry wired up to respond in an electronic way to different external stimuli, but it is not conscious of feeling anything and such words are programmed responses with no independent will or mind induced emotions. Moreover, if a robot was ordered and equipped to hold a gun and shoot someone it would not be bothered with a guilty conscience or arrested and put on trial for murder, but one who programmed it to so would undoubtedly would and if found guilty duly punished. Moreover, if a robot had genuine thoughts and feelings, hopes and aspirations as we human beings do, to pull the plug and throw it on the scrapheap when it became old and outdated should be regarded as a crime punishable by law because this would be tantamount to murder.

Therefore, it is perfectly obvious that Dennett's argument doesn't prove his point, and in fact militates against it. So we are back to the mind first argument of Locke and that by the circuitous route for the benefit of slow learners. As Bill Bryson in his book *A History of Almost Everything* gives us some indication of the magnitude of that which needs to be explained to produce a simple yeast cell which is nothing compared to the much greater size of a human cell of which there are many trillions in the human body. To build the most basic yeast cell, for example, you would have to miniaturise about the same number of components as are found in a Boeing 777 jetliner and fit them into a sphere 5 microns across; then somehow you would have to persuade that sphere to reproduce.(Bryson 2003, p.451) And even then you would have to explain the ordered complexity of a human being was not only ordered intelligently to think intelligently, but operating to many different categories of understanding, and endowed with feelings of many different kinds that take us beyond the world of physics to explain.

Sir Fred Hoyle, a highly acclaimed astrophysicist, when considering the incredible odds of producing a single protein (a very small part of a living cell) by chance, concluded that it was utterly impossible – "like a whirlwind spinning through a junkyard and leaving behind a fully assembled jumbo jet." (Bryson 2003, p.352) Bryson also reminds us that there are some 3.2 billion letters of genetic code in the human genome and these: "provide $10,^{1,920,000.000}$ possible combinations which is one followed by more than three billion zeroes after it which would take 5000 average sized books just to print that massive figure." (Bryson 2004, p.482)

It is little wonder then as that Professor Brian Silver puts it: It stretches even the credulity of a materialistic biogenesis fanatic to believe that proteins (the stuff of life) and nucleotides DNA or RNA could emerge simultaneously within the primordial soup. (Parentheses mine). (Silver 1998, p.347) And this only explains the biological complexity of a biological body which cannot of itself explain the experiential reality of a living self-conscious mind. This puts into clearer perspective the possibility of life appearing on other planets by means of blind randomness that those who talk so glibly about finding life on other planets would do well to remember. The odds set out above only represent what is needed to produce a physical body, not that which can infuse inanimate master with conscious life. "And God made man of the dust (chemicals, of the earth, and breathed into his nostrils the breath of life, and man became a living soul." These the most profound words ever spoken fully combatable with the evidence of science, so that life is a two part harmony one of ordered complexity and the order of life generating efficiency all of which add up to working of a wise creator.

Again as Bill Bryson admits, that how living things came to be so well ordered: "is one of biology's great unanswered questions." In his book *A History of Almost Everything*, he writes with regard to the coming into existence of a single protein which is but a very small part of a living cell: "... the chances of spontaneous self-assembly are, frankly nil. It just isn't going to happen." (Bryson 2004, p.351) As we have already noted, the mathematics simply cannot be made to work such is the vast and unimaginable odds involved, and even with this we still need to explain why anything exists, and how a universe came into existence and just happened to be so well endowed with all that was necessary to bring into existence a life permitting universe which is commonly referred to as the "anthropic principle."

So it seems that we are really getting nowhere with respect to explaining intelligent life on earth, with Richard Gregory a thorough going evolutionist admitting that: "The question of 'success', and 'progress' and 'fittest' biologically and socially, has never been satisfactorily answered. As a result there is an essential circularity in Darwin's Theory of Evolution." (Gregory 1993, p.172) Such circularity means that Darwinians are really getting nowhere because they are postulating incredibly ingenious mechanism of order producing efficiency which are as difficult to explain as life on earth is to explain without them. While Roger Penrose, an evolutionist and much-respected scientist, writes: "To my way of thinking ... Things at least seem to organise themselves better than they ought to, just on the basis of blind chance evolution and natural selection." (Penrose 1989, p.416)

Penrose still wrestling with the problem believes that: "... a final theory could only be a scheme of a very different nature from our present theory. There seems to be something about the way the laws of physics work that allows the laws of natural selection to be a much more effective process than it would be with just arbitrary laws." (Cited in Dennett 1995, p.447) And when we add to this the problem of how inanimate matter is turned into a living self-conscious mind of ordered profundity the problem just gets worse in which nothing is ultimately explained.

All these ingenious order producing laws add up to an elaborate process of intelligent design of vast cosmic proportions. But what many evolutionists do is to keep adding to the different order producing means and mechanisms that produce intelligent life on earth without putting all these means and mechanisms together and reckoning up the order producing sum of them to see the massively ingenious order producing process evolution really is. So what evolutionists have done is to establish that, to some degree at least, life on earth evolved, but the nature of this evolving and what it means in terms of an ingenious process of life producing efficiency has never been honestly addressed let alone explained. So the means go on and on without considering that: "The basic problem facing anyone who is looking for the origin of life is to account for the formation of a complex, *very highly organised, self-sustaining and self-replicating system* out of a mixture of chemicals that, certainly in the early days of the soup displayed none of these characteristics." (Silver 1998, p.350)

Henri Bergson philosopher and writer believes that a process of random selection is inadequate to explain what occurs within evolution and that there seems to be some sort of persistent drive towards greater individuality and at the same time complexity and this he referred to as *elan vital,* which is usually translated "life force." (Cited in Magee 2001, p.214) Bergson believed that this life force was moving towards some future potentiality even though he never declared what this might be. Arthur Koestler believing that: "It seems possible that confronted with these problems, biology is reduced to helplessness and must hand over to metaphysics." (Koestler 1978, p.273)

Koestler goes on to argue that the neo-Darwinian theory which holds that evolution is the outcome of nothing but chance retained by natural selection is: "a doctrine recently exposed to growing criticism which nevertheless is still taught as gospel truth." Koestler goes on to say that evolution in its classical form is seriously flawed and: "This lethal flaw was recognised by leading evolutionists, (Mayr, Simpson, Waddington, Haldane etc.) several decades ago, it was and is, as I said an open secret. However, since no satisfactory alternative was in sight, the crumbling edifice had to be defended." (Koestler 1978, p.170)

This would appear to indicate that there were some within the evolutionary fraternity who knew, or who at least suspected, that there was a serious problem of credibility with the standard theory of evolution operating to chance mutations and natural selection but failed to openly admit it. Rather, they continued to exude an air of confidence in a theory that was built on very shaky foundations indeed and what, in fact, were no rational foundations at all. While the idea of a wise creator was anathema and unworthy of even being considered by those whose explanation was totally inconsistent with the cause and effect of rational thinking, while the spiritual and qualitative implications of conscious life represented a reality not even worth considering.

The philosopher Arthur Schopenhauer, who was no theist, could see the ridiculous nature of the standard evolutionary theory and argued that to believe that matter in the form of chemical forces could of themselves bring about living organisms: "is not merely mistaken but, as already remarked, stupid." (Cited in Silver 1998, p.239) Even Nietzsche who wouldn't have passed over an opportunity to belittle the idea of God admitted that: "The influence of the environment is nonsensically overrated in Darwin ... the essential factor in the process of life is precisely the tremendous inner power to shape and create new forms which merely uses and exploits the environment." (Cited in Silver 1998, p.277) While Geach rightly argues: "... the elaborate and ostensible teleological mechanism of this reproduction logically cannot be explained as a product of evolution by natural selection from among chance variations, for unless the mechanism is presupposed there cannot be any evolution." (Geach 1973, p.330)

Anthony Kenny argues in his book: *Philosophy in The Modern World,* argues that evolution does not disprove the existence of God. And going on he points out that theists believe that: "... the ultimate explanation of such adaptations must be found in intelligence." *(*Kenny 2007, p.301) But for some everything just came together like magic out of nowhere, or by some ascribed to the magnificent order producing powers of nature to which no order producing significance is ultimately attached. Just call it nature and mark it inconsequential and the idea of intelligent design will go away and be overwritten with fine sounding words and an endless stream of meaningless tautologies. Or just call it science and evolution will be so cosmologically blessed it can explain the coming into existence of incredibly complex living things by means that are the very antithesis of the ordered sum of their existence. Meanwhile, the more ingenious mechanisms of biogenesis evolutionists introduce to explain how evolution works the more they dig themselves into the logic of intelligent design but their prejudices won't allow them to admit it.

Bertrand Russell might well argue that: "Whatever knowledge is attainable, must be attained by scientific methods, and what science cannot discover, mankind cannot know." If Russell means empirically based science he is completely wrong because the inquisitiveness of mind that impel scientists to do science and the intelligence by which they need to carry it out cannot be established in empirically based scientific terms. But when we include consciousness and all that this implies by way of qualitative attributes of being of which intelligence is an integral part the picture changes in which we come face to face with the evidence of a wise creator waiting for a suitable and reasonable response from us: but some of these creatures become gods onto themselves and regard themselves as wiser than their creator who ordered them into existence in the first place. But this is surely a very dangerous game for finite minds to play and there is danger and death in that decision. As a wise prophet once said: "If the light that is in you be darkness how great is that darkness."

When we leave the existential reality of being out of the equation of life we find ourselves in the darkness of a reductionist delusion where the verities of life and the rich diversity of the human experience is buried beneath a world of mundane materialism and causeless irrelevance. This ongoing saga of heterogeneous bewilderment is further revealed by Gareth Southwell an otherwise competent and insightful scientist tries to explain how that: "... while blind evolution has no intended outcome or purpose the process is not pure chance." But if evolution is not a process of pure chance surely that would make it a process of intelligent ordering by design that is anything but blind operating to a well thought-out plan and purpose which is clearly revealed in all that it has so skilfully and wondrously created by way of an ordered cosmos and intelligent life on earth. (Southwell 2013, p.70)

It seems that some want to have it both ways, which in the end results in confusion and a complete contradiction in terms, which is rather sad when scientists do such an effective and thoroughgoing job of revealing the myriad of ingenious means to which evolution operates to bring into existence intelligent life on the earth, and then fail to draw the right conclusions about the significance of it all in terms of sufficient cause and go on to attribute it all to nothing of any real order-producing significance even to nothing at all. They praise the wonderful means by which all things were ordered into existence and the best they can come up with to explain it all is by arguing that while evolution on the one hand has no "intended outcome or purpose" but it is not a process of "pure chance." But when something that produces a world of exceedingly complex living things by means other than pure chance this must of logical necessity by a process of intelligent ordering the purpose of which is seen in that which it has so wondrously produced.

This is like arguing that while a factory that makes motor cars is not operating to a process of blind chance, but the whole operation has no intended outcome or process or purpose. And why would anyone argue like this? Why to obtain a free lunch in the form of a motor car without having to pay the price for it and arguing that while it is not the result of a pure chance it has nothing to do with an intelligent manufacturer who expects to be paid for it and who will take you to court if you dare to steal or copy his ingeniously patented designs. The heart of man wants to be answerable to no one, but as moral beings it didn't work with Adam, and it will not work with us there was a price to pay, and all too soon man was in conflict with his fellowman one killing the other out of envy and jealousy as each tried to outdo the other in a sense of supercilious superiority.

Now we face a total catastrophe in global warming, it might not be out of place to seek the face or our creator for courage and wisdom to take the necessary steps to face up to this cosmic challenge not just out of bare necessity and self-interest, but out of lover for Him our creator who ordered it into existence in the first pace and instructed man to lock after and care for his creation, and also out of love for our neighbour especially in third world countries who are going to suffer in ways unimaginably if global warming is not reversed. Not to mention how it will touch us all if we are not willing to make the necessary sacrifices to avert this looming disaster.

In this the rich have a huge part to play in this so rather than amassing wealth they must learn to share it before it is taken from them in a world of conflagration that will over-run them and show no mercy as they take it from them as life becomes ungovernable as the disparity between rich and poor increases. While some companies have made more billions than their most optimistic projections anticipated, and the government is afraid to take a percentage of it in case they take a huff and refuse to reinvest while those on the bottom rung of the ladder are on the breadline. Yes we need investors that make profits, but they need to learn to share it as well as reinvesting it or allowing it in accumulate in the bank before it's taken from them and it will be taken from them if and when this looming Global Crises comes within a conflagration that will make life ungovernable.

People will not see their children starve or themselves dispossessed of the essentials of life while some live in luxury, have a house worth millions and some with two, and also with a holiday home in some exotic place and also a yacht worth millions and even some with two. The writer when shopping buys some items to put in the charity bank for those who are poor and in financial difficulties. No I don't have to do and could make excuses why not to do it, and while some might abuse it some in genuine need will benefit from it. Nurses working to save the lives of others who have scarcely enough to live and feed their children is not a just and fair society. The rich need to find a way to reinvest some of their wealth back into society before the conflagration comes and it is taken from them, a halfway house between Capitalism and Communism at least in the short to medium term.

But will we have the heart and will to make the necessary sacrifices and adjustments to avoid the serious and menacing challenges of this present age remains to be seen. But whatever happens we need to work together at all levels of society before panic sets in and everyone operates to the survival of the fittest mentality as opposed to operating for good of all at every level of society. Everyone must play their part in which sacrifices will have to be made and will increasingly have to be made but have we the moral courage and conviction to make them before it is too late.

Chapter 10
Demystifying Evolution

Matt Ridley argues that: "The genome is an information processing computer that extracts useful information from the world by natural selection and embodies that information in its designs." (Ridley 1999, p.220) However, who set up this information-processing computer up to extract useful information from the environment and embody it into its ingenious designs? Moreover, we have been informed time and time again by many evolutionary theorists that evolution was not trying to do anything and was operating to no strategic plan or meaningful purpose whatsoever. But now it seems we have a most ingenious gene machine operating purposefully on the earth to bring all the necessary means together to produce intelligent life on earth and that in ever-increasing degrees of ordered sophistication.

Nick Lane suggests that: "It has only become starkly apparent in the last few years and only to those who follow evolutionary biology, that there is a deep and disturbing discontinuity at the very heart of biology…" There is nothing in the soup that can drive the formation of the dissipative structures that we call cells, nothing to make these cells grow and divide, and come alive, all in the absence of enzymes that channel and drive metabolism. (Lane 2015, p.21 and 95) In other words, something is missing and it is not just the power to drive and empower the process, it's the lack of a plan of any king.

One evolutionist argues that natural selection in and of itself operating outside the order producing genius of DNA/RNA is not in any sense a creative process. But this means that evolution operating to the ingenious biological factory of DNA/RNA is needed to turn evolution into a process of the most incredibly ingenious order producing dexterity and we need a separate gene factory for all the different species we find on the earth. But while these gene factories and wondrously and variously described the origin of these gene factories is never explained.

In her book entitled *The Canon*, Natalie Angier while trying to bridge this gap between cause and effect writes: "As biologists like to point out, evolution is a tinkerer, an ad-hocker, and a jury-rigger." (Angier 2007, p.173) But what in precise terms and plain speaking is a jury-rigger within the context of evolution? Is it that there is something within evolution that is somehow rigging the jury of natural selection so that it can produce intelligent life on earth?

And what is an ad-hocker? Isn't this something that comes into play for a special case or who makes it up as they go along as necessity requires and ability allows to achieve a particular purpose? Something set up for a special purpose or as a special case within an overall scheme of things. But evolution we are informed has no mind and no intelligence to operate in an order producing fashion as a jury rigger or as an ad-hocker so as to channel evolution into ordered states of vast and varied complexity. An ad-hoc committee might be set up to arrange for the provision of a wheelchair ramp in a public building when the law in the middle of the building process called for such a provision. But neither the building that is being erected nor the wheel chair ramp that is a necessary adaptation to the original plans is operating to a process of blind randomness. Both have to operate intelligently and in conjunction with each other to accomplish such an ordered and integrated adaptation.

And who is doing all this tinkering we might ask? What kind of order producing tinkering could this be that is playing about with evolution to produce intelligent life on earth? This is obviously an order producing tinkering because tinkering with chaos by means of blind randomness is never going to produce anything of any ordered significance should we tinker thus for all eternity. All these are just made-up ideas subtly contrived to get an explanation between nothing and intelligent design to explain intelligent life on earth and it simply doesn't work. What we need is an order producing process of uncompromising creativity to produce the vast complexity of intelligent life on earth.

Carl Popper an eminent scientific theorist reminds us that scientific theories must be logically self-consistent and points out that if scientists do not know how to invalidate a theory then they do not know how to validate it. (Witham 2002. p.34) However, in general terms the existence and working of any phenomenon must be validated in terms of rational thinking in which the proposed cause must be able to explain the ordered sum of the effects produced. While rational cause and effect thinking is the only thing that stands between us and abounding ignorance, obscurantism and even a creeping causal insanity.

Theists believe that it is very dangerous to go against the rule of rational thinking and hold to the old adage *Ex nihilo nihil fit* = from nothing, nothing comes. The fact is that there is no evidence we can present to those who have effectively closed their minds to the causal logic of rational thinking that will convince them that exquisitely ordered things owe their existence to a process of intelligent ordering operating to the principle of intelligent design behind which there is a most intelligent and creative mind operating to a realisable purpose. So like monkeys up the banana tree they know nothing and suspect nothing with regard to the principle of sufficient cause or recognise that we need a process of intelligent ordering to produce intelligently ordered things the most complex of which is intelligent life on earth.

While Stephen Pinker believes that we cannot learn evolution until we unlearn our intuitive engineering way of thinking which attributes design to the intentions of a designer. (Pinker 2002, p.223) This is just another way of saying that we should abandon the normal course of rational thinking when it comes to evolution because evolution as he understands it can produce extremely complex living things without a process of intelligent design or the need for an intelligent designer. Well praise the good Lord and past the biscuits because that would be some neat trick, not merely beyond all human comprehension but and contrary to the whole course rational thinking. But God would not do this to confuse us, but created intelligent life on earth in a way we could understand it by joining effects to causes so that we can trace the ultimate cause back to the order producing to cause in the form of a wise creator. But according to Pinker we must throw the logic of rational thinking into the dustbin of useless ideas in order to understand evolution taking us up queer St. to an ideological dead end. But, of course, we can believe anything when we abandon the cause and effect logic of rational thinking.

While Daniel Dennett believes something the same, arguing that if we suspend our faculty of rational thinking when it comes to evolution we can avoid attributing the existence of intelligent life on earth to an intelligent and sufficient cause. But of course, there is no better way of becoming a fool than by abandoning our capacity to think intelligently and reason causally. And as we have seen how he argues that with evolution we can abandon the whole idea of sufficient cause and look for things of all: "sorts of excellence, worth and purpose that can emerge, bubbling up out of mindless, purposeless forces." Again he argues: "Let me start with regularity – the mere purposeless, mindless, pointless regularity of physics – and I will show you a process that eventually will yield products that exhibit not just regularity but purposive design." (Dennett 1995, p. 65–66) But Dennett doesn't show us how, or what he means by saying give me order and I will give you design, when if the order he is talking about can go on to produce intelligently designed living things it must have the power within it by which to do so making it a process of intelligent design.

But if evolution has nothing to do with rational thinking in which we need to explain intelligently ordered effects in terms of intelligent and sufficient causes, why then do scientists go looking for such causes if such causes don't exist? If this is the case what scientists should really be doing is forever throwing dice with the disordered chemicals of the earth and seeing how long it takes them to get as much as a single living cell. The truth is that God is the elephant in the room that everyone is trying to avoid so that such theorists dance around the topic of intelligent design like cats on a hot tin roof fearing like hell to avoid the idea of an intelligent and sufficient cause in the form of a wise creator. Therefore, Philip Johnson points out: "As long as Darwinists control the definition of key terms their system is unbeatable regardless of evidence." (Cited in Colson 1999, p.81) This is why we must force evolutionists out into the open to explain in clear intelligently constituted terms how evolution operates to bring into being intelligent life on earth without presupposing the means in some convoluted semantics that presuppose the very means that still need to be explained.

Scientists who believe that nothing of any order producing significance produced the ordered sum of everything don't need evidence because there can be no evidence for that which nothing created. For Aristotle, intellectual pursuits were described as: "the moments of happiness that the activity of the mind brings to those who dedicate their lives to intellectual pursuits (such as the wise person or the philosopher) to the blessedness that accompanies a god's activity of contemplation. This kind of life surpasses all others in every respect because it nurtures the more divine element in humanity." (Cited in Ferris The Pimlico History of Philosophy 1998, p.65, p.65)

The fact is, with intellectual pursuits we are on God territory because we could not investigate anything intelligently, or reason intelligently about anything if it was not intelligently ordered in the first place. And our subjective world of being gives us an insight into the nature and purpose of our existence and the kind of order producing Being our creator is. So this is why theists regard the standard theory of evolution as not merely philosophically naïve but simply bad science. Nick Lane enumerates some of the complexities with evolution even in its early stages of development, some of which we enumerate below.

* Bluntly put, we do not know why life is the way it is.
* There is a black hole at the heart of our biology.
* The biggest questions in biology are yet to be solved.
* Speaking of detailed mechanisms of energy … these mechanisms exert fundamental constraints on cells. But we have no idea how they evolved into existence.
* First, the broth of amino acids will not spontaneously join together to form a chain of linked amino acids, but … To get them to join together to produce living cells we first need to activate them to do so. Only then can they react to form a chain.
* It takes energy to form these amino acids in the first place.
* Enzymes speed up chemical reactions by millions of times the unconstrained rate.
* The origin of life is the origin of information, without which, all are agreed, evolution by natural selection would not work.
* The continuous flux of energy and matter is precisely what is missing from the primordial soup.
* But if minerals are no use as replicators, then we need to find the shortest and fastest route to get from inorganic to organic molecules that do work as replicators.
* Proteins or RNA requires first activating the building blocks into different order producing forms.
* Evolution, as so often, is cleverer than we are, and yet there is no innate or universal trajectory towards complex life. The universe was not pregnant with the idea of ourselves.
* If just one amino acid is out of place, a single stone in the full mosaic the consequences may be crippling degeneration of the muscles and brain, and an early death.
* I think we can reasonably conclude that complex life will be rare in the universe there is no innate tendency in natural selection to give rise to humans or any other form of complex life.
* What I would argue with more certainty is that, for endosymbiosis between two prokaryotes, and that is a rare random event, is disturbingly

close to a freak accident, made all the more difficult by the ensuing intimate conflict between cells.

* These same shuttering electrons and protons have sustained you from the womb: you pump 10^{21} protons per second, every second, without pause.

* How lucky that our minds, the most, the most improbable biological machines in the universe, are now the conduit for this restless flow of energy, that we can think about why life in the way it is.

* So he concludes with the words "May the proton force be with you!"

Therefore, it is surely the time to accept that science's mechanistic and empirically based definition of life is not merely seriously limited but fundamentally flawed. Reality for us as human beings is determined by who we are as rational beings engaging and interacting with an ordered world both in terms of our senses and our many different attributes of understanding. What we need as a solution for an evolutionary theory in crisis is to realise that behind a world of vast complexity there is an ingeniously creative cosmic mind generating the energy and directing the whole operation of evolution into order producing forms of intelligent life in the form of – a wise creator.

Einstein has said: "I believe in Spinoza's God, a deity revealed in the orderly harmony of the universe. I am moved by reverence for the rationality at the heart of reality. For me, this attitude seems to be religious in the highest sense of the word. I call it cosmic religious feeling." (Einstein, *Out of My Latter Years* 30–33; *The World As I See It*) As we have already noted, Edmund Husserl affirms that the thing of which we were indubitably certain is our own conscious awareness of ourselves so if we want to build a conception of reality on a rock-solid foundation this was the place to start. This Husserl referred to as the phenomenology of life world within which we understand the world in terms of different categories of understanding. This is the world we experience, the life world constituting who we are as conscious beings and the world of things consciously perceived by means of our senses both of which represent an all-inclusive reality that make up the warp and woof of life.

Daniel Dennett in his book '*Consciousness Explained*' writes that: "With consciousness, however, we are still in a terrible muddle. Consciousness stands alone today as a topic that leaves even the most sophisticated thinkers tongue-tied and confused. As with all other mysteries, there are many who insisted that there will never be a demystification of consciousness." (Dennett 1993, p.22) But we don't have to understand how we came into existence as conscious beings to experience who we are. We cannot deny who we experience ourselves to be unless we want to commit a dangerous form of ontological suicide and give up the ghost altogether. As rational beings we must use our rational attributes of understanding, not just to investigate and analyse the world and everything in it, but to draw the necessary rational conclusions with respect to all that we experience ourselves to be as conscious living entities endowed with different attributes of being and understanding.

Dennett writes: "That as far as we know, of course, the pedigrees of the early replicators were all pretty much the same: they were each of them the product of one blind, dumb-luck series of selections of one kind or another." (Dennett 1993, p.175) Here, we have a bottomless bog of blind dumb luck proffered to explain what only a process of credible order producing ingenuity could possibly explain. Professor Brian Silver is more professional and down to earth as he explains the same thing describing it thus:

During the nineteenth century, abiogenesis was given a boost by the successful synthesis of organic molecules from inorganic matter, but the fact that we can synthesis amino acids and nucleic acids from inorganic starting materials does not explain how life started. We are intelligent beings who can purposefully bring together chosen chemicals under carefully controlled conditions. This is very different from accounting for spontaneous formation of living systems in an inanimate world empty of intelligence. And we have come nowhere near creating life in a laboratory. [Silver 1998, p.339]

Martin Heidegger referring to life in terms of our own constituted nature of being understood: "The Ontological Priority of the Question of Being," not least because our intrinsic nature of being stands at the centre and source of all knowing and is itself an essential part of that which is to be known. This is, of course, why Plato the Greek philosopher urged people to look within themselves because the greatest secrets of life were to be found there. Within our own soul, argued Plato, one could discover both our own essence and the world's meaning and that: "knowledge of the divine as implicit in every soul." While: "that the spiritual realm was forever superior to whatever human beings tried to accomplish in the temporal world … That the spiritual alone held genuine truth and value." (Cited in Tarnas 1998, p.41–44)

Philosopher and writer Bryan Magee argues that: "there actually is something that is impossible for me to doubt, and that is that I am having the conscious experience that I am currently having, even though I may be completely wrong as to its provenance." Magee goes on: "This was what was meant earlier by saying that the subjective is indubitable in a way that the objective can never be." (Magee 2000, p.118) Moreover, that which emanates from the mind represents, "… the very language that penetrated most deeply into the human experience and our understanding of it." (Magee 2000, p.136) There is, in fact, little point in knowing everything about the world of empirically based reality and failing to recognise the profound significance of who we are as conscious beings operating intelligently within it.

The human mind represents the greatest phenomenon in the known universe and the senses are but the handmaid of a living mind as it negotiates its way through the world of other sentient beings and empirically based things. As John Polkinghorne puts it: "By a person I mean at least this: a self-conscious being, able to perceive the future in anticipation, hope and dread; able to perceive meaning and to assign value: able to respond to beauty and the call of moral duty, able to love other persons, even to the point of self-sacrifice." These, of course, are qualities of being that cannot by any stretch of the imagination be attributed the physical substance even a physical brain as we presently understand a physical brain to be. Polkinghorne again argues: "It is strange, therefore, that some scientists seem to repudiate the insights of consciousness preferring instead to remain set in the misplaced concreteness of a world of atoms and the void." (Polkinghorne 2000, p.11–12)

As a cause must be able to explain all that we predicate of the effects produced, we need a cause that can explain a complex physical body and the experiential reality of a living self-conscious mind within which we understand and operate in the world we live in. Cox and Forshaw in their book *Why Does $E=mc^2$?* can see the validity of cause and effect relationships within the context of a world of ordered complexity and write: "Causality is another seemingly obvious concept whose application will have profound consequences. It is simply that the requirements that cause and effect are so important that their order cannot be reversed … When put in these terms, nobody could argue with the requirements of causality … Cause and effect are sacred in Einstein's universe." (Cox & Forshaw 208, p.71) But this does not seem to cause them to consider for a moment that the cause that brought all things into existence both animate and inanimate needs to be explained in terms of a living life producing cause without which science would be rendered impossible and doing it to be ultimately about nothing.

As Polkinghorne asks: "Why is science possible?" And going on he rightly affirms: "Science exploits the wonderful rational transparency of the physical world, but it does not explain it. If the universe is the creation of a rational God, then it is possible to understand its intelligibility as due to its being shot through with signs that are accessible to the thoughts of creatures made in the image of the creator." (Polkinghorne 2000, p.159) And as our creator has not only created us to be biologically complex but ontologically alive with attributes of being with which we can communicate with other living creatures, and also with Him whose image we have been created at least for those who want to see it.

As John Heil in his book *Philosophy of Mind* argues that: "You can, of course, turn your back on the metaphysical issues, but to the extent that you do you are diminished intellectually and perhaps in other ways as well." (Heil 1998, p.7) So as a metaphysical reality of conscious being is an intrinsic part of the effects produced and represents the life world and reason dictates that the cause that brought us into existence is and must be a living life producing cause according to the irreversible law of cause and effect as Cox and Forshaw rightly insist. The world of being is the prime mover within the world of things and we cannot assume that conscious life is synonymous with the working of a physical brain just because we cannot explain how a physical brain can produce a living self-conscious mind. But some have a vested interest in avoiding such a holistic analysis want to reduce life to a physical phenomenon under the control of a physical brain. As we have seen Moheb Costandi explains that: "Some say that we have learned more about the brain in the past decade than we did in the hundred years preceding it. Even so, we are only beginning to scratch the surface, and a huge amount remains to be discovered." (Costandi 2013, p.3)

Our mind is that part of us in which God has shared with us something of his own essence of being with us, so those who emphasise the empirically based side of life at the expense of the spiritual side of life makes them somewhat one-sided in their analysis of life and not so sensitive to the inner world of being within which God can be known and experienced. So as the saying goes: "That which is born of the flesh is flesh that which is born of the spirit is spirit" and again the flesh profits nothing, the "spirit gives birth to life." So life is still something of a mystery, but it is mystery of life generating profundity we cannot deny that links us to that cause from which we have come. So just as we can use our senses to navigate the physical world so the spirit of life connects to the world of other living things and to the one who has infused our mind with the spirit of life and attributes of being that direct our understanding into many different kinds of experience.

There is an overlapping reality between empirically based information being fed to a physical brain by means of our senses and who we are as conscious beings that experience many different things that leave different impressions on the mind. We might see a flower and be inspired by its beauty, pluck a bunch of flowers and give it to them as a token of our affection towards another person, be inspired how they appear from a mundane looking seed of not apparent significance, and be fascinated and inspired by the One who had wisdom to bring them into being from the right chemical formula of the earth into something so delicate and beautiful. And bees that can take their pollen and produce honey out of it in an ongoing circle of life in which is everything connected to everything else leading back to a wise creator whom we can relate to in spirit and in truth. So, just as we are connected to those we love both with bonds of spiritual interconnectedness so we are forever connected to our maker who endowed us with these attributes of spiritual interconnectedness.

Moreover, whether they like to admit it or not empiricists and sceptics know very well what we mean by the word spiritual and all good dictionaries have a full and clear definition of the term and what it means. 1 – From Latin – *Spiritus* the breath of life. 2 – That which is vital in a way that matter is not. 3 – That which has psyche, essence, substance, soul. 4 – Refined in nature, pure and holy. 5 The life principle that takes us beyond the world of mundane physics. 6 – The thinking, motivating, feeling part of man. 7 – Life as distinguished from the body. 8 – Personality and vivacity of spirit. 9 – Inner man. When used aright, this is the perfect place for God and man to meet for those who want to know Him. While that which is spiritless is described as dull, apathetic, unemotional, heartless even dead the world of the spirit that makes alive to God the creator of all things.

Freud described life as consisting of the rebellious pleasure-seeking *id*, and the *superego* which sets before the mind worthy ideals and virtuous thoughts and a conscious that creates a sense of guilt when we refuse to listen. Then we have the ego, the will, or volition, that mediates between these two opposing influences within which we make a life for itself for good or ill. This, in fact may well be what life is essentially all about, and according to many religious around the world it is. Morality is not a thing that can be learned by mere abstract thinking like a mathematically equation, it can only be learned by personal experience operating in the axis between good and evil. We are architects of our own destiny but he stands upon the stage of life and in spite of the evidence he denies the existence of God is not off to a good start, because in that god-defying decision they have made themselves out to be god.

When we are having an enjoyable experience like listening to music, we are not merely being informed by our senses about different notes and noises, we are having a spiritual experience that can move and enthral us in a way we simply cannot explain. But how could the electro-chemical signals moving between the neutrons of the brain transmute into the reality of a conscious mind is not understood. Empirically based reality is dead letter until the mind takes it and makes sense of it and we respond to it in many different ways as our needs and desires determine. As Richard Tarnas observes: "Thus human reason establishes its own existence out of experiential necessity, then God's existence, out of logical necessity." (Tarnas 1996, p.279)

Jim Baggott tries to get around the importance the metaphysical dimension of life by arguing that because the metaphysical dimension is beyond the reach of science we should stick close to the methodology of empirically based science to avoid the danger of straying into what he calls fairy-tale physics that relate to the world of metaphysics. (Baggott 2013, p.1f) But our metaphysical reality of being cannot be reduced to fairy-tale physics because it none other than us as conscious beings existentially engaged in science and without which there would be no science no science. This is why we need a holistic science of life and without which we have a totally distorted view of reality. In fact, science is metaphysical research programme, intelligent minds investigating an intelligently world to more clearly understand it, and surely are bound as rational being to apportion intelligently ordered things to intelligent and sufficient causes, and living things to a living life producing cause.

So when Baggott argues that scientists should hold to empirical based science and not stray into the world of metaphysics lest we end up in the world of fairy-tale physics he could not be more wrong. The truth is that science itself is a metaphysical research programme in which scientists are called to use their intelligence to investigate many different things and to draw the necessary conclusions with respect to its nature and origin in terms of sufficient cause. It is when we fail to do this and reduce science to an empirically based research programme drawing empirically based conclusions that we end up in the world of fairy-tale physics and Baggott does this spectacularly well. As John Heilunder the heading of the *Qualities of conscious experience* writes:

> Now, however, we find ourselves face to face with a deeper mystery. The qualities of our experiences seem to differ utterly from the qualities of any imaginable material object. How then could we seriously entertain the hypothesis that conscious agents are nothing more that congeries of material objects, conscious experience nothing more than manifestations of complex material dispositions? [Heil 1998, p.207]

It is only when the human mind actively brings forth from within itself the full power of a disciplined imagination and saturates its empirical observation with archetypal insight that the deeper reality of the world emerges. The human imagination itself being part of the world's intrinsic truth and without which knowledge of the world is in a real sense is incomplete. (Tarnas 1996, p.434) Moreover, it is not only Baggott who is guilty of this grave error of judgement; many scientists do exactly the same on a daily bases. And when Baggott argues that: "What you take for your reality is just electrical signals interpreted by your brain," we are effectively being dehumanised. Wilder Penfield the father of modern neurosurgery argues that he and other scientists struggled to prove that the brain accounts for all that we predicate of a living conscious mind and had encountered concrete evidence that the mind and brain are distinct from each other, although they clearly interact. (Cited in Strobel 2004, p.249)

John Polkinghorne argues: "The impersonal should not to be given precedence over the personal or the quantitative over the qualitative, for they are simply differing aspects of our encounter with reality whose character is complex and multi-dimensional and whose different levels can be known only in ways that conform to their distinctive natures." (Polkinghorne 2000, p.12) It seems from all this that we could more readily be described as embodies spirits than physical entities. Therefore, "looking at matter tells us nothing about consciousness." So "Niels Bohr and Erwin Schrodinger have thought that biological systems, including brains, might behave in ways that are indescribable using classical physics." Schrodinger argues that: "From all that we have learned about the structure of living matter, we must be prepared to find it working in a manner that cannot be reduced to the ordinary laws of physics." (Baker2013, cp.49 and 50) In fact the subjective world of being is more indubitably real than the objective world of sensibly perceived things.

Vitalism in the most profound sense is the belief that there is something over and above inanimate matter that lies at the heart of the existence of all living things. Hegel has aptly put it when he writes: "History is essentially the history of the spirit that runs its course in time." (Heidegger 1962, p.480) While as Anil Seth reminds us: "Human self-consciousness the experience of being 'me' plays out at many different levels. These include a basic sense of being and having a body, to experiences of looking out onto the world from a particular first person perspective, and then to experiences of volition and will." (Cited in Aliens 2016, p.53) How moral being is incorporated into a physical brain we do not know but it is none the less real for all that, and as finite beings there are things we must be accept on faith in the ordered and ontological reality of all that we experience ourselves to be. Love is one of those things and no one repudiates this prince of virtues because they cannot understand how the brain generates it. And to love God and to feel his love for us is of such ineffable worth it is the crown of all experiences which to experience passes human understanding. God is not all about doom and gloom but about love and mercy grace and forgiveness and longs to make Himself known to those of a contrite heart.

Moheb Costandi writes: "Some believe that gaining a better understanding of how the brain works will provide answers to life's big questions. It will not: brain research cannot tell us everything about ourselves, or what it means to be human." (Costandi 2013, Intro.) Even the most ardent defenders of the mechanistic theory smuggle purposive organising principles into their science in the form selfish genes or genetic programs. Sheldrake 2003, p.55) In *Being and Time*, Heidegger attempts to trace out the tragic-comic effects of this repression in the history of the subject, and to demonstrate the fertility and power that is released when that repression is lifted. (Mulhall 1996, p.33) "Being itself needs accounting for" adds Heidegger, and asks how many people can be so wrong about something so close to their own natures, and adds: "such forgetfulness – particularly when one's topic is what it is to be human – is liable, were it not comic, to be so tragic in its consequences. Virtues, values and meanings are projected upon the natural world by the human mind and constitute who we are operating within that world. The soul the forgotten reality in a world of things but to which Jesus pointed out was the most precious thing a person possesses, and asks the question: 'what will a man give in exchange for his own soul?'"

Jim Baggott argues that: "We might be here because, by happy accident or the operation of some complex natural physical mechanisms we have yet to fathom the parameters of the universe just happens to be compatible with our existence." (Baggott 2013, p.283) But while the latter is self-evident, the real question which Baggott is trying to evade is, why the parameters of the universe have been so spectacularly configured to bring into existence the immense biological complexity of a working brain and then to bring that ordered compendium of a biological complexity to life endued with finely tuned attributes of being. For whatever that cause is, it none other than the author of life.

Stephen Pinker may well argue that the brain is but an extremely complicated computer of immense computational software, but when a computer his outworn its usefulness we don't bury it with tears of grief stricken sadness as we would if a family member who passed away, we without too much dissonance of mind dispose of it without too much thought as to where it will eventually end up whether to the scrapheap or to be recycled, and while it was ordered into existence it has no soul it, it is not sacred and unless we are seriously mentally disturbed we are not going to take it to bed with us. A computational machine like a computer has no conscious mind, endowed with feelings, affections, hopes, aspirations or a moral being with a distinct sense of personal identity or moral responsibility. It doesn't feel guilty if it crashes no matter how its crashing might affect the operator. It has no emotions, moral culpability, conscience, feelings, hopes and other aspirations as we humans possess, and if a robot was set up to harm someone the law would not arrest the computer and put it on trial but it would arrest one who programmed it to do so.

Pinker goes on to argue that: "It is not a matter of honouring some ineffable distinction between organisms and physical systems but of understanding what kinds of physical systems organisms, including human beings, are." But alas poor Pinker is merely presupposing the very thing that needs to be explained in terms consistent with the subject matter, and failing to see that inanimate matter irrespective of how well ordered it might be still represents a complex physical object that fails to explain the precise means by which physics as inanimate matter in transformed to become the qualitative reality of a living self-conscious being that we experience ourselves to be. Pinker fails to explain in precise causal terms how all that we know about the working of a physical brain can produce all we predicate of a living self-conscious mind endowed with different qualitative attributes of being that we invariably regard as precious and even sacred.

So Pinker is only fudging the whole issue and failing to honestly face up to the problem of the difference between physical systems and living things. Water cannot be turned into wine no matter how much water we keep adding to water or rearrange the molecules thereof. And if we turned on the water tap in our kitchen and wine came flowing out we would not pass this off as nothing that did not need to be explained, rather, we would set our mind to investigating what was going on because what we understand water to be is very different to what we understand wine to be and we would not stop until we had solved the problem. Even if we never came to understand how wine came flowing out of our water tap this would not stop us enjoying the wine, but this problem is not solved until someone can show us clearly in logical steps how water as a substance can be changed into wine.

Pinker argues that his computational model of the brain is validated by artificial intelligence because it shows that ordinary matter can perform feats that were supposedly only performable by what was mental stuff. (Pinker 2002, p.33) But artificial intelligence may be able to operate effectively within the world of physics but this is far from explaining conscious life with different attributes of understanding or the many different desires, emotions, feelings, hopes, aspirations or a sense of moral being that we as sentient beings possess. Moreover, artificial intelligence originates from human intelligence, therefore no human intelligence no artificial intelligence and human intelligence needs to be explained by a pre-existing intelligence until we get back to that ingeniously creative first cause.

Artificial intelligence is conscious of nothing, feels no pain, it has no feelings or heart-felt emotions, has no conscience, moral sensibility, hopes and aspirations. It fact robots have no fear of death, they do not weep when one of its fellow computers goes into melt down and ends up on the scrap heap having worn out its usefulness. And as we have earlier pointed out, a robot might be primed to say 'I love you' under certain external promptings but it feels nothing and these are but empty worlds and are not accompanied by the appropriate emotions and feelings. Nor has a robot any sense of gratitude to the one who programmed it into existence. It does not pay taxes even though its owner might. Moreover, Dennett goes on to say: "Surely life can be explained in terms of things that aren't alive." (Dennett 1991, p.455) But if this is so no one has discovered it, and we shouldn't waste our time looking for it because matter no matter how much of it we might have it has not the wherewithal within itself to bring inanimate matter to life.

Dennett gives us an illustration of his theory of consciousness by stating that: "Solids or liquids or gasses can be explained in terms of things of things that aren't themselves solids, liquids or gasses." (Dennett 191, p.455) But the problem with this illustration is that solids, liquids and gasses and that which goes to make up their chemical makeup is still inanimate matter when it is conscious life we are trying to explain which is a very different thing altogether to material configurations of matter no matter how varied or rearranged.

There is also the fact that identical twins do not only behave differently but are two completely distinct self-conscious human beings even though their physical brains were created by the exact same genetic code. What is it, therefore, that must be added to a physical brain to create a self-conscious reality of a living mind, and as identical twins aptly demonstrate cannot be explained by anything within the genetic code that produces two identical biologically babies but who are two to entirely different self-conscious human beings that came from the same genetic information? There is obviously another dimension that needs to be added that brings conscious life into existence over and above the working of a physical brain. On another level, Nick Lane admits that: "There is a black hole at the heart of biology…Incorporating energy into evolution is long overdue. This continuous flow of energy is precisely what is needed to produce intelligently ordered things and there is nothing in the soup that can drive the formation of disparate structures that we call cells, nothing to make these cells grow and divide and come to life." (Lane 2016, p.1–95–289) But the one thing of which many evolutionary acolytes are absolutely sure is that a living conscious mind has absolutely nothing to do with a living life producing cause. And why not we might ask? Is it because they do not want it to be so least they become obligated to one to whom they for their own reasons would prefer did not exist.

Daniel Dennett likes to boast about how a computer can learn to play Chess better than some good chess players yet they have no mind. What Dennett is trying to do is to argue that we do not need a mind-first intelligence to explain the coming into existence of intelligent life on earth because a computer has no mind yet it can engage in intelligent activity like playing chess. But what Dennett seems to conveniently overlook is that it is human beings that produce computers and without humans beings who are endowed with intelligent minds they would be no computers. Therefore, to argue that a computer can play checkers to beat a human player by changes 'mindlessly generated' is completely misleading because it was human intelligence that programmed computers to operate intelligently so we have a mind first way of order producing intelligence out of which computers were ordered into existence to operate as they do. Therefore, if there was no human mind there would be no computers unless God wanted to produce them.

Dennett goes on to describe those that produced computer programmes as the greatest minds of the century that invented computers and programmed them to operate intelligently. He explains how Samuel a computer programme producing genius was not only able to programme a computer to play chess but could programme it to learn from its mistakes to play more effectively. (Dennett 1995, p.209f) What Dennett is describing here is a process of the most programming creating genius carried out by the best brains in the computer world and then he goes on to claim that an intelligent mind had nothing to do with this which is highly disingenuous. And while computers may not have fleshy brains as we humans do they have been programmed by people with intelligent minds operating to produce artificial intelligence that emulates human intelligence. In other words, no intelligent minds no artificial intelligence and so no effective chess playing computers!

Moreover, such a computer playing chess with a human being has an advantage over the human because a human being can have a multitude of things running through their mind at any one time, momentarily lose consecration or have something else on their mind, be worried or distracted by some other concern, or suffer from mental fatigue or boredom while the computer has no such encumbrances or distractions and has nothing to do but that which it was programmed to do. And for Dennett to argue that a computer could learn to play chess and continually to improve its performance were 'mindlessly generated' he is being wholly misleading because he knows fine well that such computers did not programme themselves into existence but were programmed by some of the most intelligent minds in the world.

And when a computer stops playing chess as it was programmed that is all it can do, it cannot love, it has no emotional life, it cannot feel pain, it cannot laugh, and if it was programmed to shoot a gun and kill someone it would have no conscience about it, it has no sense of time existentially speaking and it was programmed to say I love you it would feel nothing. Those who like to think that life is nothing more than a complex compendium of inanimate matter will find that they have a very lively piece of matter on their hands. While those who say that, they cannot find a vital dimension to life is like someone forever looking for the donkey they are riding on and saying they cannot find it no matter how hard they look. At what point and by what means is a physical brain transformed into a living mind, and although we do not know how this is achieved we are the proof of it within ourselves that it does happen?

Tarnas observes: "But contemporary science has itself become increasingly self-aware and self-critical, less prone to naive scientism, more conscious of its epistemological and existential limitations." (Tarnas 1996, p.404) Fred Hoyle is most certainly right when he declares that: "A common sense interpretation of the facts suggests that a super intellect has *monkeyed* about with physics, as well as with chemistry and biology, and that there are no blind forces worth speaking about in nature." (Cited in Strobel 2004, p.78)

Some scientists may well argue that the job of the scientist is not to solve mysteries without recourse to divine intervention and to explain everything in terms of nature's own resources. But what are nature's own resources in the light of all that they have brought into existence from the starry hosts above us to the moral being within us as Kant would say. Moreover, when was it the scientist's job to explain the immense complexity of life on earth outside of a process of intelligent design or an order producing cause of any kind? If some scientists feel predisposed to explain all that exists without recourse to divine intervention they are prejudicing their own research and are presupposing what they cannot possibly know and runs against the evidence. Here is what a detective would refer to as a motive, a motive to distort the evidence to avoid a conclusion some are determined to avoid in the form of a wise creator. In fact, we as living entities are a living and finite expression of Nature's own being, the outworking of a living life producing cause actively at work in the universe.

It is little wonder that some scientists and evolutionary theorists have found so little evidence of a wise creator when they are determined not to find it, and who believe that it is wrong to even look for it and suspect not for a moment that they themselves are the living proof of it. In all this, there seems to be a sordid little plot to keep God as a wise creator out of the picture, and secular theorists in the forefront wining Nobel Prizes for trying to explain by means of intelligence that which many of them go on to argue has nothing to do with intelligence or a sufficient cause of any kind.

For some, the laws of nature seem to be a convenient repository from which to source the ingenious order producing laws that govern the universe. Therefore, nature becomes a kind of a cosmic Pandora's Box full of so many wonderfully creative laws of order producing ingenuity that seem to appear like magic out of nowhere. But in the real world when all the laws of nature are added together and given the order producing credence they deserve we are confronted with evidence that nature is a living life producing cause at work in the universe and sharing something of her own being with us in the ordered and living sum of who we are. Therefore, Mother Nature seems to be acting like the handmaid of a wise creator bringing into existence the vast complexity of intelligent life on earth. Mother Nature is a wise creator by another name, a Female version of God which makes no difference because gender is not a factor when it comes to the existence of a wise creator.

Lawrence M. Krauss in his book *a universe from nothing* argues that: "theology has made no contribution to knowledge in the past five hundred years at least, since the dawn of science." (Krauss 2012, p.144) But what kind of contribution to knowledge is it to apportion the ordered complexity of all that exists to nothing and taking some two hundred pages to do so when there is not a lot one can say about nothing. It seems that Krauss fails to realise that it is theology which is based in the belief in God as a wise creator who is the only credible explanation for a world full of the necessary and ingenious means to bring into existence an intelligently ordered world and then to fill it intelligently ordered living things. Even Steven Pinker in spite of his faults openly acknowledges that: "Nothing comes out of nothing." (Pinker 2002, p.75) Moreover, if everything came from nothing of any credible order producing significance what does that make Krauss as the result of such a pathetic process of cosmic nothingness? It seems that those who argue for a universe from nothing must not think much of themselves because as the cause is so the effects will be. (Krauss 2012, p.58)

Indeed, it seems that theorists like Krauss have too much to say about nothing and have miserably failed to understand the meaning of the word and the indisputable fact that from nothing – nothing comes turning such science into a cosmological charade in which the effects are cosmologically vast but the cause never gets beyond nothing. However, after Krauss has spent some 200 pages writing about his universe that came from nothing he goes on to say that: "by nothing, I do not mean nothing," and then goes on to talk about, how much 'energy' is contained in nothing. In this, it seems that in this Krauss has contradicted his grandiose theory of nothingness, and goes on explain how Quantum physics can do that which is logically impossible and bring something from nothing. But how it operates, to do produce this God-like miracle is not explained, but whatever it is it isn't nothing!

As we have seen in an earlier chapter, quantum physics represents a spooky action at a distance in which everything is connected to everything else by invisible threads that cannot be detected with the naked eye, quantum forces that cannot be denied and yet cannot be explained by us as human beings which seems very like God to me. (Krauss 2012, p.58) In the end, Krauss falls back on the old argument of who created the creator, but because something created may well not understand how it was created or explain the cause that brought it into existence doesn't mean that it has no cause. We as rational beings have been granted unspeakable gift of rational thinking to discern that effects have causes commensurate with the ordered sum of the effects produced but some seen to prefer the suspend their rational faculty of being because they are afraid of being confronted with the logic of a wise creator to whom they owe everything.

But according to some a sweaty mouse has better credentials by way of origin and explanation than a human being, because the sweaty mouse has at least a credible origin, but we as human beings according to some do not. This kind of thinking contributes absolutely nothing whatsoever to science but rather undermines the fundamental rudiments of rational thinking as the only true basis of good science and turns science into a cosmological farce in which nothing of any order producing significance produced the ordered sum of everything. In fact, this makes theists the only true scientists because they insist on explaining intelligent life on earth in terms sufficient to explain the ordered and living sum of it both biologically and ontologically. So we have some evolutionists who are of the rational kind in the form of theists who argue that intelligently ordered living things require intelligently constituted causes to explain the ordered and living sum of their existence, and those of the irrational kind who argue that intelligently ordered things do not need to be explained in terms of an intelligent and sufficient cause commensurate with the ordered and living sum of their existence.

Michael Denton has aptly observed that an undirected process of no order producing significance could somehow turn dead chemicals into the extraordinary complexity of living things is surely "no more or less than the great cosmological myth of our time." (Cited in Strobel 2004, p.278) Belief in God as a wise creator is really the life-blood of science because it provides scientists with a world full of intelligently ordered things to intelligently investigate and reason intelligently about. Science rests on the fundamental premise that reality both animate or inanimate is intelligible, and to be intelligible to us it has to be ordered intelligently and this is why scientists in their tens of thousands down the long years of human history have been so keen to examine the world and everything in it knowing implicitly or explicitly that being ordered intelligently it can be investigated intelligently.

Therefore, it could be said that theists are the only true scientists because they do not stop until they get to a credible explanation in terms of an intelligent and sufficient for an ordered world full of intelligently ordered things and the ontological reality of living things. Moreover, why would a person sit down to write a book about how nothing produced the ordered sum of everything which is no explanation for the existence of anything! Max Weber is more to point when he argues that empirically based science cannot provide for us values to live by and that the world's obsession with physical things tends to eliminate all sense of moral purpose from the earth. He believed that the human sciences were distinct to the natural sciences that pertain to the world of physics, and that the human sciences took us to the heart of our existence as human beings both physically and metaphysically.

Therefore, there is a logical link between scientific truth and religious beliefs in that the idea of God as a wise creator is the only conceivable way to explain an ordered world full of intelligently ordered things and to avoid the embarrassment of having to explain a world full of intelligently ordered things animate and inanimate in terms of the order producing sum of nothing. Thus, we need to help those who have not yet learned the meaning of the word 'nothing', and who seem to need help in understanding the art of rational thinking. And when we get to a true and inclusive science of life we find ourselves confronted with something truly ineffable. Therefore, the objective world of physics must be brought together with the subjective world of being if we are to have a holistic science of life. This does not mean that we can reconcile these two worlds in absolute terms because life fades into infinity beyond our own finite minds to fully understand. But as Heidegger has aptly affirmed, everyone knows very well what they mean when they use the word 'being' even though they cannot explain it in empirically based scientific terms. (Heidegger 1962, p.2)

Ravi Zacharias has argued: "The infrastructure of our society has become mindless and senseless because the foundation on which we have built cannot support any other kind of structure." (Zacharias 1994, p.21) While Margaret Mahler has argued: "As we begin to enter the storms of emotional strain and conflict that characterise the human condition, we may well have to give up some of this neat precision in exchange for a richer, deeper understanding of the verities of the human experience." (Cited in Hundert 1990, p.131)

Jim Baggott in his book entitled *Farewell to Reality* admits that: "Scientists are human; they are often selective with their data, choosing to ignore inconvenient facts that don't fit, through the application of a range of approaches that, depending on the circumstances, we might forgive as poor judgement or condemn as downright fraud. They make mistakes. Sometimes driven by greed or venal ambition, they may cheat or lie." (Baggott 2013, p.9) As long as he applies this principle to himself and examines his own motives and thinking we have no problem with this critique. As we have seen earlier Baggott tries to remove metaphysics from science when science is a metaphysical programme of investigation carried out by intelligent minds who are honour bound to draw logical conclusions from intelligently ordered effects in relation to their causes. But by limiting verifiability reality to empirically based facts, removes the need to apportion intelligently order things to intelligent and sufficient causes because such conclusions cannot be verified in empirically based terms.

Within the context of science operating in a world vast complexity luck has become the operative term, with seemingly no limits of what luck can do. But there is a limit on what luck can do operating by to pure chance within a disordered world of inanimate matter. In fact luck, for practical purposes is aimless, gormless and powerless. How it could order all things into existence and then breathe life into inanimate matter is beyond all reckoning. When it comes to luck, it is conceivable that if our parachute didn't open after jumping out of an aeroplane flying at twenty thousand feet that we could land on a huge snowdrift that cushioned our fall and as a result survived against the massive odds. However, it is inconceivable that we, the aeroplane from which we jump, the parachute that usually works to land us safely back on terra firma and the world and everything in it on which we land could come into existence by pure happenstance or an endless stream of luck. A happy coincidence can happen every now and again, but it cannot be made the basis for the coming into existence of a world full of extremely complex and intelligently ordered things from what before was once the disordered and disparate chemicals of the earth.

When we push the idea of luck too far, it becomes a form of base superstition unworthy of science and completely contrary to the logic of rational thinking. As Peter Hodgson argues that: "The resort to God is not a cloak to cover ignorance, but the logical consequences of the nature of our knowledge of the structure of the universe as discovered by empirical science." (Hodgson 1994, p.193) Moreover, a chance occurrence can have a bad outcome just as readily as a good one like being struck by lightning because we just happen to be standing in the wrong place at the wrong time. As Dr Lee Spetner in his book *Not By Chance* quotes Yves Delage who writes with regard to chance: "… we see in natural selection an inexorable force whose function is not to create but to destroy to weed, to prune, to cut down and cast into the fire." (Spetner 1997, p.175) In other words evolutionists believe in a theory that is cutting down those things unfit to survive but never explaining how complex living things were ordered sufficiently to come into existence to survive and thrive. A farmer must first sow good seed before it is worth his while pulling out the weeds.

We have seen how Richard Dawkins openly admits that: "increasing coincidence mean increasing improbability", so that we must inevitably get to a point, and that right quickly, when the possibility of luck producing complex living things of ever increasingly complexity becomes an utter and compete impossibility. Such luck reads more like a *just-so* story totally divorced from the world of rational thinking and concocted by someone with an over-heated imagination. So like in the fairy-tale, Dumbo can be made to fly by merely flapping his big ears and that with a cart load of people on board, but back in the real world it isn't going to happen.

If, for instance, two friends claimed that by sheer chance they met at an airport, and by chance just happened to be travelling to the same flight to the same destination, just happened to be allocated seats beside each-other on the aircraft, just happened to get the same taxi from the airport and their hotel, just happened to be booked into the same hotel, just happened to be allocated the same room in the hotel and just happened to fall into the same bed a rational person is going to smell a rat and conclude that the whole thing was a planned liaison and not a series of lucky coincidences at all. But for some anti-design evolutionists the luck just goes endlessly on from the beginning of time to present day and then to sanctify and bless their ill thought-out theory they call it science and they then look surprised because we are not willing to buy it.

Monkeys, although we love them, do not ask why the bananas appear on the banana tree for them to eat: they are just an endless stream of free lunches, and are taken completely for granted. So it seems that there are those who do not only believe that we came from monkeys they want us to think like monkeys. Some even go farther and attribute all that exists to nothing at all, and the statement of Aristotle seems to be the best reply to such naivety when he remarked that "nothing is what rocks dream about."

As Richard Tarnas writes: "In this perspective, nature pervades everything, and the human mind in all its fullness is itself an expression of Nature's own being, and it is only when the human mind actively brings forth from within itself the full powers of a disciplined imagination and saturates its empirical observation with an archetypal insight that a deeper reality of the world emerges." (Tarnas 1996, p.434)

Chapter 11
Fairy-Tale Physics and Just-So Stories

Once we as rational beings accept that something is intelligently ordered we know immediately and intuitively that it needs to be explained in terms of an intelligent and sufficient cause or a series of interconnected causes operating to the same end. Moreover, the claim that the argument for design is flawed because it appears to suffer from the argument if infinite regress in that we then need to explain the designer, and designer before that and so on and so forth. But this is not logically necessary at all because we must get back to that first uncaused that is necessary to explain the ordered sum of the effects produced. Either that or we must consider that what we think by way of such ordering isn't happening at all, and if this is the case where did we come from. That we came from nothing and nowhere is no explanation at all and is just a cop-out to avoid being indebted to that cause from which we have come. He who created us inculcated into our being the attribute of rational thinking so that could reflect on the origin from which we have come in the light of all that we have been ordered to be.

So any idea about having to explain the creator in infinite regress is but idle speculation not a logical necessity and could be regarded as an idle distraction from facing up to living out that which we have been created to be and to whom as moral beings we are ultimately answerable. The design argument runs like this according to David Hume:

Look round the world: contemplate the whole and every part of it you will find it to be nothing but one great machine, subdivided into an infinite number of lesser machines, which again admit of subdivisions to a degree beyond what human senses and faculties can trace or explain. All these various machines, and even more minute parts, are adjusted to each other with an accuracy which ravishes into admiration all men who have ever contemplated them. The curious adapting of means to ends, throughout all

221

nature, resembles exactly, though it much exceeds, the productions of human contrivance: of human designs, thought, wisdom, and intelligence. Since therefore, the effects resemble each other, we are led to infer, by all the rules of analogy, that the cause also resemble: and that the Author of Nature is somewhat similar to the mind of man, though possessed of much larger faculties, proportionate to the grandeur of the work he has executed. [Cited in Dupre 2007, p.152]

A monkey sitting on a shipyard wall looking at a great ocean liner being constructed would never guess that amongst the network of scaffolding, tools and equipment of many different kinds operating in the background, the apparent mess, men and materials being moved around every which way, the noise, banging, clanking, the manic manoeuvrings that a beautiful ship is being constructed. To the monkey it is nothing but an incomprehensible shambles operating to no sensibly perceived purpose.

That's the monkey, but in spite of its innocent naivety amidst the apparent bedlam of confusion a grand purpose is being accomplished in which a great sea-faring vessel is being constructed. We as human being can readily appreciate the order producing process of shipbuilding creativity going on in the shipyard, but are not so quick to recognise and give due credit to the hand of a wise creator who is behind an ordered world and our own existence as human beings. It seems that some theorists become just like the monkey and fail to see that among the massive order producing panoply of activity going on within the world of evolution and that beneath the surface an ingenious process of order producing creativity has taken place.

Christian de Duve believes that life is a cosmic imperative so that life is: "written into the fabric of the universe." (Cited in Davies 1999, p.234) Therefore, the working of nature with its vast order producing ability and life generating efficacy is just another name for an intelligent and sufficient cause indistinguishable from and synonymous with the working of a wise creator. That is why our maker put us as human beings in charge of it and told us to care for it and look after it. As one writer puts it: "Causality was obviously inspired by a general view of the universe as a rational and deterministic system." (Cited in Copleston Vol. IX, p.118)

In spite of all this, The *National Academy of Sciences* argue that because intelligent design as a concept cannot be established in empirically based scientific terms the whole idea must be rejected. But we could say the same of great ships or anything else man has created and deny that such things are designed at all because intelligent design cannot be proved in empirically based terms. But we are not all matter limited to our physically based senses, our senses are feed into an intelligent mind to be processed in relation to their significance, cause, meaning and purpose. We are not zombies engaged in science but some seem to act as if we were. Our mind brings us to life and all that we are as living entities is part of the design and needs to be explained in terms that are able to explain it.

So when The National Academy of Sciences deliberately deny the idea of intelligent design they are doing a very devious and dangerous thing which is both irrational and dehumanising leaving scientists as zombies like creatures engaged science all brain but no mind, so in professing themselves wise some have indeed become fools. We cannot get reason and rationality into a Petri dish to examine it as we would a physical object, but reason is what we use to do science and to not just ascertain the significance of what we are examining in itself but its significance in terms of a cause that is able to explain it. So *The Royal Academy of Sciences* don't seem to realise the significance of what scientists are doing when they engage in science and fail to draw the necessary conclusions with respect to the cause in relation the nature of the ingeniously ordered sum of the effects produced. So if it cannot be examined like a physical specimen in Petri dish under a microscope it isn't verifiably real at all. Such of course makes life a very dull party or really no party at all.

Thus as Hundert observes: "While Kant realised that Descartes's 'I' is not just an object but also a subject of knowledge, Kant's 'I as a subject continued to be concerned only with objects of its knowledge, while Hegel's concern is the subject of knowledge itself, which is why knowing gets subsumed within the larger context of living." (Hundert 1990, p. 52) In this all-inclusive epistemology a human being, and more especially the human mind, is the greatest reality in the known universe that needs to be investigated, understood and explained. And moreover, the reason to which it operates demands of us that effects must be explained in terms of sufficient cause and the ordered sum of a living life needs to be explained in terms of a living life producing cause just like the one theists call God.

Colin McGinn asks why it is that we cannot by means of our intellect resolve the problem of the relationship between a thinking mind and a physical brain and that perhaps it is impossible for us to resolve this problem just as it is impossible for a dog to understand Einstein's theory of relativity. (McGinn 2002, p.1820) But whether or not we can understand how a physical brain can produce a living life producing effect in the form of a living self-conscious mind we have proof within ourselves that this does take place and both must be used if we are to a comprehensive science of life. We cannot and do not deny the reality of love even though we cannot explain how it is generated and mediated to us through the working of a physical brain. We do not deny ourselves the pleasure of listening to music because we cannot understand how it has such an enjoyable affect upon us. We dare not repudiate moral sensibility as a genuine attribute of being because we cannot work out how a physical brain can convey to us such qualitative categories of understanding and the different experiences they invoke within us. We cannot deny the feeling of grief at the loss of a loved one because we cannot understand how the brain as a complex physical mass can produce such moving experiences we all feel at the death of a loved one. Such grief is evidence that life is both solemn and serious and death is something we long to overcome and to be forever with those we love.

Moreover, we would challenge materialists to inform us as to what word they would use to explain how they distinguish themselves as qualitative beings of profound ontological significance from inanimate matter and even the working of a physical brain? To make no distinction leaves the world of being unexplained in what is a subtle form of self-negating reductionism to avoid being confronted with a cause that is not only order producing but life generating. But what some can't understand as finite beings they reject because they have no one they can trust to produce in them reliable attributes of being beyond their human ability to explain. Even the existence of an inquisitive mind is a necessary prerequisite for engaging in science which cannot be validated in empirically based scientific terms. Richard Tarnas writes with respect to the Greek legacy of Socrates and Plato who regarded: "the Logos as a divine revelatory principle, simultaneously operative within the human mind and the natural world." (Tarnas 1991, p.47)

Bernard Lonergan reminds us that we have what he refers to as 'self-appropriation', that is consciousness of ourselves. (Lonergan 1990, lecture 1) This is the existential side of life that represents a world of ineffable being that that cannot be denied without denying who we experience ourselves to be which essentially to deny ourselves. Heidegger reminds us: "History, which is essentially the history of the spirit as it runs its course in time." So who we are as conscious being living in the objective world of physics is the most crucial question a person could ask, because this determines who we are as human beings and how we understand ourselves and the world we live in. But the modern scientific work of empirically based science had not only trivialised this world of being but "sanctions its complete neglect", as Heidegger argues. Therefore the way to the most essential aspects of reality is not empirical, but the study of living experience and everyone knows what they mean by it because everyone uses it constantly and know what they mean by it. (Heidegger 2000. P.2)

So what we need is a science of the existence of man of which empirical science is but is but one aspect. Cox and Forshaw remind us of the importance of cause and effect relationships within the context of science and believe that: "It is worth reflecting, however, that humans seem capable of ignoring it on a daily basis." This, they argue, is because the attribute of abstract reason is: "not a faculty we generally need too much in everyday life." (Cox & Forshaw. P.71) But it is interesting that Cox and Forshaw are none too quick to apply reason to the ordered complexity of all things which are calling out to be explained in terms of sufficient. So their science is partial and incomplete with no clear reference to a cause that explains those things they endlessly reason about, or themselves as those doing the investigating that also need to be explained in their own living life defining terms. The origin of the existence of all things is passed over in silence without drawing the necessary conclusions in terms of intelligent and sufficient causes that are needed to explain intelligently ordered things. So while the effects are ingeniously marvellous the cause is left dangling in epistemological mid-air and not explained in terms of an intelligent and sufficient cause at all.

Cox and Forshaw accept that Einstein was a genius who will be remembered as long as the universe lasts, but if it takes a genius the calibre of Einstein to reveal something of the complex workings of the universe it would surely take an even greater cause to bring into existence the ordered sum of all that exists in the heavens above and the earth beneath which scientists have the privilege of investigating in the hope of better understanding it. What we need is a science that seeks to explain an intelligently ordered world full of intelligently ordered thinks in terms of sufficient cause as opposed to leaving it all dangling from one God-almighty skyhook. We need a cause that can go beyond empirically based reality to a philosophy of the existence of man, a cause that can explain a rich ontology of being that takes us into the fullness of the life world and what it means to be rational sentient beings operating in an ordered world.

Even to know that there is a purpose to life is an essential part of that quest for human fulfilment and has been a part of the human experience from time immemorial. But Jim Baggott argues that what you take to be your reality of being is just electrical signals interpreted by your brain. (Baggott 2013, p.4) However, it can also be said that scientific facts are nothing more than electrical signals interpreted by our brain, and even pain is but electrical signals interpreted by our brain, that moral being is but electrical signals interpreted by our brain, and that intelligence is but electrical signals interpreted by the brain, love is nothing but electrical signals interpreted by our brain, and the grief we feel at the loss of a loved one are but electrical signals interpreted by our brain, and that clinical depression, an accusing conscious, and fear of death etc., are all just signals interpreted by the brain.

But how does the brain turn into a living self-conscious mind as a reality in its own right? What other dimension do we have to add to a working brain produce a living mind and how do these together produce life as we experience it to be. We don't know but we cannot deny it because it adds up to the conscious living sum of who we experience ourselves to be as human beings. As Richard Tarnas writes: "And it is only when the human mind actively brings forth from within itself the full power of a disciplined imagination and saturates its empirical observation with archetypal insight that the deeper reality of the world emerges." (Tarnas 1991, p.434) How electro-chemical signals moving across the neurons and dendrites of the brain can produce life as we experience it to be we simply don't know, but we cannot reduce life to the working of a physical brain just because we cannot explain how the brain produces the profound and irresistible reality of who we experience to be.

Jim Baggott accepts that there is a metaphysical dimension to reality but that such is beyond the reach of empirically based science to identify or explain it so the best we can do is to ignore it and limit verifiable reality to concrete empirically based scientific terms. But of course this is something we cannot do because this metaphysical reality of being represents none other than who we experience ourselves to be and takes us beyond the world of empirically based reality and determines who we are as rational beings of profound ontological reality and qualitative significance operating within the world of empirically based reality. To exercise our powers of reason tells something about the origin of the living life producing cause from which we have come and our moral being informs sets the standards by which we relate, or should relate, to the world of other living beings and things.

But Baggott wants to by-pass, or at least marginalise, this fundamental reality of being that takes us to the very heart of who we are as human beings and for scientists to concentrate on the empirical dimension of reality lest we drift into fairy-tale land. But, of course, fairy tale land is to restrict science to empirically based physics in which the heart and soul is taken out of our humanity and reason which cannot be defined empirically can is twisted and distorted until the origin of life can be described in a way that has little to nothing to do with how we experience it to be or attributed to a cause that adequately explain it. We as rational beings are morally obliged to give due credit to that cause from which we have come and use all our attributes of being to understand and experience all that we were meant to know as human beings. It's hard to deny who we experience ourselves to be but Baggott tries to argue that even when metaphysical elements are involved science is still a dialogue limited to empirically based facts. But this is anything but a holistic science of life, and who we might we ask is doing all this science and how are we going to come to healthy and holistic science of life if we reduce, or concentrate, on the empirically based reality to the exclusion that reality of being that we experience ourselves to be?

A holistic understanding of reality only comes about when we employ our full complement of faculties and categories of understanding we possess as a species by which to do so, the rational, volitional, sensory, moral, emotional, aesthetic, imaginative, inspirational and epiphanic and then the world speaks its meaning through the human mind. But the world in which modern man lived was becoming as impersonal as the world of his science earth bound and materialistic with no sense of ultimate purpose that threatens the very essence of our humanity and a failure to take seriously the looming threat that hangs over the world with global warming, because how can we take global warming seriously if we don't take life seriously and know that civilisation in in the balance. Civilisation can only be saved if we think it is worth saving and making sacrifices to achieve it, but life is so much taken for granted with its origin and significance of no real consequence so that its purpose and meaning of it all is trivialised and demeaned. How can something whose origin is an accident and its existence of no abiding relevance that makes it worth saving?

The writer is somewhat tired listening to those who never stop talking about how wonderful nature is with all its rich diversity of life, its ingenious designs and marvellous complexity of wonder working creativity but of so little worth, value or relevance in terms of cause or consequence and above all no one to thank, a thoughtless generation with an all-consuming arrogance as to reduce their creator to the order producing sum of nothing. Those who take life for granted are destined to lose it and will never do enough to save it in the face in looming disaster. But as Edward Hundert points out that a true understanding of the life world with its different attributes of being makes for a: "for a richer, deeper understanding of the verities of the human experience." (Hundert 1990, p.131) While Kuhnian philosophy of science has shown that there can be no sharp line of demarcation between scientific and other forms of rationality. (J. Wentzel van Huyssteen, 1997, p.164) In fact, the foundations of science do nor rest on empirically based foundations as some suppose, but on a holistic philosophical of life where reason rules and where being supplies the necessary ontological motivation to do science and to use it for the good of mankind. Reason within a causal vacuum or separated from out intrinsic humanity is a most dangerous and deceitful thing.

Science empirically speaking: "tell us little to nothing about our experience of subjectivity, about the astonishing emergence of personhood, and about why we have an intelligible universe. God is the name that we give to the best available evidence for all that is." As life and all that it involves represents of subjective reality of being that regulates out thinking and behaving as human beings in world, not least of which is the attribute of reason, we must therefore, if we want to get a holistic philosophy of life, objectivise ourselves as that ordered integrated complexity of life we represent as human beings and use all our faculties of being if we are to get a true and authentic science of life. All else is just a shallow patted rationalism operating in a vacuum that gets us precisely nowhere but going round in circles within a vacuum of mindless emptiness. To realise that modern science's mechanistic and materialise conception of reality is not only limited but fundamentally flawed and fails to face up to larger challenge of life as being reveals it to be. As Heidegger at the end if his life could exclaim "Only God can save us", because, no doubt, he can inspire within us that which make's life worth saving.

Jim Baggott may well argue that it is the "horse of science that pulls the cart of philosophy." But it is rather the other way round, because it is the horse of being that drives the cart of reason and determines that we reason about in the act of living and way of behaving making reason the servant of being not the master of being or that which constitutes who we are as human beings operating existentially in a physical world. So no matter how ordered and complex things scientists prove different things to be for some at least the origin never gets beyond nothing so the horse of science proves to be a very poor horse indeed and more like a blind man flogging a dead horse. And as we have seen J.I. Austin warned against over simplification in which one might be tempted to call the occupational disease of philosophers if it were not their occupation. So in the end life in all its ordered complexity and ontological fullness as the most sublime and stupendous reality in the universe is explained away into a causeless void of nothingness.

Putnam argues that: "Science is wonderful at destroying metaphysical answers but incapable of providing substitute ones, science takes away foundations without providing a replacement. Whether we want it to be there or not, science has put us in this position." (Cited in Dennett 1996, p.181) But the truth is that science does nothing of the sort because science itself is a metaphysical research programme investigating different things that prove to be ever more complex than anyone ever imagined, and within different categories of understanding which constitutes who we are and that which we reason about within the context of the life world. Empirically based science can lead to the problem in which scientists fails or to take account of themselves in the act of knowing and understanding!

While Hegel has referred to *The Phenomenology of Spirit* that takes us to the centre and soul of our existence as human beings and it is within this world of conscious being that life is lived, science is carried out, decisions are made and conclusions are drawn. We cannot get closer to the truth than '*who*' we experience ourselves to be the essential essence of which logically and ontologically demands and a living life producing explanation by way of sufficient cause.

Steven Pinker tries to explain away the significance of consciousness and refuses to accept that it is a totally different reality to that of corporeal substance in the following way: "Consciousness was like a storm raging in the brain," and that: "The intuitive feeling that we have an intuitive 'I' that sits in the control room of our brain, scanning the screens of the senses and pushing the buttons of our muscles is but an illusion. These events compete for attention" argues Pinker and, "as one process outshoots the others, the brain rationalises the outcome after the fact and concocts the impression that a single self was in charge all along" and made the decision for us but giving us the impression that it was us who made the decision, (Cited in Kaku 2014, p.35) It seems from this that the human brain is out to thoroughly deceive us by giving us the illusion that we are in control of our decisions when we really are not. This means that our decisions are a kind of an internal lottery game that has nothing to do with our own volition or conscious decisions as freethinking beings.

One wonders how this defence would stand up in a court of law if we were up for murder. "I really didn't do it your honour but my brain did it and then gave me the impression that I did it. In fact, your honour, my brain stitched me up by giving me and the court the impression that I committed the crime when my brain is like a lottery game that made the decision for me and only gave me the impression that it was me that committed the crime." If such an excuse were offered to a court of law it would not be to jail we would be going to but a lockup ward surrounded by medics in white coats. In fact, it is hard to believe that a scientist that wants to be taken seriously could even make such a claim and humbly consider for a moment that the brain is of such massive complexity and that consciousness so dimly understood and seriously consider that there was more going on within a working brain than we can presently understand. If this was in fact the case every criminal could use it as an effective defence against conviction and the world would be in a most horrible mess.

Moreover, if the brain makes a decision a split second before we were conscious of making the decision couldn't we immediately change that decision if it did not conform to our more informed and considered opinion. It is, however, quite remarkable that if the brain is making our decisions for us why they seem to systematically agree our more considered decision a moment later. There is obviously something wrong here that undermines the whole idea of free will and how the mind works in response to decisions made. It is possible that our own intrinsic nature of being is so primed and prepared to automatically make certain decisions about certain subject matter that the brain automatically fires as it is primed in this way to automatically do. And how do researchers know from within complex working of the brain which signal represent the information being presented to the brain for consideration and which signal is the response made to that information by the brain?

Sometimes the brain within a particular context can prejudge the question being asked before the whole question is fully formulated giving the impression that the answer was forthcoming before the question was fully formulated. However, the brain is such a massively delicate and intricate instrument of cognition and setting up the means to measure that delicate and intricate activity of the brain so massively complex we cannot be too cock sure that scientists have got it right. If it is not in accordance with experience and represents a contradiction in term the whole idea should be called into question. Anyway, the time lapse of about three hundred milliseconds represents exceedingly fine margins which we should not read too much into and if it was to be applied to criminal behaviour we could convict anyone and the world would be in one hell of a mess.

Panenberg argues that the concept of God remains a mere hypothesis and can never be finally justified by our experience of ourselves or the world. (Cited in Wentzel van Huyssteen (1997, p.65) However, who can say with any authority that the existence of the world in all its complexity, its colour light, beauty and life accommodating complexity is just some mighty cosmic accident? That the universe and its miraculous appearing and from which matter was formed that supplied basis chemicals from which all material things now consist is just nothing of any real significance, that the solar system in which the earth is so strategically placed and finely tuned to be life permitting and life sustaining habitat in just a massive coincidence, that the mindboggling complexity of life even in its most primitive form is so massively complex just fell into place by chance, that living things came to conscious life with manifold attributes of being by some freak accident that is proof in nothing, that the reason that is within us as part of that being demands of us that effects whatever they may be need to be explained in terms of a cause that is able to explain the ordered and living sum of them.

Moreover, we experience ourselves as those endowed with attributes of life defining substance and significance that call forth from within us a cause that can explain the ordered and living sum of these vital life-defining effects. And then we have attributes of being through which we can meaningfully relate both physically, mentally and emotionally with other living things and with that life generating cause from which we have come. So in the end we are connected to

231

that cause from which we have come, logically, physically and metaphysically as living beings to a living life producing cause which represents and generates a very special and meaningful relationship in its own right to those who are exercised thereby. As:

> Post-Kuhnian philosophy of science has shown us that there can be no sharp line of demarcation between scientific rationality and all other forms of rationality. In fact rationality in science relates to the reasonableness or a more basic kind of rationality that informs all goal-directed human action. In this sense one might have a richer theory of rationality that includes not only empirical adequacy but also compatibility with metaphysical or philosophical theories. (*Even one we would add that takes us into the of spirituality*) Parenthesis mine!
> [Cited in van Huyssteen 1997, p.164]

It seems to the writer that some people are in fact trying very hard not to believe in the existence of a wise creator. And in the final analysis the only alternative is that nothing brought into existence the ordered and living reality of all things which is no cause at all – and is in fact is a contradict in terms. We would argue that to close our minds to reason and ignore the evidence of being both of which we have evidence of a wise creator is very dangerous game for mortal man to play. If we were to suggest that something like a pencil sharpener, a radio or a motor car came into existence by chance we would be laughed to scorn and thought of as fools. A single basic and very primitive cell is more complex that a modern motor car, but it seems that there are none so blind as those who do not want to see.

Professor John Nash who was a mathematical genius who won the Nobel prize for his work in spite of the fact that he suffered a serious problem with schizophrenia in which he saw people that weren't there and entered into an involved and convoluted dialogue with these imaginary people that almost ruined his marriage and his work as a highly talented mathematician. Eventually with medication and the help of a patient and loving wife he was able to manage his problem and eventually realised that the people he was seeing were not real at all and learned to ignore them. At his award ceremony at which he received his Nobel Prize, he recounted how he had worked through many rational problems and mathematical equations and formulas in his life and drawn many different conclusions about many different things, but that the greatest thing he had learned was the equation of love, and looking to his wife in the audience he said "you are my reason, you are all my reasons."

He had discovered the greatest truth in the universe that emanates, not from the world of mathematics or the empirically based science important as these are in their own right, but it is from within our reality of being where the greatest pearls of truth are to be found. There is a sense in which we cannot always see the significance of the mind because it is preoccupied in the act of living. All reality has its origin within us and even our senses which are fed to a working mind to be sorted out in terms of an appropriate response. So what remains to be done is to give thanks to our creator who is the origin of love and gives us a sense of purpose to life and seek to connect with him and if we succeed we are made complete.

It is hard to play God when we are not him and in the end some are not willing to take anything on faith and invent their own cause in which they delight in playing devil's advocate in which everything is regarded as futile as it is meaningless and causally irrelevant and then ask for prove of that which to a rational mind is logically compelling and ontologically self-evident. Hegel believed that what we need is to develop a philosophical system which is a true ontology of being a science of the existence of man: "The study of living experience which he described as The Phenomenology of Spirit." (Cited in Hundert 1990, p.39)

Jerry Fodor argues: "To describe the mind, we need only describe the program, and leave details about the hardware out of the story." He goes on to add: "psychology will never be replaced by neuroscience," no doubt because neuroscience represents the working of a physical brain which cannot of itself explain all that we predicate of a living self-conscious mind and its qualitative attributes of being. (Cited in Papineau 2006, p.52) Scientists may talk a lot about a theory of everything, but we will never have a theory of everything until we include within that theory a comprehensive science of life by which and through which we know all we were made and meant to know as human beings.

As we have seen. Plato recognised the fact that truth did not merely lead in from without but out from within so that mind revealed within itself knowledge of its own nature which lifted the human person above sterility of a meaningless and mundane existence. It is only human beings endowed with this archetypical insight, he argued, who can see the ultimate significance of life and that their place within the world of things and delving into the essence of his own soul and the desires of his own heart could identify something spiritually sublime that reflected something of origin from which he had come and went on to endeavour to be one with it.

Like his mentor Socrates, Plato's whose attention was on the mind and soul, to moral virtue and intellectual integrity on which the world order was contracted and revealed in its most profoundest sense so that it was only natural for him to cultivate a relationship with this living source of all things. Thus knowledge of the divine was implicit in every soul but forgotten he argued, within the world temporal distractions and a mundane existence.

To try to better understand things of the mind and soul Isenberg has commented that the idea of parables could be used to help us understand spiritual nuances of understanding in contrast to empirically based things. Parables are earthly stories with deeper spiritual meaning and moral application that speak to the heart. So when Jesus was trying to enable his followers to grasp inner truths of the heart and spiritual nuances of understanding he used parables. A sower went forth to sow he taught, knowing full well that in the parable of the sower as told by Jesus the seed in question is not primarily referring to physical seeds we plant in the soil, but the seed of truth and grace as sown in the heart of a fertile mind looking for that which satisfies the essence of the soul in its quest for peace, purpose, hope and understanding what life is about.

Some of these seeds in question fall on stony ground of what was obviously a hard and unreceptive heart that is not amenable to the seed of truth and righteousness being taken up with the world of empirically based things which to them is the only truth worth knowing. Other seeds fall on shallow ground in which the seed of truth begins to grow but then withers and dies because it has no depth in itself becoming preoccupied with the world of time and sense and the things of a temporal and mundane significance. Other seed falls on thorny ground where the briars and thistles of earthly care and the deceitfulness of riches choke the word so it dies away without bearing the lasting fruit of truth and goodness that is pleasing to God and satisfying to the soul. But some seed falls on fertile soil of a humble and contrite heart and perseveres with determination in truth and goodness bringing forth fruit pleasing to God and satisfying of the true nature of the soul in its pursuit of righteousness and true knowledge of God.

An empirically based and a shallow unbelieving heart is very stony ground indeed with little fertile ground for truth of the knowledge of God to take root and bring forth fruit worthy of out station as human beings employing all its faculties of being by which to do so. To ignore this kind of inclusive epistemology, one being physiological and the other psychological one that relates to the body and the other that relates to things of the heart – the soul – in search of the true meaning and purpose to life as reflected in all that we have been ordered to be is a most dangerous philosophy of life. In this we end up in a meaningless world whose origin is attributed to luck, life that has no ultimate meaning or purpose, lives that are driven by a shallow hedonism, an environment that is increasingly mechanistic, atomised, soulless, existentially empty, and self-destructive running out of road and moving inexorably towards the end game of eventual annihilation or summary judgment.

Whether some like to acknowledge it or not the divine handiwork of creation itself now stood unveiled by science. Through science man had served to reveal God's greater glory, demonstrating the mathematical beauty and complex precision, the stupendous order reigning over the heavens and the Earth. The luminous perfection of the discoverers' of this new universe compelled their awe before the transcendent intelligence which needed to be attributed the Creator of such an awe-inspiring cosmos. Or was it all down to luck operating within a cosmic vacuum, but this answer has never really satisfied either in rational or cosmological terms and sounded more like fairy-tale physics to a rational mind in which the ineffable and multi-dimensional nature of the effects produced could not be attributed to no credible cause at all or to some crude course of cosmic blindness fumbling aimlessly in the universe. As Newton's insightful exclamation: "I think Thy thoughts after Thee Oh Lord."

As Edward Hundert argues that what we need is to move beyond objectivity and develop a holistic philosophy of life that pertains to the science of *the existence of man*, a study of *living experience* as the ground of all knowing. Or again as he puts it: "In terms of contemporary psychological jargon, a continuing core of self-consciousness is clearly required to distinguish one's self-boundaries and self-experiences from experiences coming from the external world." (Cited in Hundert 1990, p.19) We must be prepared to give up some of our neat analytical precision in exchange: "in exchange for a richer, deeper understanding of the verities of the human experience." (Hundert 1990, p.131)

A butterfly is a delicate and complex species that can soar into the sky and flutter gracefully in the wind having been transformed in a most incredibly ingenious way from being a caterpillar earth-bound and vulnerable, and even though it hasn't the faintest idea how this metamorphosis took place or how it came to be a butterfly this doesn't stop it being a butterfly in all its graceful beauty as a happy and fulfilled species. But some human beings seem unwilling to accept who they are as a species and refuse to make full use of their mental attributes of being where knowing is subsumed with the larger context of being that enables them to fly above the mundane world of empirical based reality to realise their full potential as human beings. As free beings God has given us the right to choose whether we enter into a relationship with him or not, as a forced relationship has no value or virtue. We have the rational basis to believe in God and the attributes of being by which to engage and know him but the choice is ours.

The butterfly uses its instincts and corresponding attributes of being to be what it was ordered to be and to fly as it was made and meant to fly. But alas, doubting and conceited human beings fearing to face up to the logic of their own existence with different desires and instincts intrinsic to that which makes them distinctly human balk at who they are and turn life into a purposeless charade reducible to a chanced upon arrangement of inanimate matter devoid of all meaning and empty of all purpose. The net result is that they do not fly as they were meant to fly within yet above the world of mundane physics and fail to realise heartfelt hopes and aspirations to which the human heart aspires and without which they become a bitter and disillusioned species.

There is indeed a high price to pay for those who like to play god but who are not Him. So some begin to deconstruct themselves according to their own finite understanding and what an appalling mess they make. They take nothing on faith and refuse to use all their attributes of being to know all that they were made to know and ordered to understand as a species. We are smarter than the butterfly but we are not God, and there are things we too must take on faith or spiritually die and ontologically self-destruct.

Daniel Dennett in his own inimitable fashion claims that: "Vitalism has been relegated to the trash heap of history. Unless you are prepared to declare that the world is flat." (Cited in Southwell 2013, p.91) But what would this make Dennett if he is devoid of the vital signs of life defining substance and significance and nothing more than material stuff of mere mundane insignificance and mindless irrelevance. And if this is the case from whence did he get the vivacity of spirit, determination of mind and rational capacity to write books on the origin of all things and with an infallible air of authority declare that God does not and cannot possibly exist? This sounds more like someone playing God who is not Him and making a fool out of themselves by thinking that they can be more vital and wiser than that cause from which they have come.

So as Kant believed, we must leave room for faith because we are not God and use our attributes of being by which to know Him as he can be known from within our own rich ontology of being. Some such people as those described above are those who would ban religion from schools when if nothing created the ordered sum of everything as an increasing number of theorists believe there would nothing of any real significance to teach in a world ultimate purposelessness. And if all that exists is reduced to empirically based reality there would be no one with the necessary vital signs to learn anything or respond intelligently to that which is being taught. So all schools should be closed because there is nothing of any vital substance or significance to teach so it is a matter of eat, drink and be merry for tomorrow we die.

And if the origin of life can be reduced to a mindless process of blind and blundering randomness wherein does life's special value and sacredness lie? When life is reduced to complex biological entities operating to complex physiological brains operating empirically in an empirically based world life loses its sense of sacredness and significance and begins to be treated as such. How can the sanctity of life be maintained when it is but a chanced upon arrangement of inanimate matter of no ultimate relevance that like everything else owes its origin to nothing? This is where the lubricous theory of nothingness lands us, namely in a world of chanced upon irrelevance of blind pitiless indifference.

It seems that, some who follow the logic of the survival of the fittest so rigorously they thought they could give nature a helping hand and do a bit of weeding out for themselves to build a better species and we now know where this led. This weeding out was applied to certain races, as well as those regarded as physically subnormal, psychologically weak, and those regarded as an inferior race, in kind or status. Frances Galton and cousin of Darwin coined the word *eugenics* as a policy of encouraging "good" human specimens to breed at the expense of those regarded as less worthy. Some suggested cash grants to encourage marriage and child production among the 'fit', and sterilising for those regarded as 'unfit'.

H.G. Wells could write about 'efficiency', referring to races that are not efficient will have to be kept under control by measures such as infanticide, abortion and suppression while races such as the black, the yellow races were regarded as inferior justifying their discrimination and repression because they argued that, "the way of Nature has always been to slay the hindmost." This made it easy for the German nation in their sense of ethnic superiority and social conceit to take this survival of the fittest mentality to its most logical and dangerous conclusion against the Jews who they regarded as an inferior race. However, this survival of the fittest mentality was accepted for a time in England, Japan, parts of Europe as well as in some states in America with one of its advocates in the Fabian Society, Sidney Webb, who warned of the national deterioration that would follow as a consequence of the presence in Great Britain of Irish Roman Catholics, the Poles, the Russian and German Jews.

The eugenics movement gained acceptance because evolutionists placed so much emphases on the empirical and material side of life and played down the spiritual and moral reality of conscious being that made every human being precious and sacred in their own right in spite of physical deformities, material differences or ethnic origins. The eugenics movement may well have lost it appeal, but the subtle and pernicious influence of it goes on beneath the surface eating away at the soul of our humanity, eroding our values, and robbing us of those vital attributes of being that make us distinctly human and life worth living.

So just as it was all right for cattle breeders to select the best stock to breed with and deselect the rest as unworthy of breeding so Francis Galton argued that: "Let us improve the stock of our species as we have improved that of others." (Cited in Ridley 1999, p.288) While Churchill seemed to momentarily fall for this dangerous way of thinking when he said in Parliament in 1911 that, "the multiplicity of the human race of the feeble-minded" was "a very terrible danger to our race."

Some like Hilaire Belloc and G.K. Chesterton who wrote against such shameful ideas, with Chesterton arguing that: "eugenicists had discovered how to combine hardening of the heart with softening of the head." (Cited in Ridley 1999, p.288) It was easy for those who questioned the reality and significance of the inner world of qualitative being and who placed so much emphasis on the empirically based and mundane side of life to think this way. Gareth Southwell seems right when he argues that: "The debate goes on, albeit in a one-sided way, but the continuing enigma of consciousness, for instance, which Dennett himself struggles with, suggests that the traditional scientific view still arguably fails to account for the very things that vitalism claims to explain: how material things can have purpose, consciousness and sentience." (Southwell 2013, p.91)

Rupert Sheldrake argues that: "What Dawkins does is to project on to the DNA molecules the purposive vital forces of vitalism, trying to squeeze the soul into chemical genes, which are thereby endowed with plans, purposes and intentions they cannot possibly have." (Sheldrake 2013, p.164)This is why Sheldrake goes on to describe Dawkins as: "a vitalist in molecular clothing," because he can't help using vitalist language such as that expressed in his selfish gene theory. But for some all that exists is proof of nothing and things that have their origin in nothing soon come to be regarded as worth nothing but a piece of causeless irrelevance. In all this, life becomes cheap because the living and sacred essence of the soul cannot be established in empirically based scientific terms. But why do we need to prove the existence of the soul when the life we are living constitutes the very essence of that soul which some say they haven't got and cannot find. The soul is not something we find lying around like a brick it is the living essence of who we are operating existentially and qualitatively in a physical world.

Some theorist like Thomas Nagel likes to boast that Darwin enables modern secular culture to heave a great collective sigh of relief, apparently by providing a way to eliminate purpose, meaning, and design from fundamental features of the world. But there is nothing here wherein to boast because if this is true there is no purpose to anything and all science is ultimately doing is producing an endless collection of facts about nothing. In this, scientists have done a great disservice to mankind because if life has no credible origin, has no worthy purpose and no inherent value and without any redeeming features of qualitative purpose and significance, what is the point of doing science. One would be better playing tiddly winks in concrete yard and then wondering why they are becoming so bored.

This is increasingly the world we live in, a world in which life is cheap and materially based, and when we hear of the increase of knife crime committed by young people they are really not destroying that which has a sacred living soul because the modern world has taught them that life is reducible to a chanced upon compendium of empirically based reality of no more significance than a physical entity. It is easier to dispense with life that is ultimately reducible to an accidental compilation of physics that came from nothing and ultimately means nothing. This is where the overpowering physicalism of empirically based science has landed us, and the only hope for humanity is that Nagel's understanding of Darwin was wrong and needs to be radically overhauled.

Shelling is surely right when he argues that fundamental elements of cognition which arise from within our own nature of being must be joined with verifiable facts about the natural world if we are to have a holistic philosophy of life. While Jan Swammerdam in the seventeenth century could write: "In anatomy of a louse you will find miracles heaped on miracles and will see the wisdom of God clearly manifested in a minute point." But Shelly in his Hymn to Apollo came closer to the truth in concluding that: "I am the eye with which the universe beholds itself and knows itself divine."

Chapter 12
Misleading Analogies That
Lead to Error and Confusion

Matt Ridley in his book *Genome* writes: "While some of these analogies might mislead, we are familiar with the kinds of techniques and technologies that Mother Nature employs to solve her problems and achieve her ingenious designs." (Ridley 1999, p.173) Well might Ridley suggest that some of his analogies might mislead because the description above has nothing to do with what he really believes about evolution and how it works to produce intelligent life on earth. As far as he is concerned there is no personage we can refer to as 'Mother Nature' operating to solve her problems to achieve her ingenious designs, no creative mind of any kind and no ingenious order producing cause in place to produce the ordered complexity of life on earth. So the above description of evolution by Ridley is nothing more than an elaborate fiction that enables Ridley to avoid the embarrassment of having to explain the coming into existence of massively complex and intelligently ordered living beings where no intelligent and sufficient cause exists.

But by referring to the order producing power of Mother Nature Ridley has set up his tent in creation territory where he has no right to be because he doesn't believe that Mother Nature has anything to do with an intelligently creative force operating within nature, but that living things came into existence by a process of natural selection without the need for any such creator or an intelligent and sufficient cause of any kind.

Then we are informed by Ridley that genes have: "found a way to delegate their ambitions, by building bodies capable not just of survival, but of intelligent behaviour." (Ridley 1999, p.27) But Ridley is playing with us, because he doesn't really believe that genes have ambitions or deliberately employing the necessary means to build bodies capable of survival and intelligent behaviour. But in the end Ridley is forced to come clean and asks: "How can a bunch of genes, each one a string of quaternary code, make an animal polygamous or monogamous?" Answer: "I do not have the foggiest idea, but that they can do so I have no doubt. Genes are recipes for both anatomy and behaviour." (Ridley 1999, p.37)

Then Ridley goes on to eventually spill the beans and concludes: "I wrote earlier that my genes built me and delegated responsibility to my brain. My genes did nothing of the sort. It all just happened." At last, the truth is out − it just happened so the just-happened theory meets the just–so story so that we are back to an elaborate form of fairy-tale physics in which life doesn't really need to be explained in terms of an intelligent and sufficient cause at all: "it just happened."

Ridley goes on to illustrate his theory of evolution by writing: "When a boulder runs down the hill and nearly crushes you it is less dangerous to subscribe it to a conspiracy theory that it was pushed by somebody than to assume that it was an accident." (Ridley 1999, p.310) In other words, we are getting to that point in which evolution is just a long series of accidents and nothing to do with Mother Mature and her ingenious laws and designs. So the bolder by which he illustrates the process evolution wasn't pushed, it just happened to roll down the evolutionary hill as it were and is ultimately attributed to no cause at all. And, moreover, this evolutionary accident happened over and over and over again rolling merrily down the evolutionary hill until intelligent life of many different kinds of ingenious varieties and designs appeared on the earth and that in ever-increasing degrees of ordered sophistication.

Moreover, according to Ridley to apportion the order producing ingenuity of evolution to an intelligent and sufficient cause is regarded as a nasty little conspiracy theory thought up by fools and charlatans who think that we need an intelligent and sufficient cause to produce intelligently life on earth. So that in the final analysis, according to Ridley: "the genome is the book that wrote itself", which means that we are back to a situation in which the origin of life on earth is apportioned to no intelligently constituted cause at all. The genome made up of 3.2 billion or so letters of life producing information is the book that wrote itself into existence, and did it by randomly moving amino acids about. So we are informed that a process of happy go lucky accidents managed to produce a veritable host of complex living things and that kept on increasing in complexity until the whole earth was full of living things so massively complex and intelligently ordered evolutionary theorists haven't worked it all out yet.

What then has happened to Mother Nature and her wonderful techniques and technologies operating to solve her problems and achieve her ingenious designs? It seems that she has died the death of a thousand cuts and has left us alone with nothing but an endless series of accidents to explain the coming into existence of massively complex living things increasing in complexity as they roll merrily along down the evolutionary hill by a veritable multitude of happy coincidences that have nothing to do with an intelligently constituted cause of any kind. This is just about as bad a fairy-tale story as was ever told that might fool a child but not an adult whose mind is developed to reason causally and think rationally.

The fact is that many people, even relatively well educated people, have been led to believe this ridiculous story and have trusted the so-called experts who tell them the truth about the origin of life on earth, but who long ago had forsaken the ground of rational thinking and have no credible explanation for the coming into existence of anything whether creature great or small. Some seem to have so thoroughly confused themselves they actually believe that a never-ending stream of cosmic accidents can explain the vast complexity of intelligent life on earth. It all started out with natural selection which is a theory that has never been explained, but could somehow defy the logic of rational thinking to bring into existence the vast complexity of intelligent life on earth where no intelligent order producing cause exists.

Evolutionists like Darwin wave tempted to believe that somehow life on earth was just tumbling into existence by means of blind randomness outside of an order producing cause of any kind, and just because they couldn't see any such order producing cause at work within evolution to explain it. But we now know that they were wrong and that the origin of life originated from mechanisms of intelligent order producing genius we now refer to as DNA and its working partner RNA, the origin of which has never been explained.

Ridley goes on to claim that: "A religious instinct may be no more than a by-product of an instinctive superstition to assume that all events, even thunderstorms, have wilful causes." (Ridley 1999, p.310) But thunderstorms do indeed have causes, and the one who set the world up to rain upon the earth from which thunder storms originate are a by-product of such storms. It is not superstition to believe that effects have causes, it is superstition to believe that life on earth and the earth itself is all due to a mindless process of blind dumb luck. An intelligent mind reflecting on the order and integrated complexity of all things can detect a plan of purposeful significance and profound order producing profundity operating on the earth and in the universe.

So to believe that massively complex and intelligently ordered living things have their origin in an intelligent and necessary cause is not superstition it is the result of hard-nosed rational thinking that demands of us that we explain the vast complexity of the ordered and integrated complexity of all things in terms of an intelligent and sufficient cause as opposed to believing that everything just tumbled into place by an endless stream of coincidences. The human mind itself being in all its fullness is itself an expression of nature's own being. "And it is only when the human mind actively brings forth from within itself the full powers of a disciplined imagination and saturates its empirical observation with an archetypal insight that a deeper reality of the world emerges. ... Then the world speaks its meaning through human consciousness." (Tarnas 1991, p. 434 & 435)

Ridley may rejoice in how Gregor Mendel who discovered something of how genes work to produce a wide variety of pea-plants, but conveniently failed to point out that it was not Mendel who invented, engineered or put in place the order producing genius of this information that produced these wonderfully engineered pea plants from the raw chemicals of the earth. Ridley goes on to argue that genes have: "found a way to delegate their ambitions, by building bodies capable not just of survival, but of intelligent behaviour as well." (Ridley 1999, p.27) But what ambitions are these? How could genes have ambitions, and they need an enormous amount of ordering before they came into existence to be an order producing means of immense order producing significance before they could produce the humble pea-plant? Genes are veritable factories of order producing efficiency the origin of which, outside of an intelligent and sufficient cause, has never been explained, or given the intelligent order producing credit they deserve. Therefore, Mendel had nothing to do with the origin of pea plants he only discovered what was there to be discovered in the form of a complex code of pea-plant producing information put in place by someone much wiser than Mendel or even Matt Ridley.

Ridley never explains the origin of these ingenious life producing genes but goes on to argue that with regards to life the egg came before the chicken. But then Ridley recognises a problem which he tries to explain away by writing: "Someone somewhere must be imposing a pattern of increasing detail upon the egg as it grows and develops. There must be a plan." But all the information must already exist within the egg to produce the chicken or there would be no chicken. So are we to invoke divine intervention that imposed such order producing detail into the egg to produce the ordered sum of the chicken? But just when Ridley is about to make a breakthrough in his thinking he fudges the whole issue and goes back to arguing that the order must be imposed from within the egg itself without explaining how the order producing information got into the egg to produce the chicken which means that he has explained precisely nothing, taking us back to the 'just happened' theory that produced the ordered sum of the chicken every other living thing.

So who or what is imputing all this order producing detail into the egg? Is it divine intervention, is it magic, is it a miracle, is it a mystery, or is it an illusion? But of course for Ridley as it is for other evolutionists it is none of these things because wonder of all wonders and mystery of all mysteries – nothing did it. Ridley can neither explain the order producing information within the egg to produce the chicken or how the chicken came into existence before the egg existed. Then he argues that: "The reason for this confusion is that the genome is the book that wrote itself, continually adding, deleting and amending over four billions of years." (Ridley 1999, p.123) Well praise the good Lord and shout hallelujah because that would be some trick that no one but good Lord himself could perform. But back in the real world and without divine intervention it is perfectly obvious that nothing could write itself into existence before it existed and adding and deleting by means of blind randomness would never produce the ordered complexity of anything.

Thus we have an enormous black hole of mindless irrationality that lies at the very heart of the classical theory of evolution and theorists getting paid for writing gobbledegook and calling it science. As Gerard Schroeder points out: "We are the universe come to life," so that we are again confronted with a life producing creativity operating on the earth an all-encompassing wisdom that pervades the universe. So that God is what mind becomes when all that exists passes beyond the scale of our human comprehension.

Then we are informed by Ridley that: "Mutation is random but selection is not." (Ridley 1999, p.237) But one doesn't need to be an Einstein to realise that if mutations are random we are never going to have anything of any ordered significance to select. Ridley boldly quotes from Richard Dawkins in defence of his theory when he argues that we are survival machines – robots blindly programmed to preserve the selfish molecules known as genes. But anyone with their thinking cap on realise "blindly programmed" is a contradiction in terms. A process that is programmed to produce intelligently living things is something that is achieved by blindly moving what was originally in a state of primordial disorder. Blindly shuffling molecules about is never going to produce the ordered complexity of anything should we shuffle thus so for evermore. It seems to the writer that this kind of thinking is not looking for the truth as it really is but truth as they would like it to be. Confuse the situation enough with fancy words, elaborate verbiage and fine sounding theories and people will believe anything.

It is true that Ridley advances ideas that are helpful for us to understand how adverse circumstances the chemistry of the body operates to produce depression and to even shorten life and so on, but the origin of these complex reactions go unexplained as to how chemicals can produce such reactions that affect the mind in the way they do. In the end, Ridley doesn't really know whether the chicken produced the egg or the egg produced the chicken or which came first, but in the end neither is explained.

Ridley goes on to declare that there is no such thing as free-will which he regards as a necessary fiction, but it is a fiction all the same and that whatever way we act no matter how evil or reprehensible we are but acting in character, merely expressing the many determinisms that made us who we are. (Ridley, 1999, p.309) But this pre-supposes that we as human beings in normal circumstances have no part to play in what we become or what we do, and are forever fixed with no choice in the matter and we will act in accordance to what our antecedence has made us to be for good or ill.

Certainly if a child's upbringing is seriously deficient and abuse is taking place a child will be adversely affected, but this doesn't mean that in normal circumstances human beings have no choice in what they do or what they become. In normal circumstances, human beings have a conscience that guides us in our behaviour and has the capacity to understand moral concepts and the differences between good and evil. We can't, for instances, teach a lion not to kill because such runs against its very nature of what it is as a lion, but we as human being are wired up to be moral beings and to know, or learn to know, the difference between what is acceptable behaviour and what is not, together with a conscience to challenge and correct us.

According to Ridley therefore, Hitler who was a Fascist and a mass murderer was only doing what came naturally to him according to his own antecedence and was not therefore responsible for his actions as a mass murderer.

So if Hitler had survived the Second World War we would merely give him a slap on the wrist because he was only acting out what he became because of the many different events that made him what he became. And if this is the case, what right has one section of the community to impose their will on another if each and all are merely acting out who they are or who they became and have no real choice in the matter? (Ridley 1999, Cp.22–23)

Moreover, what is going to happen when everyone who commits a crime no matter how hideous or evil discovers that there is no such thing as free will and everyone is only acting in character no matter how evil the act or shameful the crime? Such a philosophy of life gives every scoundrel, crook and villain a cover for their crimes and us no basis to condemn those who have no free will and therefore cannot be held morally accountable for their actions. Empirically based scientists have great difficulty incorporating qualitative attributes of moral being into a physical brain because qualitative attributes of being cannot be identified, explained or verified in empirically based scientific terms. We don't know how the brain can generate moral being but moral beings we are, and the only exception to this is feral children, brain damaged people or seriously abused children whose mind has been detrimentally affected and psychologically damaged they have not acquired a moral conscience.

We have no way of explaining how moral concepts are produced by all that we understand the working of a physical brain to be the difference is so stark and profound and every reason to believe that there is more going on within our own brains than the complex working of the a physical brain no matter how complex or neurologically sophisticated and that there is another dimension to our existence, a spiritual dimension that is ontologically rich, qualitatively profound and existentially exciting, and morally challenging. Bryan Magee agreeing with Kant argues that there is: "a part of reality that is not of the empirical world is rationally demonstrable, and is therefore known by us with certainty." (Magee 2000, p.195) This is the case because we are the living proof of this onto ourselves. Heidegger also points out that: "An understanding of Being is already included in conceiving anything which one apprehends as an entity," and this applies: "Whenever one cognises anything or makes an insertion, whenever one comports oneself towards entities, even towards oneself." (Heidegger 1962, p.22)

In other words, we know perfectly well who we are as conscious beings actively and consciously operating in the world of physics even though we cannot understand its origin in precise technical terms or how a physical brain can produce a qualitative state of being, something precious and sacred it cannot be expressed in empirically based terms no matter how complex we conceive a physical brain to be. We would suggest that Darwin's wife was making a legitimate point when writing to her husband urging him not to be too much influenced by: "things which cannot be proved in the same way, and which if true are likely to be above our comprehension." (Spencer 2009, p.39) This seems a timely and appropriate observation because our inner reality of being cannot be identified or verified in the same way as empirically based things and must be taken on faith or we ontologically self-destruct and existentially die.

And so it proved with Darwin, there was something about the origin of life he didn't understand, a God-like gene machine operating on the earth beyond the naked eye to see operating effectively to bring into being intelligent life on earth. An order producing blueprint comprising of some 3.2 billion letters of how bring into being a single human into being. So Darwin was wrong and his wife was right, she had the wit to be faithful to reason in which effects must be explained in terms of sufficient cause, but sometimes these causes in an extremely complex world go beyond the finite understanding of the human mind to comprehend and so a modicum of faith and little humility is called for which proved to be right in the case of Darwin's wife when in 1962 Crick and Watson discovered DNA the secret behind the origin of all life on earth biologically speaking at least.

Robert Audi rightly observes that: "The most crucial kind of knowledge is not about our bodies but about our minds." (Audi 1999, p.74) Otherwise, we become what Kant referred to as a: "plaster-cast of a man", all matter and no mind, all physics and no soul, an empty vessel full of its own emptiness on its way from nothing to nowhere. Heidegger argues that the: "Question of Being" has been "forgotten" when being is not close to us, even that which is closest: we are it, each of us – we ourselves. And yet while the means of its appearing within us is a mystery to us, the essence of it is self-evidently transcendent as is the author of it. But there is a universal tendency to take it all for granted, and in fact there is a: "dogma has been developed which not only declares the question about the meaning of Being to be superfluous, but sanctions its complete neglect." (Heidegger 1962, p.2)

While Colin McGinn suggests that: "The existence of animal life seems like an eruption from nowhere until we understand the process of evolution by natural selection." (McGinn 2002, p.209) But this really doesn't explain anything because it begs the question as to what kind of a process evolution by natural selection really is that it could bring into existence the vast biological complexity of a biological body and then infuse a biological brain with the qualitative reality of conscious being complete with different categories of understanding to which is attached are different feelings that binds us in different ways to those various things perceived. Even the brain which is the vast control centre of our thinking handles all this information is a wonder of organised complexity in itself. The late Stephen Hawking indicates that: "The odds against a universe like ours emerging out of something like the big bang are enormous ... I think clearly there are religious implications whenever you start to discuss the origins of the universe. But I think most scientists prefer to shy away from the religious side of things." (Cited in Boslough 1992, p.55)

But why should scientists shy away from that which is so logically compelling and crucial to our understanding of the origin and meaning of life on earth? But for some God as a prime mover is not allowed to get a foot in the door least they might be answerable to Him as moral beings. Again it has been naively alleged by scientists that God is not a testable hypothesis, supposedly because they cannot get him into a Petrie dish to be examined under a microscope. But of course the idea of God is a testable hypothesis, because all that exists needs to be explained, and when that which represents that which we cannot deny but extends beyond our own finite minds to fully understand and explain God as a wise creator comes logically and forcibly into play the one that produces that which we cannot deny but goes beyond own ability as human beings to fully understand or explain. Our intelligence points to an infinity of wisdom indicative of and synonymous with the idea of a wise creator.

We might fly in a jet airliner that takes us to our desired destination without understanding all that is needed to order it into existence and keep it in the air, but if we didn't believe that someone has it all worked and knows how to produce such a flying machine as an effective mode of transport we would never travel in one or trust ourselves to such a thing. The universe and the world we live in is something the same, we accept that there is an order producing intelligence operating in the universe beyond our own finite ability to fully understand, but we should accept that our maker has given sufficient reason to trust Him in the ineffable complexity of all that exists and to land us safely in that place he has postulated to our consciences to be our final destination, at least for those who remain faithful to Him.

Einstein aptly remarked that: "what we know is little what do not know is vast" so that all that exists goes beyond our finite mind to fully understand into an infinity of wisdom before our finite eyes. The fact is that the idea of God has been part of the human psyche from time immemorial and as Giambattista Vicoa seventeenth-century philosopher argued that there has always been beliefs shared in common by all peoples, namely belief in providence, the existence of an immortal soul, and the recognition of the need to regulate and keep under control human passions. (Cited in Watson 2005, p.827)

Richard Dawkins may argue that: "We can give up belief in God while not losing touch with a treasured heritage." But what kind of a treasured heritage is it to believe that nothing produced the ordered sum of everything, that hopes of immortality so passionately held nothing but false hope an idle fancy, life regarded as so very sacred dumped into the earth to be forever forgotten, a creator who brought us to life but who had no ultimate purpose for us, attachment to loved ones and longing to be reunited forever with them mocked and betrayed, death the ultimate victor and all else figments of a deluded imagination. There is no treasured heritage here, but Dawkins is not God for he would make a very poor god, even no God at all who cannot even give a credible explanation for his own existence and certainly not for the existence of intelligent life on earth. At the end of his book *The God Delusion* Dawkins writes: "… I am thrilled to be alive at a time when humanity is pushing against the limits of understanding. Even better, we may eventually discover that there are no limits." This seems like a good argument for the existence of God, but it seems that Dawkins is so busy playing God he has failed to even consider the fact that he is not Him. (Dawkins 2007, p.387 & 420) John Heil asks: "How then could we seriously entertain the hypothesis that conscious agents are nothing more than congeries of material objects, conscious experiences nothing more than manifestations of complex material dispositions?" (Heil 1998, p.207)

While Matthew Alper trying to assess the truth about spiritual experiences within the context of belief in God goes into all manner of mystical experiences, ecstatic states of the mind, near death experiences, drug induced states of mind, speaking in tongues, and religious extremes of different kinds he is setting up straw men and shooting them down and thinking how good a God-destroying marksman he is. Spiritual experience and belief in God as a wise creator goes far deeper than such experiences described by Alper above, and are more psychologically profound, rationally compelling and experientially real than these extreme manifestations of different spiritual states which merely lie at the more extreme and superficial end of religious experience.

Dawkins talks about learning what our selfish genes are up to so that we might have a chance to upset their selfish plans and designs and learn to be unselfish, generous towards the common good. But if genes have produced us both body and mind how could we act in a way that contradicts that which these selfish genes have created us to be? Bryan Magee whom we respect as a scientist, in his book *The Confessions of a Philosopher,* admits that there is nothing he wants more to believe than that he has an immortal soul and the prospect of annihilation terrified him. But that which created him must have created within him these heart-felt hopes and fears, but in spite of the fact that he so passionately holds them this he doesn't seem to act upon them or use the appropriate means to expedite his hopes and remove his fears. He rather seems to prevaricate and begins to question himself, arguing that such ideas could just be what he wants to believe and have nothing to do with truth. But alas poor Bryan, has the longings of our own heart nothing to do with the truth of who he is as a human being? Does who we are and how we think nothing to do with who we are as human beings and that which we have been created to be with different needs, heart-felt hopes, and aspirations nothing to do with the truth of who we are have been created to be as a human being?

Birds build nests, sit on the branch of a tree and sing their happy song at the joy of being alive, and some fly to different countries in the winter to find a better environment in which to live, they do not argue within themselves or with each-other about their existence or why they are the way they are, they follow their instincts and aspirations and behold it works and as a result they are a happy and fulfilled species. But some human beings will take nothing on faith and think they know better than their creator and so begin to deny who they are and repudiate those attributes of being that make them distinctively human. Are we as human beings proof of nothing, and refuse to follow our own inborn instincts to where they naturally lead, or are we so wise in our own conceit we take nothing on faith no matter how logically compelling or experientially desirable it might be?

A bulldozer doesn't know that it owes its existence to an intelligent bulldozer producing manufacturer to be an effective functioning bulldozer, but we as rational beings do because we know as rational beings that a bulldozer needs to be explained in terms of an intelligent bulldozer producing cause and could not possibly fall into place by shuffling the iron ore particles about. Does a monkey have to know how it was ordered intelligently into existence to be an effective functioning monkey? The answer is obvious. We as rational beings have been let into the secret of the origin of life in that we know as surely as reason can teach it to us that monkeys as complex living entities need to be explained in terms of an intelligent monkey producing cause just as bulldozers need to be explained by an intelligent bulldozer producing cause behind which there is a bulldozer producing mind.

The same applies to ourselves, and if we refuse to accept the idea of a wise creator because we cannot understand all that our creator is we are treading on very thin ice and rising above their station as finite beings who must take their position as creature before our creator and know that a measure of faith is called for and that he who by means of an intelligent mind has created us can fulfil all that he has put in our heats to hope for and aspire to be as human beings. In fact, trying to explain all that exists outside of an intelligent and sufficient cause proves exceedingly more difficult than explaining all that exists in terms of an intelligent and sufficient cause in the form of a wise creator.

The philosopher Nigel Warburton believes he is being ever so logical when he argues that: "If the series of effects and causes is going to stop somewhere, why must it stop at God? Why couldn't it stop earlier in regression, with the appearance of the universe itself?" (Warburton 1999, p.18) But this would leave the universe and everything in it hanging from one God-almighty skyhook. So it seems that Warburton wants to back-pedal into an ideological backwater of causal insignificance and refuse to trace the order producing current of life producing creativity back to the source from which it flows. But repudiating the idea of a wise creator solves absolutely nothing and lands us with an even greater problem of having to explain how an intelligently ordered world full of intelligently ordered beings and things came into existence outside of an intelligent and sufficient cause of any kind which seems more irksome and causally ridiculous than the idea of a wise creator who to whom they owe everything.

What do theorists like Warburton put in place of an intelligent and sufficient cause to explain a world full of intelligently ordered things which go beyond his finite ability as a human being to fully understand? Why absolutely nothing which is a cowardly ideological cop-out this is. But such would rather risk being accused of being unreasonable and irrational than facing up to the logic of sufficient cause in the form of a wise creator who as moral beings they would be ultimately accountable. Intelligently ordered things cannot be explained away by an infinite regression of reductive absurdity until the cause becomes nothing.

Thus Huxley writes: "For myself as no doubt most of my contemporaries, the philosophy of meaninglessness was essentially an instrument for liberation … and liberation from a certain system of morality." (Huxley 1937, p.269–273) Here we are getting to the root of the problem for some at least, in which antagonism to the idea of a wise creator is motivated by the desire to be free from obligation to a wise creator to whom if he existed we would be ultimately accountable as moral beings. Thus, all evidence of God's existence is suppressed and vigorously denied and the weakness of this argument is that reason has to be turned on its head to make it work leaving such theorists with no means to explain the ordered sum of anything let alone their own existence.

Michael Brooks in The New Scientist Publication *Chance* quotes Clare Wilson who tries to explain evolution in the following way: "Earth, several million years ago: a cosmic ray from space blasts into the atmosphere at close to the speed of light. It collides with an oxygen atom, generating a shower of energetic particles, one of which knocks into a DNA within a living creature. The DNA molecule happens to reside in a developing egg within the ape-like animal living in Africa. The DNA is altered by the collision causing it to change or mutate and which the resulting offspring is slightly different from its mother." (Cited in Chance 2015, p.43)

The odds against such a thing happening by such freak accident as that described above is so utterly absurd it puts the idea into the category of farce. We are back to fairy-tale physics again and such an unlikely event would have to occur a veritable multitude of times before we have the simplest living thing let alone an ape-like creature already in existence as that described above. And then we have to explain how the ape-like creature evolved into a human being by such a bazaar and unconvincing sequence of events. The idea that such an event could take place within the delicate balance of interacting variables going on within the microscopic workings of DNA is utterly unconvincing and we haven't explained the origin of the DNA that produced the ape-like creature which is already in existence. It is something akin to supposing that an explosion taking place in a printing factory could produce a well-written book, and then by subsequent explosions could make intelligent updates to the book until we have something like Encyclopaedia Britannica. Such descriptions show signs of desperation issuing from the workings of a deranged mind. It is little wonder that one writer concedes: "Everyone agrees that evolution occurs, but nobody understands how it works."

There are big problems with the standard theory of evolution and more scientists are admitting it: "while other scientists do not openly advertise the big problems with evolution, correctly assuming that creationists will use them for political advantage." (Cited in Witham 2002, p.8) Therefore, there is nothing simple under the sun that doesn't need to be explained in terms of an intelligent and sufficient cause. As we have seen: "It stretches even the credulity of a materialistic fanatic to believe that proteins (the stuff of life) and nucleotides (DNA and RNA the means by which living became increasingly complex) emerged simultaneously, and at the same point in space, from primeval soup." We know that adds Silver: "There are no systems more ordered than living cells and their components." (Silver1998, p.347 and 351) So here we have thousands upon thousands of scientists operating at many different avenues of scientific research and increasingly discovering how unutterable complex and intelligently ordered life really is and heaping great praise on those who make new discoveries about such things and then insist that the existence of all these things and much more has nothing to do with a process of intelligent ordering or the working of a wise creator.

We know of those who want something for nothing, but it seems there are those who want everything for nothing because they are determined not to be beholding to anyone most of all to a wise creator to whom they owe everything. As the saying goes, he who takes away reason to make way for a new revelation is destined to end up in error and confusion. So just like some of the Greek philosophers of old who as writers were wholly justified in believing that a transcendent mind was the source of cosmic order and that there was a rational teleology which lay as the basis of the universe's existence.

Chapter13
A General Overview of Two
Opposing Worldviews

The brain is generally been regarded as a unique physical organ of the body because as a physical organ it seems to pass over from performing a physical function to producing a metaphysical state of conscious being with different attributes of understanding. But as we have already indicated, how a qualitative reality of conscious being that constitutes that reality I experience as me emanates from the working of a physical brain is simply not understood. In fact the mind seems to be a qualitatively rich and ontologically profound body of being that is precious, sacred, ineffable and sublime and with many different categories of understanding inculcated into it. It could be said that within the conscious reality of our mind and being we are already in contact with our creator but some can't see it and some don't want to see it. Life is precious and our loved ones are precious to us and when a member of our family dies we mourn, and if murdered we are angry and want justice.

Is it too much to ask that we consider that life is no accident and that it is a veritable miracle life defining wonder that takes us on the journey of life and that as the greatest gift in the known universe. That we should consider saying thank-you for this gift to the one from whence it came and start a conversation with them within the bounds of our own understanding so just as a relationship with another human being is, or can become, precious with deep feelings of attachment so it is with the one who endowed us with this world of being the relationship can be felt as no other can be felt as being relates to being and in this the circle of life is compete in ever increasing degrees of experiential enlargement, confidence and intimacy. What keeps this from happening is not lack of evidence, but man playing God and who wants no one to interfere with their lives or disrupt their plans whatever they are being sovereign over their own destiny – or so they think. To be answerable to no one and too proud to bow their head in an arrogant gesture of defiance taking it all for granted.

So life is reduced to a physical organ we call the brain that just fell into place by some series of freak accidents beyond our comprehension that really mean nothing in terms of cause and less in terms in terms of purpose. But to a discerning mind this must be a huge risk because the cards are all stacked against them, rationally, biologically, morally and existentially. Just as the living is more than food and the body more than clothes so life in more than nothing.

The idea that there is a distinction between a working brain and living self-conscious mind can be seen in the fact that Identical twins are made from the same DNA information, yet from the day they are born throughout their lives until the day they die they are two autonomous self-conscious individuals living separate and independent lives. As Professor Susan Greenfield writes: "Identical twins will also show signs of distinct perceptions and thoughts that make it clear they are individuals with their own private consciousness, even though their genetic make-up is exactly the same. If individuality is not accountable by genes, it must, at least in part, be due to some other factor in the brain that is not shared even by descendants of the same egg." (Greenfield 1997, p.122) Therefore, what is happening when two distinct self-conscious beings originate from the exact same genetic information? Identical twins are in all essential aspects physically identical, but in terms of conscious being they are wholly distinct and autonomous human beings living their own independent lives. If life is explained in terms of the information within the genome, how is it that while identical twins the product of the same genetic information are two wholly distinct human beings in terms of being and personal identity?

This means there is a missing dimension to life that takes us beyond the working of a physical brain, a mystery, some might call it a divine spark, that lifts life into a different dimension of profound spiritual reality of a self-conscious reality of being beyond all that we define and understand a physical brain to be. Something ineffably rich, qualitatively profound, something that we regard as sacred, something that is quintessentially us, something, or more appropriately, someone, who mourns for when a friend or member our family die, different cords of love and affection that bind us to friends and family that does not equate with all we understand a physical brain to be, a sense of moral being that sets standards by which we live by and feel obliged to punish those who don't conform. We have feelings, instincts, passions and different hopes, at least for those who are willing to admit it for immortality. We are more like embodied spirits than biological constructions physically moving through the world by means of our empirically based senses.

We cannot deny who we experience ourselves to be without committing a form of ontological suicide, and there is nothing we are more certain of that who we experience ourselves to be and that there is a dimension to life that takes us beyond all we understand a physical brain to be. As we have seen, Moheb Costandi affirms that: "And yet, despite centuries of speculation by philosophers and, more recently, neuroscientists, we still have little idea of what consciousness actually is, or how the brain generates it." (Costandi 2013, p.76) As has been rightly observed, if you were to blow the brain to the size of a mill, or even for that matter the size a city, and walk around inside you would find anything resembling who you experience yourself to be, me.

So there is something essentially missing when we equate life as we experience it to be with the working of a physical brain, and interacting in conjunction with the brain in a most profound and psycho-dynamic dimension of reality lifting life into a dimension of spiritual reality of being operating through and interacting with a physical brain in ways we simply do not understand. This would imply that this reality of being is operating through the physical brain to execute its will in the world and operating to many different categories of understanding by which to do so and activating the body to respond in different ways to different things perceived. Who is it who falls in love with another human being, goes on to marry them and live with them hopefully for the rest of their lives.

When doctors try to treat people in different ways for various mental problems they are not doing so to fix a biological problem, they are doing so help a living person. The writer will speculate that, just like the monumental discovery of DNA by Crick and Watson in 1962 marking a giant breakthrough in our understanding the origin of the biological complexity of life on earth, scientists will one day discover that which explains the difference between a working brain and a living self-conscious mind different in form and substance to all that we presently understand a physical brain to be no matter how biologically complex it might be. Unless, of course, the good Lord doesn't want it to be and insists that we take life in all its ontological fullness on faith and expects us to act accordingly as the profound and serious substance of subject matter demands.

It is obvious that we are born as free spirits endowed with different attributes of being, or to put it another way, existential potentials which are honed and developed by upbringing and education and experience. Each species operates to its own nature of being and existential potential, and so we cannot teach a lion to do maths or not to kill other animals and its brain is the means whereby it activates its biological body to hunt its prey without having a conscience about it. So each species has its own nature of being and mental potential operating dynamically with, or in conjunction with, the working of a physical brain to execute their will in the world. We would remind the reader that theorists, and more particularly brain specialists, admit that consciousness is still a mystery and: "In spite of centuries of speculation by philosophers, and more recently, neuroscientists, we still have little idea of what consciousness actually is, or how the brain generates it." And moreover, Moheb Costandi affirms: "Some believe that gaining a better understanding of how the brain works will provide answers to life big questions. It will not: brain research cannot tell us everything about ourselves, or what it is to be human." (Costandi 2013, intro & p.p156) Ben Dupre writes:

> We are all immediately conscious of our consciousness – that we have thoughts, feelings, desires, that are subjective and private to us, that we are actors at the centre of our world and have a unique and personal perspective on it. … So how can something as strange as consciousness conceivably exist in a physical world that is being exposed by science? How are mental phenomena explicable in terms of, or otherwise related to, physical states and events in the body? These questions together form the mind-body problem, arguable the thorniest of all philosophical issues. … For there is one thing – at once the most obvious and most mysterious thing of all – that has so far resisted the best efforts of scientist and philosopher alike (to solve): the human mind. [Dupre 2007, p.28]

Pinker holds to a computational model of the mind which he thinks is confirmed by artificial intelligence. But artificial intelligence in not a conscious entity with sentience, conscience, moral approbation, feelings of different kinds, hopes and qualitative attributes of being even though it might be wired up to use words that as if it did. One might kick a life-like robot on one its artificial legs and it could be wired up to make as artificial response by way of protest, but it feels nothing and is a machine with a complex motherboard and an integrate arrangement of wires programmed to perform different physical manoeuvres. The mind is what the brain does he argues, but a conscious mind is very different from all we understand a physical brain to be and science proves and we know it by experience.

Moreover, computers need to be explained in terms of an intelligent and sufficient cause so who or what ordered us as complex living beings into existence in a universe absent of intelligence which question takes us back an intelligent and sufficient life producing cause. Pinker goes on to argue: "It is not a matter of honouring some ineffable distinction between organisms and physical systems, but of understanding what kinds of physical systems organisms, including human beings are." (Cited in Rose Alas Poor Darwin 2000, p.132) But this statement presupposes the very thing that needs to be explained, namely how complex physical systems so that matter no matter how complex or intricately arranged does not equate with all we experience ourselves to be as living entities of self-conscious reality of being with feelings and sentiments that make life sacred.

In a desperate attempt to avoid the idea of a wise creator some theorists have failed completely to come up with an intelligent and adequate explanation for intelligent life in earth and in this they have done a great disservice to mankind who are worthy of better and which leads a subtle form dehumanisation. Fraud for all his weakness discovered what the Scriptures had always taught, namely that in life we are confronted with a selfish self-centred pleasure seeking *id*, and a *Super-ego* that holds before us a higher life of goodness, virtue and moral purpose, and then we have personal sense of self called the *ego* seeking to mediate between these two extremes and how they, or more correctly we, do it determines our integrity or otherwise as human beings. Our maker wants us to do right for its own sake not because we are forced to do so, and to love him by our own volition not because we are bullied into it which would be a slave morality and an overpowering subjugation. So is this really what life is about and what we make of it determines our integrity as human beings, we can throw it away and live for the day or make something of ourselves worth preserving or throw it all away.

Pinker believes that if we make the physical brain complex enough as a physical organ that it will somehow transmute into a living self-conscious mind complete with qualitative attributes of being. As we have seen, Schrodinger a highly acclaimed scientist regards consciousness as distinct to the body and believes that: "From all we have learnt about the structure of living matter, we must be prepared to find it working in a manner that cannot be reduced to the ordinary laws of physics." (Schrodinger, 1956) Professor Brian Silver, talking about his youthful fears of death, found solace in the fact that as life is so profound and creation so inexplicable then anything is possible. Going on he writes, "… in the Slough of Despond I found hope": in the complete inexplicability of creation I asked John Dunne's question: "How can something appear out of nothing? For if that was possible, which it appeared to be, then anything was possible even life after death." (Silver 1997, p.463)

Bryan Magee talks about his fear of annihilation and longing for immortality but feels he cannot trust his desires and feelings as if they meant nothing in real terms. But he surely fails to realise that they come from a well of being intrinsic his existence as a human being, God's calling card we might say waiting for a reply of faith from him. Such thoughts hopes and desires do not come out of nowhere they come from the well of being deep within the human mind. While Noam Chomsky argues that we have an innate cognitive endowment by which we engage the world around us, to master language, to become culturally sophisticated, socially integrated and with hopes and aspirations that constitute who we are as human beings.

Socrates and Plato made peace with themselves by paying resolute attention to the mind and soul, a spiritual realm of being that constituted the life world which they believed was forever superior to the physical world within which one could discover their own essence and the worlds meaning. A world forever superior to knowledge of the world of empirically based things, a world of being much neglected according to Heidegger, but which doesn't need to be validated, defined or explained because everyone uses it continually and already understand what they mean by it, being there just like one's life, a rich ontology of being within which a richer and deeper reality of the world emerges where the human imagination itself becomes part of the world's intrinsic truth. Life is not just lived from the outside in, but from the inside out and meet within us to produce the ordered and integrated sum of the human experience.

As modern empirically science advanced in leaps and bounds revealing the ordered and integrated complexity of the physical world so that through science man was revealing God's greater glory in the wonders of creation in which everything was revealed in all its finely tuned precision revealing something of the stupendous order reigning over the universe which compelled a sense of wonder and awe-inspiring reverence. But within two centuries the tables were turned, God was not a testable hypothesis so could not be validated by science while the spiritual doctrines of religion did not sit well with the physical world of science so that God increasingly became an unnecessary and untestable hypothesis. With the theory of Darwinism and the fact the earth with the help of modern methods of looking more deeply at the solar system the Bible seemed to be wrong when it seemed to teach that it was the earth that revolved round the sun and not the sun round the earth. The universe was now a machine a self-regulating mechanism of force and physics. While metaphysics was unnecessary and outdated as religion and metaphysics continued to decline into relative obscurity.

But at the beginning of the twentieth century the classical laws of Newtonian cosmology began to break down under what became known as quantum mechanics in which the certainties of classical science were seriously undermined. Einstein declared: "All my attempts to adapt the theoretical foundations of physics to this new knowledge failed." Solid Newtonian atoms were now discovered to be largely empty, hard matter no longer constructed the fundamental substance of nature with matter and energy being interchangeable. Subatomic phenomenon displayed a somewhat ambiguous nature being both particles and waves. Scientific observation of the exceedingly small deep within the atom could not take place without affecting the nature of the reality under investigation. It is as if the scientist became part of the experiment in some mysterious way with the energy from the brain affecting the subject matter deep within the atom suggestive of the idea that there was a deep link between mind and matter. As Sir James Jeans suggested, the physical world was not so much a great machine as a great thought.

Could this mean that matter and mind are interlinked deep within the atom for the intervention of a thinking mind to have such an affect upon it when investigated so? A signal, as we humans now know, can carry information that can produce different affects depending on the how that information is processed by way of receptors and processors so that a telephone becomes a means of communication, and in the case of a television to produce live pictures on the screen as representations of life itself. So also the brain becomes alive with different attributes of being and understanding according to how it was wired up to do through the exceedingly complex working of the physical brain which takes that information turns it into life as we experience it to be. Thus matter thought to be hard unyielding metallic substance gave way to a more complex two-part process operation deep within the atom which somehow was related to the human brain.

Moreover, it became apparent that not only was there something more complex and involved going on within the wider context of the universe, a spooky action at a distance as it has been referred to be in which everything in the universe was interconnected by invisible threads – a spooky action at a distance as it has been described. Teleportation or entanglement which allows information to be communicated instantaneously no matter how far the particles are apart thus breaking Einstein's belief that nothing can travel faster than the speed of light. Both these facts reveals that there is more going on in the universe and deep within the atom than anyone had ever imagined which could have profound implications with respect to intelligent life on earth. As Joanne Baker writes with respect this whole new world of quantum physics: "The more we have learned, the stranger the quantum universe has become. Information can be 'entangled' between particles, raising the possibility that everything is connected by invisible threads. Quantum messages are transmitted and received instantaneously, breaking a taboo that no signal could travel faster than the speed of light. … Elementary particles pop in and out of existence and once-familiar substances like light seem impossible to pin down, behaving like waves on one day and a stream of bullets the next." (Baker 2013, p.3)

Some are willing to talk about Quantum cosmology: Quantum tunnelling, Quantum biology: "effects such as wave-particle duality, tunnelling and entanglement may play important roles in living organisms." (Baker 2013, p196) As Erwin Schrodinger argues: "From all we have learnt about the structure of living matter, we must be prepared to find it working in a manner that cannot be reduced to the ordinary laws of physics. … With its tangled network of neurons and synapses, the brain is one of the most complex systems known. No computer can match its processing power. Could quantum theory explain some of the brain's unique qualities?" (Baker 2013, p.199–200)

As quantum theory developed, a number of ways of creating consciousness has been proposed, from collapsing wave functions to entanglement, but we are still far from learning how this works. As Baker writes: "Speculation is rife about whether we might experience consciousness due to quantum tickling of the microscopic structures in the brain, collapsing wave functions or entanglement."

(Baker 2013, p.200) Scientists have found tiny proteins called microtubules which are found deep inside neurons of the brain which they believe might have something to do with consciousness but more experiments need to be carried out to test the theory. Whatever is going on it is apparent that the world of the exceedingly small is governed by quantum physics and the large by classical physics. Edwin Schrodinger one of the leading thinkers on Quantum physics believes that consciousness is separate from the body though related to it. This to the writer seems perfectly obvious.

But the fact remains, that conscious life needs to be explained by means capable of explaining it and if, as we now know. there is are communications going on in the universe that we previously did not think possible and even seem to be impossible to explain so it seems that there are things we must accept on faith even though we cannot explain them and we haven't explained life on earth until we can demonstrate that we have the means by way of sufficient cause to explain it. It is not reasonable to deny the power of an infinite Being just because we cannot comprehend their operations especially when they have given us so much evidence of their existence. It is as if the world fades out and ultimately eludes us in terms of its operation, but the heart of man is that sacred place where our maker has ordained for God and man to meet. Scientists are trying desperately to explain how a working brain is turned into a living self-conscious mind but so far have failed, but it would serve them better it they were to use it to the full so that they might know all they were meant to know and experience as a human being.

The present worldview argues that life is but a cosmic accident and our existence as human beings is reducible to the working of a physical brain that fell into place by chance and no ultimate purpose. This we would suggest is no basis for building a world of moral integrity and social responsible and that the world will reap a bitter harvest from such a philosophy of life. Some argue that teaching children to believe in God is tantamount to child abuse. But teaching our children that there is no meaning or purpose to life is child abuse and then wondering that they then live lives commensurate with such a vacuous and meaningless philosophy of life on a journey from nothing to nowhere. It is child abuse to encourage children not to use their intelligence to trace their origin, and the origin of all things, back to an intelligent and sufficient cause in the form of a wise creator without which we leave them in a world devoid of all meaning and bereft of all purpose, a God-forsaken world of 'blind pitiless indifference' as Dawkins calls it.

Some make excuses because of so much suffering and inequality in the world. But Voltaire, commenting on the Lisbon earthquake that killed so many people argued that: "Men do themselves more harm on their little molehill than nature does. More men are slaughtered in their wars than are swallowed up in earthquakes." So is suffering God's checkmate to mans' abiding arrogance and mans' inhumanity to man to humble those who would rise above their station. Voltaire went on to argue, that we should cultivate 'our own garden' by removing the evils from the earth, and not just to use our reason but all our faculties of being to reform society and play our part in removing injustices and inequalities in society. God did not create the injustices and inequalities on the earth human beings did by refusing to take our place as the creature before our creator and to live in equity and justice with our fellow man as we are called by our maker to do.

There are those who go to bed at night with more money in the bank than any reasonable person could ever spend in a life-time or even in some cases a hundred lifetimes, while children in the third world die of hunger, deprivation, and lack of clean water, in wars that are an affront to our humanity and from diseases that are curable in the West. And while some bemoan the hunger and deprivation of the third world and blame God for not doing someone about it while their money sits making interest in the bank with the massive multinational conglomerates taking the resources of the third world to make themselves rich and then throwing them their crumbs and calling it charity.

Jesus likens the kingdom of God to a vineyard owner who went into a far country leaving his stewards to look after his vineyard. But while the master was away his stewards played up and began to abuse their position, mistreat their servants, were unbelieving and became utterly corrupt. And even when he sent his Son to correct them and to show them the error of their ways and what manner of people he wanted them to be, they decided to kill him and to take over the vineyard for themselves and to live as they liked in God-defying arrogance.

But the vineyard owner was not dead just because the corrupt minds of men want him to be, and by entrusting them with his vineyard in his absence and leaving them to make their own choices, especially in the axis between good and evil, each person makes their own choices that decide the kind of people they become and therein their true nature is revealed and their destiny determined.

But if our Maker was forever breathing down our necks with an imposing authority of an overpowering Deity everyone would be going through the motions of obeisance and obedience because they had no option but to do so and would have bowed and scraped before their maker hoping to extract some favour and curry some advantage from him to give them the edge over their fellowmen with whom they were in competition.

If their master (or maker) has ruled over them with a rod of iron, they would have had no occasion to object or the freedom to reveal the true nature of their hearts. So in his absence each man's heart is revealed and their nature determined by the choices they make and when their Lord returns armed with the evidence of who they really are and how they acted in his absence every tongue will be stopped and only those who lived by faith in obedience to their Lord would be vindicated.

Sense-based information can reveal to us the existence of an apple, its colour, shape and size, but this does not explain its coming into existence, why we have an appetite to eat it, the capacity to enjoy it, the fact that it would be wrong to steal it. Therefore, there is much about our existence as human beings that simply cannot be established in empirically based scientific terms. So just as a child does not need to know how the differential of a bus works for the bus to get them where they want to go, so we do not need to know how the mind works to produce a living self-conscious reality of being that makes us moral beings on the journey of life.

Sartre referring to life could exclaim: "No! No! No! I know the ship is going down, but let's descend to the lower bunk and play our last game of poker." (Cited in Zacharias 1994, p.67) Not much here that provides us with a philosophy of life to be proud of or to live by. Rupert Sheldrake points out that: "There has been almost no progress in understanding how the brain produces subjective experience although many details have been discovered about the activities of different regions of the brain." (Sheldrake 2013 p.128) Einstein once declared: "All means prove but a blunt instrument, if they have not behind them a living spirit." (Ferris 1989, p.830) Therefore, while the means whereby we were created to be conscious moral beings may be hidden from us in clear and precise causal terms, the reality of who we are as conscious beings most certainly is not and is immediately known to us because it is, after all, who we experience ourselves to be and we cannot get closer to the truth than that.

One feels like asking how vital life would have to be before some would be willing to consider that it is something that issues from a vital and living source like that of a wise creator? Stephen J Gould who isn't a creationist is a tireless opponent of the idea that evolution can explain mind and morality. (Cited in Pinker 2002, p.132) A butterfly may sit upon a branch wavering precariously in the wind, but it has this notion that it would like to fly. It can't explain it or work it out but it out but it can't get the thought out of its mind. So in an act of faith and by employing every ounce of its energy it does that which it was designed to do and comes naturally to it and behold it has wings and by exercising them it can fly. But the proud and conceited hearts of men want proof of who they are when their very nature of conscious being is the proof they need and by exercising their faculties of being as they were meant to be used we can fly as we were meant to fly above the mundane world of empirically based reality to fulfil the ultimate purpose for which we were created. But if the butterfly insisted on knowing how its wings work, if they are big enough to give it enough lift to get it off the ground and keep it in the air, where it came from as a species and where the idea that it wants to fly originated came from – it will never fly. It will simply go on wondering, speculating and perishing never realising its full potential as a butterfly.

Augustine has pointed out that, there are things we need to take on faith in order to know, so that by exercising all our faculties of being and following where our instincts lead we discover all that we are made and meant to know as human beings. But it seems that some would rise above their station and think it is beneath them to even consider the idea that there is someone operating in the universe much wiser than them, or take the necessary steps at their disposal by which to know Him. Richard Dawkins describes us as living in a world of "blind pitiless indifference." What a sad and sorry kind of a man that would make, the wonder of life itself, complexity beyond our human understanding, a world of colour, light, variety and beauty and no one to thank and is proof of nothing. Taking Dawkins' statement at face value, we have nothing but a gospel of despair.

Some like James Rachels seems to think he is making a very profound statement when he argues that we were "created from animals." (Rachels 1990) But even if this were true, who created animals in all their wonder, complexity and variety, and who created human beings and endowed them with reason so that we might know that the ordered and living sum of all things needs to be explained in terms of a wise creator? Owen Gingerich speaking of DNA brings us down to earth when he argues: "So it is the game plan of science to find these clusters, these hierarchies, those pathways, catalytic ways in which life can form, in which these mutational jumps can occur and can build up to macroevolution. But the fact is that these pathways are there is what I consider to be part of God's design." (Cited in Witham 2002, p.126)

When we are confronted with something as ineffably real and wonderfully challenging as life which we cannot fully in finite terms explain, rather than trying to explain it away we would do better to see it as evidence of something very special and truly ineffable at work in the universe. Pascal has observed that: "Consciousness seeks constantly for its fulfilment in an essence which transcends it." But it seems that some are determined to reason themselves out of all causal relevance and meaningful significance and yet will weep with deep sorrow at the death of a loved one which seems quite misplaced if life is nothing more than a chanced upon compendium of corporeal substance that appeared on the earth by a long series of lucky flukes operating to no good purpose.

Richard Tarnas gets nearer the truth when he writes: "In this perspective, nature pervades everything, and the human mind in all its fullness is itself an expression of nature's essential being." (Tarnas 1991, p.434) Richard Tarnas again referring to the modern world of materialism argues: "The world in which man lived was becoming as impersonal as the cosmos of his science. With the pervasive anonymity, hollowness, and materialism of modern life, man's capacity to retain his humanity in an environment determined by technology seemed increasingly in doubt." (Tarnas 1991, p.363) While Albert Camus postulated his philosophy of "despair" with his greatest satisfaction in life was to refuse to give in to this despair and fight against it being stubbornly unwilling to give into it – a struggle he was destined to lose.

When the idea of a wise creator is repudiated and a process of mindless randomness is deemed to be the explanation for the existence of the world and everything in it all sense of meaning and purpose is removed from the earth and those who hold to this philosophy of life rush like lemmings to annihilation hoping that the cause that brought them into existence won't be there to meet them on the other side. Alexander Pope has put it: "Know then thyself, presume not God to scan: The proper study of mankind is man." In truth, to know God is not to understand all that God is in all his ineffable fullness, but to accept all that we experience ourselves to be and to use and utilise those qualitative attributes of being we possess as a species whereby to relate and get to know Him, thereby to become one Him and therein it realise our full potential as human beings.

Richard Dawkins affirms that: "religion is like the disease of smallpox only harder to cure," which is both vicious and offensive, is not grounded in rational thinking and comes close to a hate crime. Bertrand Russell may well have said that if God were to ask him why he did not believe in him he would reply by saying: "not enough evidence." This means that he must not have thought much of himself as providing evidence of nothing of any order producing significance. Yet he whose existence is proof of nothing by way of a credible origin or sufficient cause had the audacity to think they are clever enough to pronounce on the origin of all things and write books about it. Moreover, we would suggest that to argue as Russell does is like standing at the top of Mount Everest while at the same time denying the existence of mountains.

A single subatomic particle such as the 'god particle' seems for some to be of immense scientific significance with its discovery worthy of the Nobel Prize. But for some the vast complexity of all things from the starry hosts above us to the moral being within us seems to be of so little significance in terms of a cause it can be attributed to no cause at all and the maker of all things doesn't get a look in. Einstein writing to Max Born in September 1919 about the ultimate meaning and significance of life could write: "However if someone asks to what purpose we should help one another, make life easier for each other, make beautiful music or have inspired thoughts?" He would have to be told: "If you don't feel it, no one can explain it to you. Without this primary feeling we are nothing and had better not lived at all." (Ferris 1989, p.809)

Einstein believed: "The man who regards his own life and that of his fellow creatures as meaningless is not merely unfortunate but almost disqualified for life." (Cited in Blanchard 2000, p.339) Jesus could affirm: "The kingdom of God is within you," so that within ourselves we have proof of God if we want to see it and are willing to use our attributes of being through by which to know Him. As Augustine would say: "Do not wish to go out, go back into yourself truth dwells in the inner man." While Brian Cox and Jeff Forshaw in their book *Why Does E=mc²?* refer to Einstein as one who represents the greatest achievement of the human intellect, so much so that "Einstein will be remembered as long as there are humans on the earth." (Cox and Forshaw 2009) So while a human being who discovers something about some particular details about the natural world is deemed worthy of the Nobel Prize, but He who created the ordered sum of all things is not even recognised as an intelligent and sufficient cause at all and can be reduced to the insulting sum of nothing. Einstein affirms:

> those convictions which are necessary and determinant for our conduct and judgments, cannot be found solely along this solid scientific way … Objective knowledge provides us with powerful instruments for the achievement of certain ends, but the ultimate goal itself and the longing to reach it must come from another source … On the other hand, representatives of science have often made an attempt to arrive at fundamental judgments with respect to values and ends on the basis of scientific method, and in this way set themselves in opposition to religion. These conflicts have all sprung from fatal errors … To this there also belongs the faith in the possibility that the regulations valid for the world of existence are rational, that is comprehensible to reason. I cannot conceive of a genuine scientist without that profound faith. The situation may be expressed by an image, that science without religion is lame, religion without science is blind … So it seems to me that science not only purifies the religious impulse of the dross of anthropomorphism but also contributes to a religious spiritualisation of our understanding of life.
> [Cited in Ferris 1989, p.829f]

It is true that the pagan gods of years ago were indeed poor explanations for an ordered world and different phenomena on the earth, but these were at least attempts at an explanation by those who at least had the wit to know that the world and different phenomenon needed an adequate explanation. And while Steven Pinker may argue against the idea of a blank slate mind, but fails to explain the ordered and life generating realty of it or how it as the most complex reality in the known universe fell into place by nothing but blind chance. His blank slate brain was so huge it was wide as the sky as he called it, but it was still a blank slate for all that, an empirically based slate as wide as the sky, lifeless and devoid all that we experience life to be.

Hundert points out that: "By discovering the mind's 'participation in the act of knowing' Kant developed an entire philosophical system highlighting the mind's contribution to the world of physics which Hegel and Husserl referred to as The *Phenomenology of Spirit,* without which there would be no science and certainly no science of life." (Cited in Hundert 1990, p.38–39) Daniel Dennett accepts that: "Human consciousness is just about the last surviving mystery" of the universe. With consciousness, however, we are still in a terrible muddle. Consciousness stands alone today as a topic that often leaves even the most sophisticated thinkers tongue-tied and confused. "... what in the world can consciousness itself be. How can living physical bodies in a physical world produce such phenomena? That is the mystery." (Dennett 1991, p.22–25)

Although Dennett tries to demystify conscious life in the end of his book *Consciousness Explained,* we feel that we are no closer to understanding the nature of consciousness in all its ineffable reality of being at the end of the book than we were at the beginning of the book. And when Dennett makes the claim that "science is good at destroying metaphysical answers" he could not be farther from the truth, because every time scientists use their minds to engage in science they are up to their necks in the metaphysical reality of being and if they would use the rational part of it as it was meant to be used they could do nothing but conclude that they owe their existence to an intelligent life-producing cause capable of explaining all that they experience themselves to be. So when Dennett argues that science is good at undermining metaphysical explanations he could not be farther from the truth because science is a mental and metaphysical search for truth by means of intelligent and inquisitive minds is a clear manifestation of the very metaphysical proof he is trying so hard to deny.

Therefore, human understanding does not merely point to the existence of a life producing cause at work in the universe, but we ourselves are that proof. While Bohm argues that: "Just as photons are waves and particles and we observe each under different circumstances, so mind and matter are projections onto the world as a deeper order. They are separate aspects of life: being complementary, looking at matter tells us nothing about consciousness and vice versa." (Cited in Baker 2013, p.202) In the final analysis we can neither ultimately explain the world of physics which end in the imponderables of Quantum physics or the ineffable world of conscious being so that it all points to idea of an all wise creator which we as human beings must ultimately accept on faith. God doesn't want us to believe in Him because we have to because that would make for a forced and slave morality, but because we want to and when we use our faculties of being through which to know Him we can know him as he has ordered and ordained it to be. Augustine was not wrong when he argued: "Do not wish to go out: go back into yourself. Truth lies in the inner man." At least for those who have the sense to see it and the will to use it!

Wittgenstein realising something of the multi-dimensional nature of being argued that the philosopher's job is to lay all before us and not to place our own narrow interpretation upon it, to wrest or manipulate it in a vain attempt to make it conform to one's own preconceived ideas. Therefore, we need to call: "attention to facts one has known all along, but that are so obvious as to be ignored," to see reality as being just there just like: "one's life." (Cited on Pimlico History of Philosophy, 1999, p.641) It seems to the writer, however, that some theorists are like so many frustrated fish frantically trying to find the water they are swimming only and claim they cannot find it.

Husserl was surely right when he argued that consciousness must take full account of the 'life-world' as well as things perceived by our senses and these two worlds come together to produce reality as it really is. This is not a case of us knowing God in all his transcendent fullness, but God condescending to reveal himself to us in terms we can understand and placing in us attributes of being that overlap with his own nature of being whereby we can relate to him in faith and love and who can fulfil those hopes and aspirations he has put in our hearts which he alone can fulfil.

But for Bertrand Russell: "we are an accidental collision of atoms and only within the scaffolding of these truths, only on the firm foundation of unyielding despair, can the soul's habitation henceforth be built." It's good to remember that Russell is not God because what a pathetic God he would make; while he owes his existence to a cause so pathetically wanting one wonders how he could be such a wise creature coming from a cause so pathetically devoid of all wisdom and understanding. But God is not afraid of reason and rational thinking because he is the author of it, the fount of all wisdom the author of an ordered world we can reason about and who challenges us in the Scriptures to: "Come let us reason together says the Lord." And when we take up this challenge on the basis of reason and the reality of our own being the existence of God becomes a powerful argument within an ordered world and our own being an instrument through which we can relate to him.

But while reason is the thing which many scientists most like to boast, when it comes to applying it to the ordered and living sum of all that exists, the very thing in which they like so much boast turns out to be their 'Achilles heel'.

Chapter 14
A Brief Tribute to That Cause
Some Call Nothing

We engage the world around us as living subjects rich in attributes of being and understanding. As we have already noted, how a physical brain can generate such a profound reality of being we simply do not know and as Moheb Costandi argues, some believe that getting a better understanding of how the brain works will provide answers to life's big questions. It will not: "brain research cannot tell us everything about ourselves, or what it means to be a human." However Kevin Nelson observes that not knowing how the brain works to produce this profound reality of being emanating from within us may not really matter, it's how it impacts us and how we the experience of life to be in experiential terms that really matter. Life as we experience it to be is profoundly different from all we understand the brain to be even the causal link between the brain and conscious life is still a mystery. This means that conscious life and all that it entails is really a miracle because we cannot deny it and yet we cannot explain it.

This endless stream of consciousness is turned off by the brainstem and we go to sleep and turned on again when we are awakened. Consciousness will never fully understand itself even if we were to look inside our own head and even examine our brain we will not find anything resembling who you experience yourself to be. However, the spiritual reality of conscious experience cannot be measured empirically although brainwaves operating across the neurons and synapses of the brain can be detected by special electronic instruments. Mark Henderson suggests that those who apportion life to intelligent design are those who simply say: "I don't understand, so God must have done it" as opposed to seeing "how science can explain it." (Henderson 2008, p.5) But science has not explained it, and even if science could explain it, how would this mean that God as a wise creator had nothing to do with it? The fact is that man had nothing to do with the own coming into existence. This means that we are a living miracle unto ourselves, because something in the form of conscious life is an experiential reality that cannot be denied but yet is not explained in a way that encapsulates the ordered and living sum of it by apportioning it the working of a physical brain.

So the idea that the mind is a mysterious form of matter secreted by the brain trivialises life and presupposes the very thing has yet to be explained because the cause proposed is not capable of explaining all that we experience ourselves to be. This is what David Hume referred to as "disease of the learned" which caused him to conclude that: "I am confounded with all these questions, and begin to fancy myself in the most deplorable condition imaginable, inviron'd with the deepest darkness, and utterly depriv'd of the use of every member and faculty. Hume's disease of the learned which took him into bowels of despair could exclaim that to the philosophical sceptic, is in a man of letters is the first and most essential step towards being a sound, believing Christian", and that "faith and the grace of God alone could provide the certainty we mistakenly seek by human means … thus we can be grateful that nature breaks the force of sceptical arguments." (Cited on The Pimlo history of Western Philosophy 1998, p.457–460) Unfortunately there is little to no evidence that Hume ever took his own advice and was as a philosopher perhaps too conceited to ever do that which he could not ultimately understand in human earthly terms. Of course nature is not merely that which governs the laws of nature external to us, but the laws of nature operating within us that make us truly human and can deliver to our own consciousness more that the physical laws of nature.

Steven Pinker argues that we: "need to listen to the voice of our species", but the voice of our species is communicated through the mind in all its spiritual reality and existential fullness, part of which is the ability to reason which compels us to conclude that effects must be explained in terms of a cause that able to explain them. Thus, we are confronted with a living life producing cause in the ordered and living sum of who we experience ourselves to be and we are called to relate to that cause as creature to creator. We do not have to go looking for God he can be seen in the awe-inspiring reality of the cosmos, in the exceedingly complex nature of life on earth in general, and experienced within the ordered and living reality of who we are as human beings existentially profound and spiritually endowed. This means that the origin of life comes alive within us to share something of their own nature of being with us in all that which we experience ourselves to be as living entities of profound ontological substance and significance.

It can be said of this cause that in them we live and move and have our being and as the Apostle Paul could declare "is not far from us." Thus as the saying of God through the prophet Isaiah should serve as a warning to mankind when he declares: "My Sprit shall not always strive with man." Even David Hume admits that causation: "is the cement of the universe", undoubtedly because it binds everything together into a united and coordinated whole and only then can we have intelligently ordered things for intelligent minds to investigate and the mind being the most profound and revealing part of that research.

Natalie Angier in her book on evolution entitled *The Canon* speaks of the: "majestic might of natural selection" which has brought into existence the massive complexity of intelligent life on earth, but in the final analysis this majestic might of natural selection ends up being nothing to do with intelligence, intelligent design or an intelligent and sufficient cause of any kind. Therefore, evolution by natural selection, eulogised, praised and venerated by so many as the order producing genius behind the ordered complexity of all living things is then denigrated, insulted and reduced to a process of no order producing significance whatsoever blundering aimlessly through primordial chaos. Thus, the majestic might of natural selection is insulted, denigrated and repudiated being nothing more than some cosmic idiot both blind and brain dead and so causally insignificant it can be referred to as nothing.

Moreover, Angier who thinks of herself as being so accomplished and scientifically astute originated from a process of mindless futility and causal irrelevance. And if we want to credit the order producing power of evolution to Mother Nature, then either Mother Nature is another name for a wise creator or is acting as the order-producing agent thereof. Nature comes alive within us as human beings to share something of her own nature of being with us in the conscious and living sum of who we are – but even with this some don't get it.

When an increasing number of evolutionists write books on how wonderful nothing is and don't seem to realise just how far they have drifted into the dangerous by-path meadows of a mindless obscurantism. And when we refuse to buy into the twisted logic of this absurdity we are regarded as scientifically illiterate. One has to wonder how such theorists could regard themselves as being so wise and scientifically astute when they came into existence by means so causally insignificant and mindlessly irrelevant. Thus, we are fed a plethora of fine sounding words full of pseudo-scientific prognostications that on the surface sound superficially impressive but that evaporate into a causeless irrelevance and endless tautologies that ultimately mean nothing in real terms. But theists true to their own being can detect a Godlike intelligence in the order producing power of creation, and in the ordered and living sum of *who* they experience themselves to be and seek to be one with it. They love this kind of holistic epistemological as they love life itself because by it and through it they come to terms with who they are and the cause from which they have come.

It has been alleged that theists are not open to alternative explanations for intelligent life on earth other than the idea of a wise creator, but to date we haven't seen any reason based alternatives to seriously consider. Theists are willing to go with that form of evolution that sticks closely to reason and rational thinking and are willing to see in this form of evolution the means by which a wise creator operated to bring into existence an ordered world and then filled it with living things. There is no shame in honest doubt, only when we are unwilling to use our God-given intelligence operating to the cause and effect logic of rational thinking to alleviate that doubt do we become blameworthy. And scientists are increasingly discovering the incredibly ingenious means by which God through the laws of nature produced intelligent life on earth, but far as some are concerned a penny tin whistle has better order producing credentials than we as human beings who according to some ultimately have no credible cause at all. The Scriptures remind us that: "*The just shall live by faith*", not faith divorced from reason but validated by it insofar as we as human beings can reason.

When we have a true and authentic science of life, we have the necessary elements that make for of a true and authentic science of religion with God as a wise creator at the very centre of our philosophy of life as the only conceivable way to explain an intelligently ordered world full of intelligently ordered living things. Arthur Koestler sums up the situation: "In the meantime the educated public continues to believe that Darwin has provided all the relevant answers by the magic formula of random mutations plus natural selection quite unaware of the fact that random mutations turned out to be irrelevant and natural selection a tautology." (Koestler 1978, p.172) Certainly, all that exists is an awful lot of something for nothing to explain and the very idea reminds one of what Scriptures say that: "in professing themselves wise some have become fools."

In fact, we would dare to suggest that some theorists are operating in bad faith because if they had any sense of integrity as rational beings they would at the very least admit that a wise creator is a real and distinct possibility in a world of such awe-inspiring complexity and life-generating presence. There is a sense in which we as living beings are already in touch with the living God in the ordered and living sum of who we are, if we only had the sense to realise it and the wit to tap into it. Therefore, it seems that we need an 'evolution for slow learners', in which some need to understand what Matthew Tindal concluded long ago, namely that God is the: "creator of the awe-inspiring universe that moves in accordance with his eternal laws." A scientist who beholds the wonders of the universe and contemplates with any degree of sincerity the miracle of life and walks away and says how wonderful nothing is, is not worthy of their calling as a scientist or a human being.

And as C.S. Lewis has observed that nature has seen to it that: "Creatures are not born with desires unless satisfaction for those desires exists." We have an appetite to eat food for instance, but we can never test the validity of that desire until we act upon it and eat, and low we find it enjoyable and it supplies us with energy to keep us alive. The same applies to our thirst for knowledge of God who is the rewarder of them that diligently seek him and by exercising the appropriate attributes of being we can find and know him.

But we cannot complain if we fail to use all our faculties of being as they were meant to be used and find ourselves dying of thirst because we refuse to drink from the fountain of life because we cannot fathom the depth of the well. Marianne Taylor argues that the idea of God is pseudoscience because it cannot be falsified. But the idea of God as a wise creator can most certainly be falsified, because if we find that the world is intelligently ordered and we as human beings ordered intelligently to think intelligently and who can investigate the world and everything in it intelligently is clear evidence that behind the world and everything in an order producing intelligence. But when we reduce reality to empirically based facts, reason itself is qualified out of existence leaving us as witless zombies incapable of drawing rational conclusions about anything. Thus these same people can apportion the ordered sum of everything to the order-producing sum of nothing and scientists investigating the world of by means of intelligence things whose existence they claim has nothing to do with an order producing intelligence. So in professing themselves wise some have indeed become fools and in their keenness to rid the world of God as a wise creator have landed themselves in a fool's paradise.

Alan Guth argues that: "it is said there's no such thing as a free lunch, but the universe is the ultimate free lunch." (Cited in Barker, 2013, p.145) Really! Alas poor Guth, the universe is only a free lunch if you don't have to explain it and the spectacular appearance of it and the multitude of order producing and life generating means that followed it. Many scientists want the privilege of making rational judgments about the universe but refuse to accept that things need to be ordered intelligently before they can make rational judgements about anything. Such theorists are locked into an infernal contradiction in terms that can only be reversed when they face up to the logic of sufficient cause in the form of a wise creator. Such theorists cannot hide behind nothing forever because sooner or later the truth will catch up with them when the nothing that produced them comes looking for them.

Lawrence M. Krauss entitles one of his books, *a universe from nothing.* Then he entitles another of his books, *the greatest story ever told.* But how could nothing result in the greatest story ever told? What is the purpose of this story? Well there really isn't one. What is the story line of this greatest story ever told, well it is about how a world crammed full of luck and fairy-tale stories produced the ordered and living sum of all that exists. How does the story end? Why it all ends in tragedy really: One day, if mankind does not first blow themselves to smithereens in some manically inspired nuclear war, or destroy the world by global warming, the sun will burn itself out and explode as a massive fireball to form a supers-nova that will incinerate the whole earth and everything on it. So perhaps this is not so great a story ever told after all.

But there is a different version of this story and it is much more exciting, even a more convincing story, so much so because it is underpinned by rational thinking and meets the deep needs and hopes of the human heart. It is a more credible story with a highly acclaimed author whose language is based in the cause and effect logic of rational thinking. It has a much more authentic story line in keeping with life as we experience life to be. It is a story of a wise creator who operates by means of sufficient cause to achieve a noble and worthy purpose. What we make of this story reveals whether we are true searchers after truth or forever running from it.

The word nothing comes from the Latin *nihil,* and literally means *'nothingism'.* In the Disney film *Lion King*, Simba the rebellious young Prince loses his way in the world after losing his father in tragic circumstances for which he partly blames himself. In his grief, he loses the will to take over from his late father and wanders aimlessly in the world with his ne'er-do-well friends. All hope of ever realising his true destiny as the son of the late king is well nigh lost forever. Until he is challenged by his late father who appears to him in a vision saying: "remember who you are because in forgetting who you are you have forgotten me." We don't have to explain God to believe in him, we just need to remember who we are and to live out all that we have been created to be and ordered to know as human beings and it leads us right to Him.

As Plato argued: "To discover *kosmos* (order) in the world was to reveal *kosmos* in one's own soul" so in the thought life of man, the world spirit reveals itself. The belief that the universe is governed according to a comprehensive regulating intelligence, and that the same intelligence is reflected in the human mind rendering it capable of knowing the cosmic order, is a fundament principle of reality. This in turn called for an explanation for the origin of this cosmic order and the mind of man who can reflect upon it. So the Logos was a divine revelatory principle, simultaneously operating with the human mind and in the natural world so that in the thought life of man, the world spirit reveals itself. That intelligence is reflected in the human mind which attributes of being reveal the nature of that creator and the ultimate purpose of our existence as human beings. Thus the Logos was the divine revelatory principle from which all things have come and this is reflected in mind of man (nous) revealing the kind of creator our creator he is. John in his gospel in the New Testament uses the same word Logos to describe the incarnation in which God came amongst us in the flesh described as the son of God to reveal in earthly human terms the kind of being that his Father was and the kind of people He wanted us to be both in relation to Himself with our fellowman.

We don't have argue over who he was, but we are honour-bound to listen to Him and give Him a fair hearing, and if we see in him something inspiring and worth emulating and dare to follow him he will lead us to that to which the human heart aspires and all that we hope for and long for as human beings. His words were so authoritative, awe-inspiringly challenging, morally compelling and personally pertinent to the human condition in a world looking for hope and satisfaction we cannot ignore him – we must follow him or kill him – if not in the flesh but in our own hearts. This is not to say that other religions have not contributed to our understanding of God, but put the best of it together and it all points in the same direction.

We would argue that Charles Colson and Nancy Pearcey are right when they point out, that instead of being intimidated by attacks made in the name of science we can show that the very existence of the scientific method and all it has accomplished is a powerful argument for the truth of intelligent design underlying of which there is a grand designer. (Colson and Pearcey 1999, p.425)

One of the saddest things about this whole scenario is that the Church Jesus Christ became one of the most overbearing, arrogant, oppressive, and persecuting institutions the world has ever seen and we are only now beginning to get over the gross misrepresentation of Christ and the message he preached and lived out while here on earth. But we shouldn't judge something by the worst example of a thing, but by the best, and this takes us back to the original autographs where we find rich nuggets of truth still waiting to be found.

Plato described knowledge of the divine as implicit in the soul but forgotten. So he urged people to look within to "know thyself," and know who they really were and argued the: "The philosopher, or searcher after truth, must permit themselves to be inwardly grasped by the most sublime form of Eros – that universal passion to restore a former unity, to overcome a the separation from the divine and become one with it." While Heraclitus believed, that *logos* was a rational principle governing the *cosmos* and the human mind was a living and finite reflection of this fact! (Cited in Tarnas 1996, p.45) So the force of reason and the call of being draws us back to God as that origin from which we have come, with Plato believing that with a resolute attention to the mind and soul, to moral virtue as well as intellectual truth the world order itself has been contracted and revealed. (Cited in Tarnas 1965, p.47)

Chapter 15
A Win-Win Critique Where
Science and Religion Meet

It is alleged that when it was discovered by Copernicus that the earth moved round the sun and not the other way round which the Scriptures seemed to teach they were proved to be wrong. However, this is way it appeared from an earth-bound point of view before scientists with the help of the telescope and their God given intelligence discovered that it was the earth that was revolving around the sun spinning as it went. The Scriptures were obviously addressing those who were living within the context of the prevailing worldview of their own life and times, and it would have been utterly confusing if they had not done so. With modern scientists operating with more sophisticated instruments such as the telescope, scientists began to see the bigger picture with respect to the movements of the stars within the solar system.

The theologian Charles Hodge could see that when it comes to the world of physics, we should accept the findings of good science even if this meant aspects of Scripture that pertained to the physical universe needed to be updated in the light of modern scientific insights. He gave an example of this when it was discovered that the earth moved around the sun and not the sun around the earth so that is now universally accepted by both theists and scientists alike. Moreover, the primary purpose of the Scriptures was not to declare on the workings of the universe like a scientific handbook, it was a guide for God's people as to how they should live as moral beings before their creator and in relation to their fellowmen. What would it matter whether the sun was moving around the earth or the earth around the sun if people were living profligate, shameful and meaningless lives?

With new scientific discoveries, the minds of men could be further enlightened with respect to the universe and the working of the Solar System, but moral principles and human relationship were founded on unchangeable principles of personal responsibility and social morality. A.J. Ayer may claim that: "Philosophy is virtually empty without science", but what use is empirically based science if there is no purpose to life and human beings have no moral direction in life and living selfish and purposeless lives? What we as human beings need above all else is a true and authentic science of life. There is a philosophy of science whereby scientists investigate a world of empirically based things, and there is a philosophy of life within which scientists have the intelligence and determination of will to carry it out and other attributes of being whereby they live life that takes them beyond the world of physics into the world moral and spiritual attributes being.

Moreover, scientists such as Copernicus, Galileo, Kepler, Bacon, Boyle, Newton and many others believe that science strengthened belief in God because it showed more clearly the order of the universe and the vast complexity of life on earth which proved to be more intricate, complex and involved than anyone had ever imagined. One of the fathers of modern science Francis Bacon has argued: "A little philosophy inclined men's mind toward atheism, but depth philosophy brings their minds back to religion." One of the reasons for this is undoubtedly because science was increasingly discovering how massively complex life really is even in its most basic cellular level which increasingly revealed the need for the manifest wisdom of a wise creator.

Those who insisted on interpreting the six days of creation in Genesis as six twenty four hour days (commonly referred to the literal historical method) which made the age of the earth some six thousand or so years old which did not allow anything like enough time for life to slowly evolve as science was revealing it to be. However, this is all very well if this is the way the Scriptures are meant to be interpreted, but the Scriptures do not make this claim. The six days of creation in Genesis need not be interpreted as what we now know as six twenty four hour days and it is obvious that there were no such twenty four days until the Solar System was set up at the end of creation.

Henry Morris point's out the word *yom* in the Hebrew translated day can and often does refer to a period of time as opposed to a twenty-four hour day. Many translators do not even translate *Yom* as day in case it is confused with a solar twenty-four day as opposed a period of time. In the King James version of the Bible, the word *yom* is translated 65 times as the general 'time' as opposed to the word day, and in many occasions when it is translated 'day' is obviously referring to a 'period of time'. An example of this can be seen in the reference to the 'day' of the Lord which is referring to a period of time when God will manifest himself among mankind which is clear reference to a period of time and not a single day. And on different occasions when the Scriptures use '*yom*' as 'in that day' which is referring to a period of time and more especially to a thousand years of the *Millennium Reign* when peace would reign on the earth.

Augustine the fourth century theologian argued the days in the Genesis account of creation do not represent solar twenty four days, as did Origen a third century theologian. Basil a fourth century theologian and Thomas Aquinas in the 13th century argued the same way. Likewise Jewish writers, Plilo and Josephus, and obviously these early writers cannot be said to be writing to comply with modern science because these arguments made before science revealed more clearly the true age of the universe. Biblical Scholar A.H. Strong in his systematic theology and Gleason Archer in his Encyclopaedia of Bible Difficulties, argues that the events of Genesis 2:15–22 could not possibly be referring to a literal twenty-four hour day.

Moreover, Gleason Archer an authority on Semitic languages argues that in Genesis 1 omits the definite article before each creation day which then reads day one which in Hebrew prose often means a figurative or poetic form of speaking. Moreover, some Biblical scholars refer to what they call the gap theory in which they suggest that there could be a huge period of time between verse one and verse two of Genesis which describes the nature of things before creation proper began. C.I. Scofield was one such theologian.

Theologians, however, are generally agreed that the Scriptures need to be interpreted in different ways sometimes referred to as parabolic, metaphorical, allegorical, poetic, symbolic, figurative, literal and spiritual. In other words, the Scriptures must read as they were meant to be read in the light of the context and the nature of the subject matter. We have also have anthropomorphisms in which God has to explain certain things in human terms to make them more understandable to us as finite beings. It is said, for instance, that after creation God rested on the Seventh Day, but this implies that God was tired and fatigued after all that hard weeks work of creation and needed to lie down and rest a while. But God was not tired or fatigued as we humans understand it. This is God coming down to our human level of understanding to make himself understood to us as finite beings. Thus we have anthropomorphism.

Moreover, God had to speak in terms those to whom he first revealed himself could understand in a pre-scientific age where there would be little point in speaking in elaborate and involved scientific terms that an ancient and scientifically primitive people would simply not have understood. This is why the theologian John Calvin uses the word *balbutive,* which when translated means *baby talk* to describe the Genesis account of creation in a way that those back then would have understood it. If Moses or even Jesus were to have used modern terms like quantum physics, a quantum vacuum, deoxyribonucleic (DNA) or dendrites and so on they would have immediately confounded their audience, but that would come later when men by means of their God-given intelligence would discover how unutterably complex life really is and used the appropriate modern scientific terms to describe it. The writers of Scripture had to relate in simple and generalised terms so that people in a primitive, unsophisticated and pre-scientific age could understand.

We have to modify our understanding of creation in the light of good science, but moral theology and the underlying issues of life do not change and the purpose of life must always be an underlying consideration forced upon us as rational beings so that the human mind in all its vital and life-defining fullness is an expression of nature's essential being. While different attributes of being revealed in more particular terms who we are as human beings, and what duty God requires of man as moral beings. So just as we are accountable to man-made courts as moral beings so we are ultimately accountable to our maker who made us moral beings. So to know the truth as man can know it is to know ourselves and the true nature of the soul. John Calvin, Henry Ward Beecher, James Denny, Carl Henry, Cornelius Van Till, Frances Collins and by way of implication, Charles Hodge, B.B. Warfield, and Bernard Ramm all believed that the canon of Scriptures cannon always be taken literally in earthly human terms because our knowledge of the physical universe is always changing as scientists make new discoveries about its nature and function almost on a daily basis.

But the underlying purpose of life remains and to know what that is we need to know who we are as human beings operating existentially within the physical world and thereby make a life for ourselves worthy of our maker as moral beings and living in fellowship with him. So *Logos*, was the mind behind the ordered sum of all things, while *Nous* was the human mind of man which is the dynamic and living expression of that creative mind so that Logos and was a revelatory principle simultaneously operative in the human mind and in the natural world. Thus, the highest quest of the philosopher was to grasp and be grasped by this supreme rational-spiritual principle that both ordered and revealed itself both in the natural world and in the human mind.

Bernard Ram regarded some forms of: "fundamentalism as functioning within a basically pre-Enlightened paradigm." And that: "the days of retreating into obscurantism are over." (Cited in Hicks 1998, p.115) This was obviously because the world revealed by science was revealing that the earth was much older than it appeared to be as described in the Bible and some insisting on interpreting the Scriptures as they were revealed in a pre-scientific age which could be confusing and seemed to call into question the accuracy of Scriptures. The physical world is but the theatre in which life is lived out the details of which were incidental, while the purpose of Scripture was taken up with life and the relation of man to their maker and being responsible to Him as to how lived with their neighbour and looked after the earth as he commanded them to care for and look after. Einstein recognised that: "The harmony of natural law ... reveals an intelligence of such superiority that compared with it all the systematic thinking and acting of human beings is an utterly insignificant reflection." While science was revealing that the universe and life on earth was more exceedingly complex than anyone ever imagined, revealing more clearly the power and wisdom of God the creator. While Schleiermacher argued that the existence of God is held to be grounded in human experience. Truth, therefore, is not just that which is propositional but experiential, not merely cognitive but existential.

While Henry Ward Beecher, a conservative theologian who could regard evolution as a phenomenon guided by God which was much more impressive and suggestive of design than a single original act of creation. (Cited in McGrath 1999, p.192) So the wonders of creation not only warrant the existence of a wise creator but in fact demand it. Reason points us to God as creator and being draws us to Him. Thus as Plato has argued: "Only a society founded on divine principles and governed by divinely informed philosophers could save mankind from its destructive irrationality, and the best life was the one directed away from the mundane life and towards the world of eternal ideas." (Cited in Tarnas 1996, p.44) While Peter Hicks writes: "Reason must be applied to every aspect of our lives if we are to have a holistic science of reality as it is for us as human beings."

There are some however, who genuinely get lost within the complex maze of interacting variables revealed to us by many different avenues of scientific investigation and fail to see the implications of it all. But for some they simply don't want to see it, and in fact are determined not to see it no matter what evidence we present them with. This is why Jesus said: "Eyes and you see not, ears and you hear not lest you see with your eyes and hear with your ears and understand your hearts and are converted." This is why Plato urged people to 'know thyself' because only in self-knowledge can one discern who they really are and live a life that is true to the nature of the soul.

The philosopher's job is to free the soul from a deluded condition of a shallow materialism and to bring to mind knowledge of the true causes and sources of all things and to become one with it and therein true satisfaction as it was meant to be is served and accomplished. It could be said that the Greek legacy as given expression in such philosophers as Socrates, Plato and Aristotle showed that when mankind used their powers of reason within the context of their own being operating within what was obviously an extremely complex and ordered world it pointed to the existence of a wise creator. This drew out from them the desire to know him and looking within themselves they found the means by which to relate to him as conscious beings to a living life producing cause called God. This was further reinforced by mankind's quest for happiness and fulfilment and a sense of emptiness emanating from within until that sense of purpose was realised and established in the form of a wise creator.

Socrates and Plato met this challenge be using the faculties of their own mind and being to engage and pay homage to this being of awesome wonder and endeavoured to be one with it, and so to be at peace within themselves having permitted himself to be inwardly grasped by the most by sublime form of Eros – that universal passion to restore a former unity, to overcome the separation from the divine and to become one with it believing that knowledge of the divine was implicit in every soul but forgotten or distorted by other passions of the mind that led man away from God. Plato likened this highest philosophical vision to that of a lover and to be grasped by the most sublime form of ethos. The goal of philosopher in search of the truth was to free the soul from its deluded condition in which it was deceived by false and finite imitations of what was truth and did not serve the true nature of the soul in its search for fulfilment and happiness.

But of course such inspired ideas and abstract reasoning was only open to the few and closed to those who had neither the time nor inclination to engage in such abstract thinking, and even Socrates was condemned for spreading his message and ordered to commit suicide – which he readily did. The world waited for a more direct and simplified form of revelation, one that could not be missed or misunderstood, and which Christians believe came in the incarnation of God in Christ who revealed God's will to men and called all men everywhere to repent and to live the live that was becoming mankind as moral beings and glorifying to God their maker.

This God to the surprise of many loved the whole world, which was too much love for some. He too like Socrates was condemned to die, but even in his death his power and virtue was not defeated and lived on in the life of his followers who continued to carry on the message he had initiated on the earth. So that in a sense we are within excuse, the message was so profound it was life transforming and yet so profoundly simple a little child could understand it.

That message was all but lost as even the Church of Christ became a victim of its own pride and conceit became a persecuting magisterium caught up in its pomp, prestige and earthly glory being endowed with great wealth it lost the power and virtue of its master to become the very antithesis of all they were called to be and even to be at war within itself. Meanwhile, amidst the confusion of the modern world taken up with things, and deceived into believing that God is dead and foolish enough to believe that nothing created the ordered sum of everything the world grinds on to oblivion. But amidst the confusion and, conceit and reckless hedonism the voice of God can still be heard for those who want to hear it and a written witness to that truth for those who wish to read it. As Einstein has remarked: "A theorist goes wrong in two ways: 1: 'The devil leads him by the nose with a false hypothesis (*For this he deserves our pity.*) 2: His arguments are erroneous and sloppy (*For which he deserves a beating*)."

Bibliography

Alper, M. (2006) *The God Part Of The brain,* Illinois: Source Book Inc.

Alston, W. (1993) *Perceiving God*, London: Cornel University Press.

Angier, N. *The Beautiful Basics of Science*, London: Faber and Faber.

Appignanesi, R. (2006) *What Do Existentialists Believe?* London: Granta Books.

Argyle, M. (2000) *Psychology of Religion.* Routledge.

Jones, H, (2008) AQA – *An Introduction to Philosophy.* London.

Audi, R. (1998) *Epistemology*, London: Rutledge.

Audi, R. (1999) *The Cambridge Dictionary of Philosophy*, Cambridge University Press.

Baggott, J. (2013) *Farewell to Reality*, London: Constable.

Baker, J. (2013) *50 quantum physics ideas you need to know*, London: Quercus Editions Ltd.

Blanchard, J. (2000) *Does God Believe In Atheists,* Darlington: Evangelic Press.

Bowler and Morris (2005) *Making Modern Science*, University of Chicago Press.

Brockman, J. (2006) *What We Believe But Cannot Prove*, London: Pocket Books.

Broocks, R. (2013) *God's Not Dead*, Nelson.

Brooks M. (2015) *Chance: The Science and secrets of luck, randomness and probability*, London: Profile Brooks.

Brown, S. (2001) *Philosophy of Religion,* London: Routledge, London.

Brown, C. (1968) *Philosophy and The Christian Faith*, Illinois: Inter Varsity Press.

Bynum, W. *A Little History of Science.* (2012) Yale University Press.

Cole, J. (2007) *Scientists Confront Creationists*, London: Norton and Company.

Carroll, S. (1992) *Classics of Moral and Political Theory*, Edited by Morgan, M.L., Hackett Publishing Company, Inc.

Collins, F. (2007) *The Language of God*, London: Pocket Books.

Costandi, M. (2013) 50 ideas you really need to know – the human brain, London: Quercus.

Colson, C. and Pearcey, N. (2000) *How Now Shall We Live*, London: Marshall Pickering.

Copleston, S.J. (1994) A History of Philosophy: Vol. II–III–VI–VII–VIII.

Copleston, S.J. (1994) A History of Christianity: Vol. IX. Image Bools.

Darwin, C. (1971) *The Origin of Species*, London: Dent.

Davies, B. (2000) *Philosophy of Religion a guide and Anthology*, Oxford: Oxford University Press.

Dawkins, R. (1986) *The Blind Watchmaker*, London: Penguin Books.

Dawkins, R. (1976) *The Selfish Gene,* Oxford University Press.

Dawkins, R. (1997) *Climbing Mount Improbable*, London: Penguin.

Dawkins, R. (2006) The God Delusion. *Black Swan.*

Davies, B. (2000) *Philosophy of Religion.* Oxford University Press.

Davies, P. (1999) *The Origin of Life*, London: Penguin.

Dennett, D. (1995) *Darwin's Dangerous Idea*, London: Penguin.

DK Books, *The Science Book* (London 2014).

DK Books, Science – But Not As we Know It. (London 2015).

Sosa, E. and Jaegwon, K. (2000) Epistemology: Blackwell, Oxford.

Gribbin, J. (1999) *Almost Everyone's Guide to Science,* Phoenix London.

Davies, B. (2000) *Philosophy of Religion,* Oxford.

Gardner, J. (1997) *Sophie's World*, London: Phoenix, London.

Gould, S. (2001) *Rocks of Ages*, London: Vintage.

Greenfield, S. (1997) *The Human Brain*, Orion Publishing Group.

Gregory, R. (1987) *The Oxford Companion to the Mind.* OUP.

Gregory, R. (1993) *Mind in Science*, London: Penguin Books.

Hawking, S. (1988) A Brief History Of Time: Bantam Press.

Herron, F. (2000) *Show Me God,* Wheeling: Day Star Publications.

Heidegger, M. (1962) *Being and Time*, Oxford: Blackwell.

Heil, J. (1998) *Philosophy of Mind*, London: Routledge.

Heinze, T. (1973) *Creation vs. Evolution*, Glasgow: Baker.

Hawking, S. (1988) *A Brief History Of Time*, London: Bantam Press.

Henderson, M. (2008) *50 genetic ideas you really need to know*, London: Quercus.

Hedges, C. (2002) *War Is a Force That Gives Us Meaning*, First Anchor Books, Anchor Books.

Hicks, P. (1998) *Evangelicals and the Truth*, Leicester: Inter Varsity Press.

Honderick, T. (1990) *The Philosophers.* Oxford University Press.

Hodgson, P. (1994) *Winds of the Spirit*, London: SCM Press.

Hundert, E. (1989) *Philosophy, Psychiatry and Neuroscience*, Oxford: Clarendon Press.

Johnston, P. (1976) *A History of Christianity*, New York: Penguin London.

Jones, S. (2000) *The Language of the Genes*, London: Flamingo.

Kaku, M. (2014) *The Future of the Mind*, UK: Penguin Books.

Kenny, A. (2007) *Philosophy in the Modern World*, Oxford: Oxford University Press.

Prichard, D. (2010) Knowledge, Routledge.

Koestler, A. (1978) *Janus: A Summing Up*, London: Picador, 185 and 172.

Krauss, L. (2012) *A Universe from Nothing,* London: Simon and Schuster.

Levene, L. (2010) *All the Philosophy You Need to Know.* Michael O'Mara Books.

Lennox, J. (2007) *God's Undertaker Has Science Buried God*, Oxford: Lion.

Law, S. (2007) *Philosophy*, London: DK.

Lloyd, C. (2012) *What on Earth Happened?* London: Bloomsbury.

Locke, J. (1961) *An Essay Concerning Human Understanding.* Dent.

Lonergan, B. *Collected Works of Bernard Lonergan*, London: University of Toronto Press.

McGinn, C. (2002) *The Making of a Philosopher*, London: Scribner.

McGrath, A. (1999) *Science and Religion*, Oxford: Blackwell.

The Pimlico History of Western Philosophy, London: Pimlico.

Magee, B. (2000) *Confessions of a Philosopher*, London: Phoenix.

Magee, B. (2001) *The story of Philosophy*, London: DK.

Mautner, T. (2000) *Dictionary of Philosophy.* Penguin Books.

Mulhall, S. (1996) *Heidegger and Being and Time*, London: Routledge.

Inwagen, P.V. and Zimmerman, D.W. (ed.) (1998) Metaphysics, *The Big Questions.* Blackwell.

Martineau, J. (ed.) (2011) Sciencia. Mathematics Physics Chemistry Biology.

Morgan, M. (1992) *Classics of Moral and Political Theory,* Hackett Publishing Company.

M.H. (1974) *Scientific Creationism*, Creation Life Publications.

Nelson, K. (2011) *The God Impulse*, London: Simon and Schuster.

Noll, M. (1995) *The Scandal of the Evangelical Mind,* Eerdmans.

Osman, J. (2011) *100 Ideas That Changed the World.* London BBC Books.

Papineau, P. (ed.) (2004) *Philosophy*, London: Baird Publishing.

Petto, A. & Godfrey, L. (2007) *Scientists Confront Creationists*. W.W. Norton.

Pinker, S. (2002) *The Blank Slate*, London: Penguin Books.

Plotkin, R. (1999) *Philosophy Made Simple,* Oxford.

Plotkin, H. (1998) *Evolution in Mind*, London: Penguin.

Polkinghorne, J. (2000) *Faith, Science and Understanding,* SPCK.

Rachels, J, (1990) *Created From Animals*. Oxford University Press).

Rovelli, R. (2015) Seven Brief Lessons on Physics, Penguin. Ratzsch, D. (2000) *Science and Its Limits*, Leicester: InterVarsity Press.

Ridley, M. (1999) *Genome*, London: Fourth Estate.

Schroeder, G. (2001) *The Hidden Face of God Science Reveals the Ultimate Truth*, London: Touchstone.

Spencer, S. (2009) Darwin and God. S.P.C.K.

Rahner, K. (1976) *The Foundations of Christian Faith*, Crossroads Publishing Company.

Rose, S. and Rose, H. (ed.) (2000) *Alas Poor Darwin*, London: Vintage.

Rotmann, C. (1998) *Dictionary of Important Ideas*. Hutchinson, London.

Scharfstein, B. (1980) *The Philosophers.* Oxford: Oxford University Press.

Scruton, R. (1995) *A Short History of Modern Philosophy*, London: Routledge.

Sheldrake, R. (2013) *The Science Delusion*, London: Coronet.

Silver, B. (1998) *The Ascent of Science*, New York: OUP.

Spencer, N. (2009) *Darwin and God*, London: SPCK.

Southwell, G. (2013)*50 Philosophy of science ideas you really need to know*, London: Quercus.

Spentner, L. (1998) *Not By Chance*, New York: The Judaica Press.

Stevens, R. (1983) Freud and Psychoanalysis, Open University Press.

Strobel, L. (2004) *The Case for a Creator*, Zondervan Grand Rapids.

Tarnas, R. (1991) *The Passion of the Western Mind*, London: Pimlico.

Taylor, M. (2010) *I Used to Know That General Science*, London: Michael O'Hara.

Thompson, M. (2000) *Philosophy,* London: Hotter & Stoughton.

Tudge, C. (2000) *In Mendel's Footnotes*, London: Vintage.

Popkin, R. (1999) *Pimlico History of Western Philosophy,* London: Pimlico.

Ferris, T. (1989) *World Treasury of Physics, Astronomy, and Mathematics*, London: Little, Brown and Company.

Thompson, M. (2000) *Religion and Science*, London: Hodder and Stoughton.

Warburton, N. (1999) *Philosophy the Basics*, London: Routledge.

Watson, P. (2005) *Ideas, A History from Fire to Fraud*, London: Phoenix.

Wentzel Van Huyssteen, J. (1997) Essays in Post-foundationalist Theology.

Witham, A. (2002) *Where Darwin Meets the Bible,* Oxford University.

Zacharias, R. (1994) *Can Man Live Without God*, Nashville: Thomas Nelson.